THE COMPLETE BOOK OF
CACTI
&
SUCCULENTS

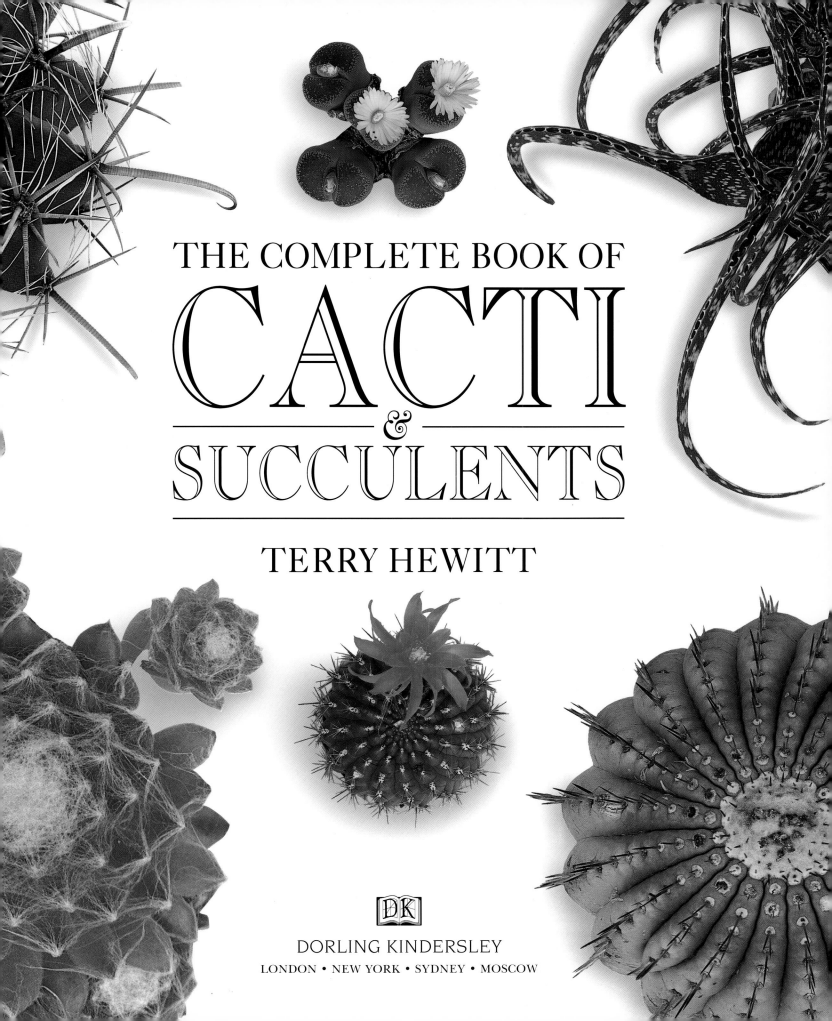

THE COMPLETE BOOK OF
CACTI
&
SUCCULENTS

TERRY HEWITT

DK

DORLING KINDERSLEY

LONDON · NEW YORK · SYDNEY · MOSCOW

A DORLING KINDERSLEY BOOK

Project editor
Annelise Evans

Art editor
Jo Grey

Editor
Blanche Sibbald

Senior editor
Rosie Pearson

Senior art editor
Tracy Timson

Senior managing editor
Daphne Razazan

Managing art editor
Carole Ash

Senior production controller
Rosalind Priestley

Main photographer
Peter Anderson

First published in Great Britain in 1993
by Dorling Kindersley Limited,
9 Henrietta Street, London WC2E 8PS

First paperback edition, 1997
2 4 6 8 10 9 7 5 3

Copyright © 1993 Dorling Kindersley Limited, London
Text copyright © 1993 Terry Hewitt and Dorling Kindersley Limited

A CIP catalogue record for this book is available
from the British Library

ISBN 0-7513-2419-1

Reproduced in Singapore by Colourscan
Printed by C & C Offset Printing Co.,Ltd, Hong Kong

CONTENTS

INTRODUCTION

ANATOMY AND DISCOVERY

STYLE GUIDE

PLANT CATALOGUE

A photographic guide with details of size, shape, flowers and cultivation needs

CARE AND CULTIVATION

INTRODUCTION

TO MOST PEOPLE, cacti and succulents are their great aunt's jade plant (which survived all these years despite her) or the cowboy cactus seen in films. At my nursery, Holly Gate, it is a pleasure to see the dumbfounded look on the face of the uninitiated when presented with an array of such a varied group of plants as that of cacti and succulents. Should the plants actually be in flower, the visitor is inevitably amazed by their beauty and is often converted into a life-long aficionado on the spot.

Some plants have a tiny diameter and yet produce large flowers that can completely obscure the plant itself, others may be towering columns or large spiny globes or have long, leaf-like stems. Gnarled old trunks, "living stones", colourful rosettes or cacti with dazzling flowers all bewilder the newcomer. The range is so diverse that anyone with a love of plants will find at least one group of interest.

Many cacti and succulents are quite tough and much easier to grow than people suspect. They are ideal plants for the beginner and grow well as pot plants indoors, in a conservatory or in a greenhouse. In warmer climates, they can make a splendid contribution to the planting in a garden. Through this book, I hope to share some of these plants with you. The information and advice that is given in the text and illustrated in the many colour photographs, most of which were taken at Holly Gate, should prove useful to both beginners and enthusiasts.

I am fortunate in having had the opportunity to make my hobby my work (and it is still my hobby). Over the years, I have met many cactus collectors from different parts of the globe and most are keen, friendly and generous. While some can be dogmatic, most are eager to discuss the plants and share their knowledge. Their fervour is contagious and I have made many good friends across the world.

In my opinion, the only "experts" who know all about cacti and succulents are those people who possess approximately 20 plants. As soon as you have acquired a few more species, you begin to realize that you do not know as much as you thought. As the collection expands, you discover that in fact there is more and more to learn about the subject. When you have amassed a large collection, you recognize that plants, like people, do not always obey the rules that have been laid down for them.

Plants in the wild are not conveniently labelled, so a universal system of botanical names was devised for them. Unfortunately, cacti and succulents are notoriously difficult to classify into neat groups. They are extremely adaptable plants that often hybridize very readily and, in the wild, vary hugely in form according to local conditions. Plants from different groups that grow in the same habitat can evolve, or converge, to look very similar. On the other hand, plants of the same species that live in different regions may diverge in appearance until they look as if they belong to completely different groups.

Individual botanists also emphasize different plant characteristics when they are classifying cacti and succulents, which often leads to clashes of opinion and confusion about the identity of a particular plant. Until very recently the classification of the cactus family had been based on an old system, which was constantly updated, with plant species being lumped together under the same name and then being separated out again by various botanists.

Common names are just as confusing because they are based on local cultures and are often applied inappropriately or to more than one species. For example, many succulents in the *Agave* genus are called aloes although they are botanically distinct from the *Aloe* genus and both *Crassula arborescens* and *Dudleya brittonii* are known as silver dollar plants.

Precision in nomenclature is not important to the beginner, but the keen grower, in order to choose plants, needs to be able to distinguish between plants that seem to differ, or those that look the same.

To make matters easier, for all plant names in this book I have followed two major authorities. The Convention on International Trade in Endangered Species of Wild Fauna and Flora (CITES) recently sponsored the CITES *Cactaceae Checklist* (compiled by David Hunt, Royal Botanic Gardens, Kew, 1992), which reduces the number of cactus species from over 6,000 to just over 3,500 species. For succulents, I have adhered to the classification system used in

Hermann Jacobsen's *Lexicon of Succulent Plants* (Blandford Press, 1974), which is still widely used. I have also included in the index any old plant names, or synonyms, which may still be in use. These are cross-referenced to the current names used in the book's Plant Catalogue, so that relevant information is not missed for want of a name.

The important thing is to have fun growing cacti and succulents. Once you have accumulated a few plants, a great deal of satisfaction can be achieved by sowing a few seeds and watching them grow and flower for the first time. Batches of seedlings can show a marked variability and it is often hard to decide which of them to part with when thinning them out.

To ensure their continued survival, collection of many wild species is now banned. Many of those species that are threatened by extinction are more likely to be at risk from climatic changes, urbanization, pollution or agricultural expansion than from collecting, but there is no need to endanger wild populations still further by taking specimens from their habitats. The more cacti and succulents that are propagated and grown in cultivation, the better they are understood, and by entrusting specimens to enthusiastic amateurs, the chances of survival for rarer species is increased.

Lastly, a warning: once bitten by the cactus collecting bug there is no known cure!

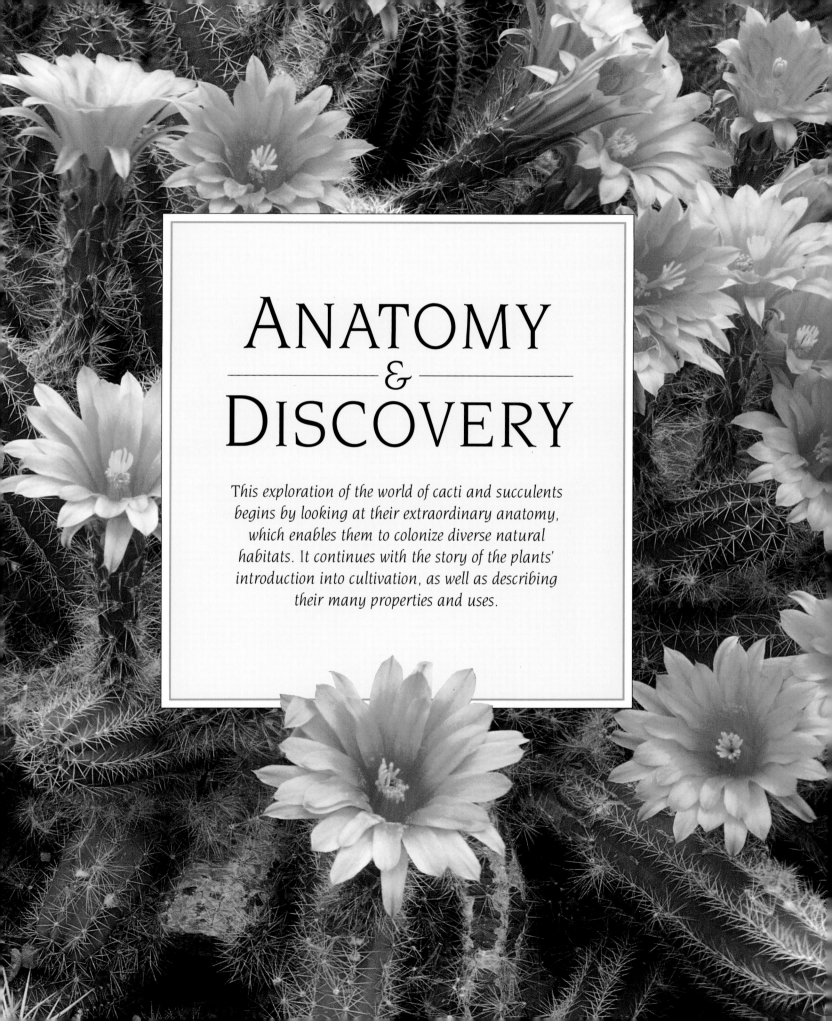

ANATOMY
&
DISCOVERY

This exploration of the world of cacti and succulents
begins by looking at their extraordinary anatomy,
which enables them to colonize diverse natural
habitats. It continues with the story of the plants'
introduction into cultivation, as well as describing
their many properties and uses.

WHAT ARE CACTI AND SUCCULENTS?

SUCCULENT PLANTS, INCLUDING the cactus family, have a highly specialized anatomy to enable them to survive prolonged drought. All are able to store moisture in fleshy tissue in their stems, roots or leaves and most have developed distinctive features to help reduce water loss and withstand their hostile habitats. They can also cease active growth and become dormant in severe conditions. The bizarre appearance of these plants reflects a unique evolution, in which plant form, function and survival are inextricably linked. Cacti are distinguishable from other succulents by their areoles, or pad-like buds (see below).

STEM SUCCULENTS

These plants retain large volumes of watery mucus in their swollen stems, which are most often round, columnar or barrel-shaped. Nearly all cacti are stem succulents and do not have any leaves, so reducing moisture loss through evaporation. The stems contain chlorophyll used in photosynthesis.

Some jungle cacti are epiphytes, which anchor themselves by their roots to other plants or in crevices where there is decaying vegetation. These stem succulents do not need to conserve moisture in the humid shade of the jungle. Instead, they mostly have flattened stems with a large surface area to absorb as much light as possible.

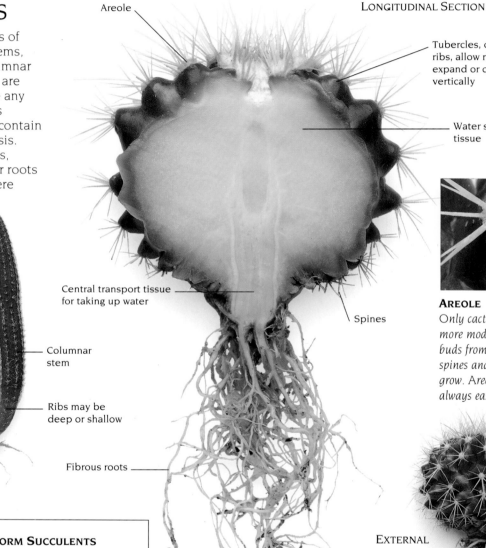

Areole

LONGITUDINAL SECTION

Tubercles, or notched ribs, allow ribs to expand or contract vertically

Water storage tissue

Central transport tissue for taking up water

Spines

Columnar stem

Ribs may be deep or shallow

Fibrous roots

RIBBED STEM

Stem succulents are often ribbed like a concertina, allowing them to expand or contract sideways as their water stocks are restored or depleted.

AREOLE
Only cacti have one or more modified, pad-like buds from which shoots, spines and flowers grow. Areoles are not always easily visible.

EXTERNAL VIEW

CAUDICIFORM SUCCULENTS
Some succulents that grow in very harsh habitats with thin soil have a caudex, or swollen base, formed from both root and stem. This provides the plant with greater capacity to store moisture. Such plants are known as caudiciform, but the term is used more broadly for any succulent with a swollen stem or root above ground.

GLOBULAR STEM SUCCULENT
A sphere is the optimum shape for a stem succulent as it has the smallest possible surface area in proportion to volume, keeping water loss to a minimum.

ROOT SUCCULENTS

A number of succulents survive prolonged dry conditions by storing water underground in their tuberous, or swollen, roots. As the roots are below the soil, moisture loss occurs relatively slowly and there is less risk of damage to the plant from grazing animals or bush fires. The leaves or stems of many root succulents are deciduous; other species' top-growth is shed during long droughts and then regenerates from the roots. The stems or leaves can be thick and fleshy, providing the plant with additional water-storing capacity, as in *Senecio coccineiflorus*, shown below. Root succulents with large tubers such as *Brachystelma* are grown in cultivation with the tuber exposed to guard against rot.

WATER-SEEKING ROOTS

Most cacti and succulents live in deserts and must be able to collect moisture from dewfalls or sporadic rains quickly, before the precious water evaporates. Many have very shallow, but extensive, fibrous root systems that spread out just beneath the soil surface, enabling the plant to take up water from a wide area. If the ground becomes damp, the plants immediately form new root hairs to collect water. Epiphytes produce aerial roots from their stems to seek out moisture in dry conditions.

EXTERNAL VIEW

Fleshy leaves

LONGITUDINAL SECTION

ROOT SUCCULENT
This succulent's main water-storing tissue lies in the tuberous roots. It also has a fleshy stem and leaves.

Succulent stem

Swollen, potato-like storage roots

Fibrous roots

Simple leaves have few pores to reduce evaporation

LEAF SUCCULENTS

This large group includes the cactus *Pereskia* and many succulents, which vary greatly in form, from *Senecio rowleyanus* with bead-like leaves to the dagger-like foliage of many *Haworthia*. These plants store water in their thick fleshy leaves, which shrivel in drought and swell up again when water is available. In very long droughts, the leaves are shed.

Some leaf succulents, such as *Lithops*, that live in very arid habitats consist of little more than a pair of united leaves. Most of the time, they are buried in the soil with just the leaf tips exposed to the sun. Their stone-like appearance camouflages them from grazing animals.

Window

Leaf pair

New leaf bud

PROTECTIVE "WINDOWS"
Calcium oxalate in the translucent cells at the leaf tips diffuses the hot sun before it reaches the plant body.

Fleshy leaves store water

LEAF SUCCULENT
Many leaf succulents have virtually no stems, forming low rosettes of overlapping leaves, which help reduce evaporation from both the plant and the soil beneath.

SURFACES

Cacti and succulents have developed a wide range of surface textures. These often striking features are the result of adaptation to different habitats, but they have similar protective functions. For example, some species from high altitudes or areas with fogs have a felted or hairy surface that helps to trap moisture from the air. In drier regions, highly coloured foliage filters out the strong light. Succulent leaves and cacti stems have few stomata, or surface pores, to minimize water loss. Unlike other plants, these pores are closed by day. When the temperature drops at night, the pores open to absorb carbon dioxide, which is used the next day for photosynthesis, or food production.

Leaf with powdery bloom

Waxy leaf

Downy leaf

Glossy stem

LEAF AND STEM TEXTURES
Some leaves have a leathery or glossy surface, others a waxy coating. Leaves with a very thick waxy layer appear to have a powdery bloom. All these surfaces reduce evaporation and help to deflect the sun's rays. Fine hairs act as insulation against extreme heat or cold. Other species have more conventional barky stems.

Bark-like stem

SPINES AND THORNS

Nearly all cacti and some succulents have spines, which are modified leaves. Cacti spines grow from areoles (see p. 10) and detach easily, but succulent spines grow directly from the stem tissue. Spines vary greatly in shape, texture and length: some are short and bristly; others are softly curved but viciously barbed. They can be coloured in various hues from white, red or yellow to black. Although spines provide a defence against predators, their main function is to condense moisture so that it drips on to the ground above the plant roots. Woolly, hair-like spines also help to shield plants from cold or fierce sun. Some succulents have thorns, which are either modified flowers, leaf stalks or leaf buds.

PSEUDOCEPHALIUM
This mass of woolly spines grows on one side of the stem. Only Melocactus (see inset) and Discocactus have a true cephalium on the crown.

NEEDLE-LIKE SPINES
Many cacti, especially globular species such as Parodia, have fine, straight, sharp spines, which are often strikingly coloured.

FISH-HOOK SPINES
Broad curved spines with a sharp point are coloured red or yellow on many barrel cacti.

TEETH AND SPINES
The sawteeth and terminal spines on succulent rosettes are out-growths of the leaf margins.

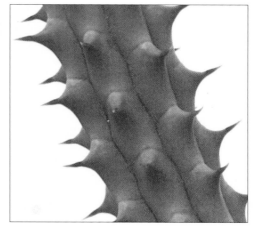

THORNS
Some succulents, such as Huernia, develop thorns that grow directly from the stem tissue.

FLOWERS

In very arid regions, where long dry spells enforce a dormant state for most of the year, many cacti and succulents have developed a very short growing season. Once rain falls, they burst into growth, forming leaves, flowers and seeds in less than a month. Cactus flowers have evolved in several ways to attract pollinators. Most desert cacti are day-flowering and produce brightly coloured, unscented blooms that attract flying insects. Many jungle cacti have large blooms that open at dusk; these are pale and richly perfumed so that pollinating moths can easily locate them. By contrast, some night-flowering species have foul-smelling, fleshy flowers that are attractive to bats. Others have tubular flowers to accommodate the long beaks of hummingbirds. Some succulents have cacti-like flowers but others possess more conventional flowers. Sometimes succulents bear tiny flowers surrounded by petal-like leaf bracts.

FRUITS AND SEEDS

Once the flower has been pollinated, it withers and the ovary develops into a fruit containing seed. Many cacti have fleshy fruits or berries. Succulent seeds and fruits are very diverse and are distributed by water, wind, insects, birds or rodents. *Mesembryanthemum* seeds are sealed in woody pods, which open when dampened by rain so that some of the seeds are washed out to germinate while water is available. If the pods dry out, they close up until it rains again.

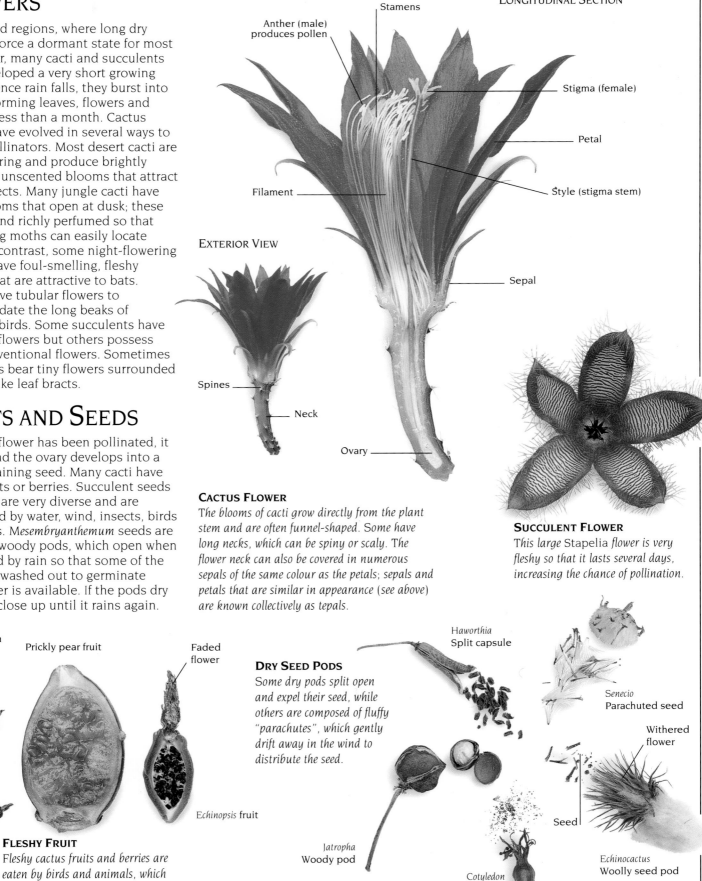

LONGITUDINAL SECTION

Stamens

Anther (male) produces pollen

Stigma (female)

Petal

Style (stigma stem)

Filament

Sepal

Ovary

EXTERIOR VIEW

Spines

Neck

CACTUS FLOWER

The blooms of cacti grow directly from the plant stem and are often funnel-shaped. Some have long necks, which can be spiny or scaly. The flower neck can also be covered in numerous sepals of the same colour as the petals; sepals and petals that are similar in appearance (see above) are known collectively as tepals.

SUCCULENT FLOWER

This large Stapelia *flower is very fleshy so that it lasts several days, increasing the chance of pollination.*

Rhipsalis stem with berries

Prickly pear fruit

Faded flower

Echinopsis fruit

FLESHY FRUIT

Fleshy cactus fruits and berries are eaten by birds and animals, which disperse the seeds in their droppings.

DRY SEED PODS

Some dry pods split open and expel their seed, while others are composed of fluffy "parachutes", which gently drift away in the wind to distribute the seed.

Haworthia Split capsule

Senecio Parachuted seed

Withered flower

Seed

Jatropha Woody pod

Cotyledon Dust-like seed

Echinocactus Woolly seed pod

NATURAL HABITATS

CONTRARY TO POPULAR BELIEF, succulents and cacti do not inhabit only conventional deserts. They have a rich range of habitats, from snow-clad Alpine slopes and arid Colorado plains to humid jungles in the Amazon basin. They grow in conditions that often seem inimical to survival and indeed their success partly depends on lack of competition from other, less robust plant life. Looking at their habitats reveals much about their evolution and cultural needs.

DESERT PLAINS

In harsh dry habitats, cacti and succulents reign unchallenged, enduring great temperature extremes of scorching days and freezing nights. Although a few can survive without water for years at a stretch and live in true deserts, which have less than 25 cm (10 in) of rainfall a year, most grow in semi-deserts, which receive sporadic rainfalls between droughts. Semi-deserts have very poor soil with sparse vegetation and rocky outcrops, rather than pure sand. The rainfall is sometimes augmented by heavy dews or coastal mists.

Cacti and succulents may grow in small pockets, as on Argentine savannahs, or in large colonies (see right). On dry plains and plateaux, known as chaparrals in Mexico or veldt in South Africa, small plants like *Haworthia* thrive in the shade of grasses and scrub, and even survive occasional bush fires.

Desert cacti and succulents have the capacity to conserve moisture and withstand drought, by becoming dormant, and to produce new growth in favourable conditions. This growth pattern can be copied by keeping the plants dry in their dormant period and watering them in the growing season.

DESERT IN BLOOM, above
A rare fall of rain can stimulate a dramatic spurt of growth, with every succulent plant rapidly flowering and setting seed before returning to a semi-dormant state.

ARID LANDSCAPE, right
In the parched desert of Baja California in Mexico, colonies of Pachycereus cacti tower over low succulents and scrub. The thick columnar cacti stems can store enough moisture to enable them to survive long droughts.

SNOW SURVIVAL, below
An occasional desert snowfall insulates the cacti against the night cold and, when the snow melts, provides their roots with water.

MOUNTAINOUS DESERTS

In mountainous terrain, including high plateaux, screes and rocky slopes, the soil is often very thin, does not retain much water and has a high mineral content that can be toxic to non-succulent plants. In a mountain desert like the Andes, conditions vary dramatically with the altitude and so, too, do the native cacti and succulents. On high peaks, plants are exposed to intense sunlight, night-time temperatures as low as -20°C (-4°F), fierce winds and snow. Above the cloud layer, there is often no rain but the plants gain moisture from melting snow. Only small globular or creeping cacti and succulents can survive such conditions, but lower down, where the slope affords some shelter, larger succulents and columnar cacti can grow. Here, the cloud belt diffuses the harsh sunlight and provides some moisture. On dry overcast foothills below the clouds, small cushion cacti predominate.

As a shield from the harsh cold and brilliant sun, many cacti in mountain regions have a dense coat of woolly spines, and succulents develop thick waxy skins. Low-growing succulents also grow in many rocky habitats in temperate regions. *Sempervivum* species colonize the alpine parts of Europe, and many *Sedum* thrive in much of the Northern Hemisphere. Even the soil-less wastes of lava rock in the Galapagos Islands provide a home for cacti such as *Brachycereus nesioticus*.

ROCKY FOOTHOLD
In mountain regions, cacti like these Mammillaria *and succulents often lodge themselves in rocky crevices where enough water collects for them to survive. The rocks also provide shelter from winds and retain the heat from the sun. Cultivated plants can be grown in this way, tucked into wall crevices or even between roof tiles.*

CACTI BY THE SEA

Although rarely thought of as coastal plants, cacti such as these Pachycereus *grow on rugged mountain foothills overlooking the sea. In this type of terrain, they can obtain vital moisture from the sea mists that roll in over the shore.*

HIGH-ALTITUDE HABITAT

Few plants can grow in the hostile conditions found on high rocky slopes like these in Mexico. Columnar cacti that branch at the base and robust barrel cacti are able to withstand the strong winds that sweep across exposed hillsides.

JUNGLES

Although most cacti and succulents grow in arid deserts and mountain areas, many species inhabit subtropical and tropical rainforests such as those in Central and South America, Africa, Sri Lanka and the West Indies. Here, the climate is constantly hot and humid and sunlight is filtered through a thick tree canopy. Cacti and succulents are amply provided with moisture from the atmosphere and regular rainfalls, so they have adapted to survive a lack of light rather than water, although they can survive periods of drought. Similarly, in cultivation, these plants are best grown in humid light shade.

Many jungle cacti such as flamboyantly flowered *Epiphyllum*, and some succulents like *Hoya*, which grow in northeastern Australia, are epiphytes. They anchor themselves to the stems of other plants or grow in pockets of decaying leaves. Often they inhabit the upper branches of trees where there is more light. Other species have a climbing or scrambling habit, which enables them to grow over or through other plants toward the light.

A few succulents inhabit the gloom of the forest floor and some small cacti such as *Gymnocalycium* grow in the broken shade of rainforest margins.

AERIAL CACTI, above
In Venezuelan and other tropical rainforests or jungles, epiphytic cacti such as Aporocactus swathe the branches of trees with their long trailing stems.

JUNGLE GIANTS, right
Tree-like succulents that grow on the jungle floor, such as Espeletia schultzii, often have a mass of broad leaves to maximize absorption of the limited light that is filtered through the thick canopy of foliage above them.

DISCOVERY AND DISTRIBUTION

ORIGINALLY, CACTI GREW ONLY on the American continent. Succulents were native to many regions from northern Europe to the Far East, although most were concentrated in southern and eastern Africa. As the map shows, exploration and trading over the last four centuries and natural distribution enabled cacti and succulents to establish in new habitats across the world.

MAJOR EXPEDITIONS

In the late 15th century, the race to find fresh sea routes to India and its riches gave rise to a surge in European exploration and so to discovery of new plants. Christopher Columbus is reputed to be the first to have taken cacti to Europe; he found weird, leafless plants in the West Indies (*Melocactus* and *Opuntia*) and presented them to Queen Isabella of Spain. Meanwhile, the Portuguese discovered a wealth of succulents in Africa and India. Like da Gama (see box), Bartolemeu Dias landed at several bays in southwestern Africa and found *Aloe* and *Gasteria* species, among many others. Spanish missionaries colonized Central and parts of northern South America in the next two centuries and sent cacti to Europe on their trading ships. In the 17th century, the Dutch East India Company, which was formed to exploit trade routes to the African Cape, shipped many succulents to Holland and thence to the Royal Botanic Gardens at Kew.

As interest in cacti and succulents grew, botanical expeditions became more frequent. Between 1777 and 1787, King Charles III of Spain sponsored several major expeditions to America. Captain Arthur Phillip, founder of Sydney, introduced *Opuntia* cacti into Australia in 1788 to establish a cochineal dye industry (see p. 25). But the high-point for explorers such as Thomas Bridges (see box) and botanists who specialized in cacti and succulents came in the 19th century. The botanist Thomas Nuttall travelled widely, from North Dakota to New Orleans, San Diego and the southern U.S.A., while he was based in Philadelphia. He discovered many new species, including some *Coryphantha*.

More recently, Dr Joseph Nelson Rose collected cacti in almost every South American country, as well as the West Indies, Baja California and the southern U.S.A. He donated many new species to the Ministry of Agriculture and the Carnegie Institute in Washington. Even today, new species are constantly being introduced into cultivation.

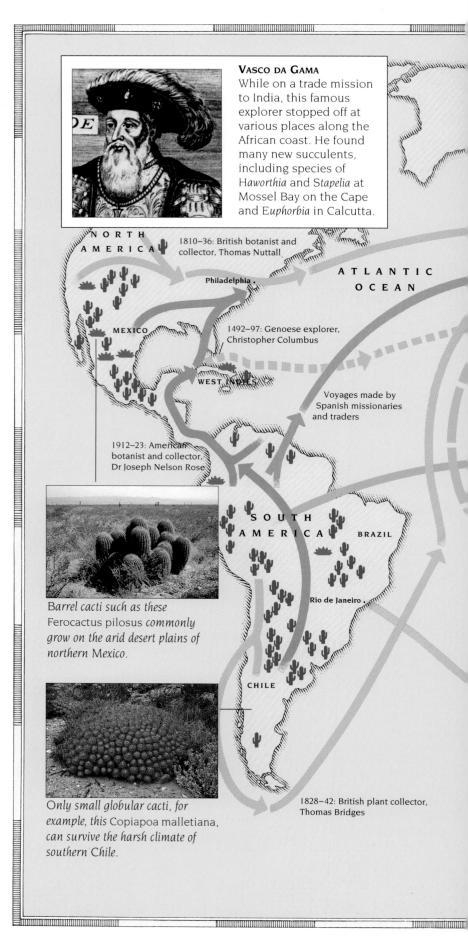

VASCO DA GAMA
While on a trade mission to India, this famous explorer stopped off at various places along the African coast. He found many new succulents, including species of *Haworthia* and *Stapelia* at Mossel Bay on the Cape and *Euphorbia* in Calcutta.

NORTH AMERICA

1810–36: British botanist and collector, Thomas Nuttall

Philadelphia

ATLANTIC OCEAN

MEXICO

1492–97: Genoese explorer, Christopher Columbus

WEST INDIES

Voyages made by Spanish missionaries and traders

1912–23: American botanist and collector, Dr Joseph Nelson Rose

SOUTH AMERICA

BRAZIL

Barrel cacti such as these Ferocactus pilosus *commonly grow on the arid desert plains of northern Mexico.*

Rio de Janeiro

CHILE

Only small globular cacti, for example, this Copiapoa malletiana, *can survive the harsh climate of southern Chile.*

1828–42: British plant collector, Thomas Bridges

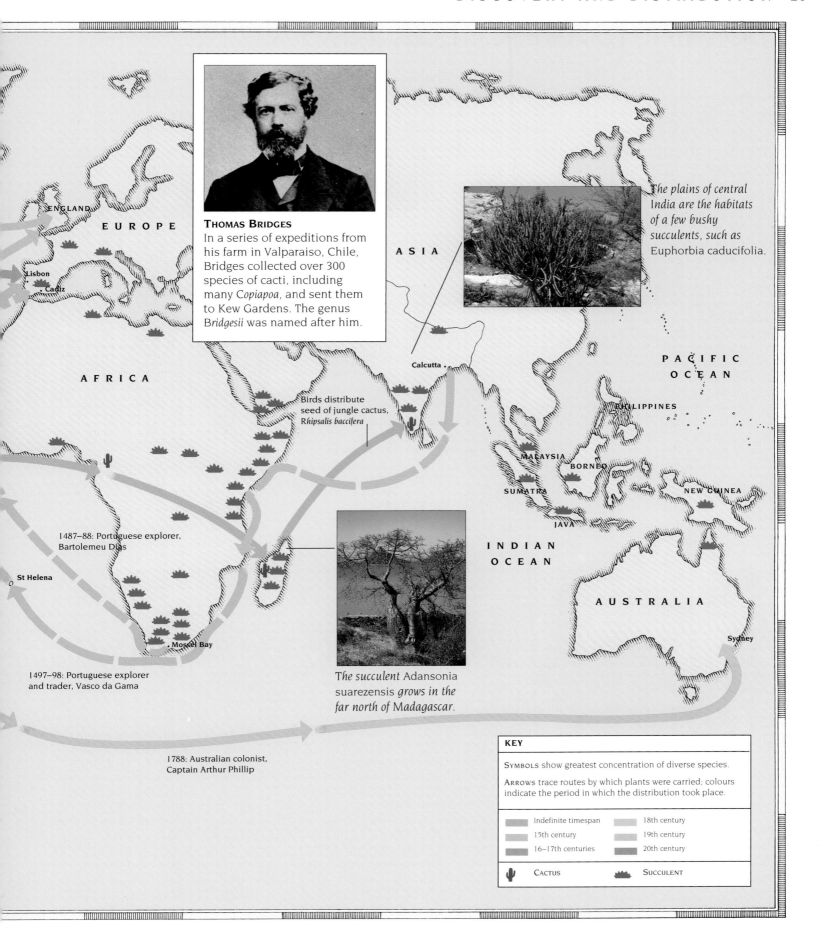

THOMAS BRIDGES
In a series of expeditions from his farm in Valparaiso, Chile, Bridges collected over 300 species of cacti, including many *Copiapoa*, and sent them to Kew Gardens. The genus *Bridgesii* was named after him.

The plains of central India are the habitats of a few bushy succulents, such as Euphorbia caducifolia.

ENGLAND

EUROPE

Lisbon

Cadiz

AFRICA

ASIA

Calcutta

PACIFIC OCEAN

PHILIPPINES

MALAYSIA

BORNEO

SUMATRA

NEW GUINEA

JAVA

Birds distribute seed of jungle cactus, *Rhipsalis baccifera*

1487–88: Portuguese explorer, Bartolemeu Dias

St Helena

The succulent Adansonia suarezensis *grows in the far north of Madagascar.*

INDIAN OCEAN

AUSTRALIA

Mossel Bay

Sydney

1497–98: Portuguese explorer and trader, Vasco da Gama

1788: Australian colonist, Captain Arthur Phillip

KEY

SYMBOLS show greatest concentration of diverse species.

ARROWS trace routes by which plants were carried; colours indicate the period in which the distribution took place.

Indefinite timespan		18th century
15th century		19th century
16–17th centuries		20th century

CACTUS	SUCCULENT

BOTANISTS AND COLLECTORS

BEFORE EARLY EXPLORERS such as Columbus stumbled upon these strange plants in their native habitats, all cacti and many succulents were known only to the local native populations. A few plants were first introduced into Europe in the 15th and the 16th centuries as curiosities, but once more species were described and classified by botanists in the 17th century, interest in the plants increased. Wealthy collectors sponsored botanists to search out new species with which to build up public and private gardens. Cacti and succulents are still collected today, but attention is focused on conservation.

ANCIENT CIVILIZATIONS

Cacti were well known to the Inca civilization in Peru, the Aztecs of Mexico and the North American Indians long before European explorers and collectors discovered them. The plants were familiar elements of their everyday environments and were frequently incorporated into their cultures, having religious significance as well as many practical uses. The Indians were well acquainted with the intoxicating effect of the sap of some cacti and the ancient cult which uses the cactus *Lophophora* in its ceremonies still exists today.

In Africa, the Bantu, Bushmen and Kaffir tribes have exploited the many indigenous succulent species for centuries, finding many different uses for them (see pp. 24–5). No African religious rites involving succulents, however, have been recorded.

FOUNDING OF A CITY

According to legend, an Aztec priest dreamed that Huitzilopochtli, the God of the Sun, told the Aztecs to build a capital city where they saw an eagle perched on a tall cactus. They did so, in 1325, as recorded in an Aztec manuscript of 1541(right), which shows the site of Tenochtitlán, the new capital, and the ten Aztec tribes that built it. The town became Mexico City and the symbol of an eagle and a cactus is still used on its flag.

CLASSIFICATION

Many of the earliest recorded cacti and succulents appear in English herbals of the late 16th century. The most famous of these is John Gerard's *The Herball or Generall Historie of Plants*, published in 1597. In his book, Gerard described four cactus species: the "Hedgehogge Thistle", which was in fact a *Melocactus*; the "Torch or Thorne Euphorbium", a *Cereus*; the "Thorne Reede of Peru", another *Cereus*; and the "Indian Fig Tree", now known to be an *Opuntia*.

Many of the succulent plants gathered by early travellers were classified by the Swedish botanist Linnaeus in his *Species Plantarum* in 1753. Other botanists of the time who mentioned cacti included Philip Miller, whose *Gardener's Dictionary* of 1731 classified cacti into four genera, and Richard Bradley, who saw many new species of succulent sent to Amsterdam by explorers and traders. In 1718 he published his *History of Succulent Plants*. Like Gerard, Bradley described *Cereus* as a torch thistle, but he also lists the "star-pointed ficoid or fig marigold", known today as *Trichodiadema stellatum*.

Cacti and succulents were shipped to Europe in increasing numbers as trade routes opened up because the plants could survive long sea voyages without soil on their roots. The Royal Botanic Gardens at Kew first sent a collector, Francis Masson, to South Africa in 1772. He sailed with Captain Cook on the ship *Endeavour*, and in three years gathered over 100 succulents for classification, including some *Euphorbia*, *Stapelia* and many *Mesembryanthemum* species. The period 1845–83 was a fruitful time for discovery and the recording of cacti and succulents and many new species were named after collectors and botanists of the time, such as Humboldt, Engelmann, Bridges (see p. 21) and Wislizenus. This also led to much confusion of names.

A major work of classification, *The Cactaceae*, published in four volumes in 1919–23 by Britton and Rose (see p. 20), and Curt Backeberg's six-volume *Die Cactaceae* in 1958–62 did much to rationalize cacti names. On succulents, Jacobsen's *Lexicon of Succulent Plants* (1974) remains an invaluable reference.

HOW THE CACTUS GOT ITS NAME

Carolus Linnaeus (1707–78) created a universal system of botanical plant names, based on Latin and Greek, that is still in use today. Linnaeus first chose the Greek word kaktos, *meaning thistle, to name the cactus family.*

Great Collectors

The first private collections of cacti and succulents were created in the 17th century, when plants and seed became available. Only the wealthy owners of heated orangeries could provide the necessary conditions of light and warmth. The Hortus Medicus garden in Amsterdam was set up at this time, mainly to grow medicinal plants for doctors. As early as 1820, greenhouse gardens were all the rage. Most collectors were noblemen, such as the English Dukes of Devonshire and of Bedford, who could afford to build large greenhouses and heat them with steam.

By 1835, the German Prince Salm-Dyck had one of the best collections of cacti and succulents in Europe. He studied his plants carefully and painted fine portraits of them. The Russian Prince Kotschoubey of St Petersburg funded many collectors. In 1830, one of them named an *Ariocarpus* cactus after the Prince and sold another *Ariocarpus* for 1,000 francs, which far exceeded the value of the plant's weight in gold.

In 1850, the craze was at its height; the general public flocked to admire the strange plants at gardens such as Kew and huge sums were paid for cactus plants. But by the century's end, the increasing cost of funding expeditions and a new enthusiasm for orchids led to declining interest in cacti and many fine old collections were broken up.

GARDENERS OF PRIVILEGE
Until the 20th century, most gardens and major collections of cacti and succulents were owned by the wealthy, who became patrons of botanists in return for new species for their gardens.

Gardens and Conservation

EXOTIC COLLECTION
One of the most famous botanical gardens with a collection of cacti and succulents is the steeply terraced Jardin Exotique in Monaco.

Today, interest in cacti and succulents as both garden and indoor plants is as strong as it ever was and there are national cactus and succulent societies in many countries. Botanists continue to discover new species in the wild and their research uses modern technology, such as electron microscopes and computers, to provide an increasing store of knowledge about the strange anatomy of these plants.

Impressive collections of cacti and succulents have been established in various parts of the world, in both private gardens and botanical institutions. Among the best known are the Huntington Botanical Garden, California, the collection at Zürich in Switzerland, the Palmengarten in Frankfurt, Germany, and the oldest surviving collection at the Royal Botanic Gardens, Kew. A collection in Brisbane, Australia has also been established.

As with many other groups of plants, the conservation of cacti and succulents has gained increasing importance in this century. Greater control is required to protect endangered species in the wild, not only from unscrupulous collectors and smugglers, but also from ever-expanding numbers of grazing herds and from land development, climatic changes, pollution, and the depletion of natural pollinators.

The collection of some species of cacti and succulents from the wild is now illegal in many countries. Bodies such as the International Union for the Conservation of Nature, or I.U.C.N, encourage growers to raise rare species from seed, rather than buy plants that may have been taken from the wild.

PROPERTIES AND USES

THE APPEAL OF CACTI AND SUCCULENTS lies in their intriguing and unusual appearance, but many of these astonishing species also have a hidden value. From ancient times, they have been used as a source of food, drink and medicine and even for making tools and constructing buildings. Their use in the future promises to be even more diverse. The cactus *Cereus hildmannianus* may have the potential to absorb harmful radiation from VDU screens, and the stems of certain *Opuntia* can be processed to produce an alcohol fuel, which could be used in place of petrol; unlike fossil fuels, cacti are a renewable resource.

FOOD AND DRINK

Few plants look less edible than cacti and succulents, so it is surprising to learn that many species are cooked and eaten as vegetables, while others produce mouth-watering fruits. The best known fruits are from *Opuntia ficus-indica* (prickly pear); the yellow, white or red fruits are commonly sold in Mexican markets and are also available in Australia and many Mediterranean countries. The claret cup hedgehog cactus, *Echinocereus triglochidiatus*, has fruits that become pink when ripe and are made into a delicious jam.

On the high plains of Bolivia, the cactus *Neowerdermannia vorwerkii* is cooked and eaten in the same way as potatoes, and in Mexico, the flat joints of young stems of *Opuntia subulata* are peeled, cut up and boiled to make *nopalitos*. The tubers of *Ceropegia* and *Brachystelma* form part of the diet, in the southern African bush, of the Bantu and Bushmen tribes. Some cacti and succulents can even be made into sweets: pieces of the aromatic, sweet-sour flesh of *Ferocactus wislizeni* are candied in a sugar solution.

Perhaps the most internationally well-known product is tequila, the fiery distilled liquor from Mexico that is made from the boiled and fermented hearts of *Agave* plants. *Agave* species are the source of another local alcoholic drink called *pulque*, which is made from the hearts' sap.

PRICKLY PEAR
The ripe fruits are eaten raw or made into jam; the yellow fruit (above) is the sweetest.

TASTE OF TEQUILA
Tequila is traditionally drunk neat, accompanied by a pinch of salt and a squeeze of lime.

NATURAL BEAUTY
Clear sticky Aloe sap is used in moisturizers, aftershaves, skin preparations and shampoos.

COSMETICS AND MEDICINES

Succulents and cacti, like many other plants, have been used since ancient times as a source of cosmetics and medicines. The healing properties of *Aloe* species were known to the Greeks and Romans who used them to treat a variety of ailments, from serious wounds to mild skin complaints. These same properties are recognized today; the mucilaginous sap from freshly split leaves can be applied directly to the skin to soothe minor cuts and burns.

The *Aloe* is also a popular natural ingredient in cosmetics; its sap is added to a wide range of beauty products. *Aloe barbadensis* (syn. *A. vera*) is the most commonly used species in the cosmetics industry and it is cultivated extensively in Florida, Texas and the West Indies.

Queen of the night, the night-flowering *Selenicereus grandiflorus*, also has therapeutic properties. Its freshly cut blooms are used in the preparation of medicines for improving blood circulation and the cactus is cultivated widely in South American countries for this purpose.

In the early 20th century, the fleshy tuber of *Testudinaria elephantipes* was used as a source of cortisone, an anti-inflammatory agent. Many *Testudinaria* species are still used today in the manufacture of the contraceptive pill.

A small species of cactus, *Lophophora williamsii*, known as *peyote*, was valued in the past for its medicinal uses as a treatment for disorders such as rheumatism and asthma. The Aztecs believed that this "sacred mushroom" had mystical powers because it has hallucinogenic properties. Although it is still used today by some North American Indians in their religious ceremonies, possession of the cactus is now illegal in many countries.

PRODUCTS AND MATERIALS

Cacti and succulents have other unexpected uses, most of which have been developed throughout the Americas and in Africa where the plants have always grown wild. For example, the cactus *Oreocereus celsianus*, a native of Argentina and Bolivia, has fine, soft, hairy spines that are gathered and used like wool to stuff pillows and bedding.

Commercially, the most important succulent is *Agave sisalana*, which is used to make rope, as well as twine, sacking and rough matting. It is grown widely in Kenya and also in Madagascar, where forests have been cleared to make way for large *Agave* plantations.

In the past, succulents provided the Indians from northern Mexico with a way to catch fish: the stems of *Stenocereus gummosus* were crushed and thrown into the water to release their toxic sap, stupefying the fish, which could then be scooped up easily by hand. In southern Africa, the poisonous sap of *Euphorbia cereiformis*, E. *heptagona* and E. *virosa* was boiled into a syrup and then applied to arrow tips for hunting.

Perhaps the oldest tradition of cultivating cacti for specific uses dates back to the Aztec civilization, which

flourished in Mexico from the 14th to the 16th century. *Opuntia coccenillifera* was grown by the Aztecs as a host plant for the cochineal beetle, a type of mealy bug. Large quantities of the female insects were crushed to produce a rich purple dye, which was used for colouring royal and ceremonial robes. Male beetles yielded a brilliant scarlet dye. When the Spanish arrived in Mexico in the 16th century, they set up their own cactus plantations and sent the dye back to Spain. Today, cochineal dye is produced extensively in South America for use as an organic food colouring and in lipsticks.

DYE FROM THE PAST
In this 16th-century illustration, Spanish overseers supervize the collection of cochineal beetles for dye.

IMPLEMENTS AND CONSTRUCTION

Almost every part of both cacti and succulents can be exploited for practical purposes. In South America, some cactus spines are used as toothpicks and to make combs, while the long sharp spines of the columnar cactus *Cereus hildmannianus* are used as sewing needles. In Mexico, the curved spines of *Mammillaria bocasana* were employed for many centuries as fish hooks.

The Mexican succulent *Calibanus hookeri* has grass-like leaves that contain a substance similar to soap. This substance, combined with the roughly serrated leaf edges, makes the leaves extremely effective as pot-scourers. *Calibanus hookeri* also yields a plentiful supply of tough leaves, which are ideal for thatching roofs.

In Namibia, the flammable resinous coating of *Sarcocaulon burmannii*, a small shrubby succulent, has earned it the

nickname of "bushman's candle", because the whole plant can be set alight and used as a torch.

Some cacti are surprisingly strong and have woody stem tissue that makes a good construction material in regions where wood is difficult to obtain. In the treeless area along the Bolivian border with Argentina, *Trichocereus pasacana* is used to build houses and also for firewood; in Venezuela, *Pilosocereus* species serve the same purpose.

The columnar habit and fierce spines of some cacti and succulents make them valuable for hedging. *Euphorbia milii*, known as the crown of thorns, is commonly used in this way and is often seen planted as an impenetrable barrier along the centre of wide roads in Madagascar, while in Mexico, the large columnar cactus *Pachycereus marginatus* is grown as a formidable fence.

A LIVING FENCE
Some columnar cacti, such as Pachycereus, *are planted in rows to form a barrier.*

STYLE GUIDE

A dazzling sample of the beautiful shapes and
flower colours of cacti and succulents leads into
a section on how to exploit the decorative qualities
of these plants both indoors and out. Practical
projects show step-by-step how to create imaginative
arrangements in different types of container.

CACTI SHAPES

THE DECORATIVE APPEAL OF CACTI lies predominantly in their strange forms. They bear little resemblance to conventional "leafy" plants, ranging in shape from tiny globes, creeping, candle-like stems and squat barrels to huge, branching candelabra. Their stark profiles give them a sculptural, almost abstract quality, making them striking as feature plants and ideal subjects for the visual drama of a formal composition. The shape of a cactus may be highlighted by spines and the plant body fluted with deeply indented ribs or studded by chunky, divided ribs known as tubercles.

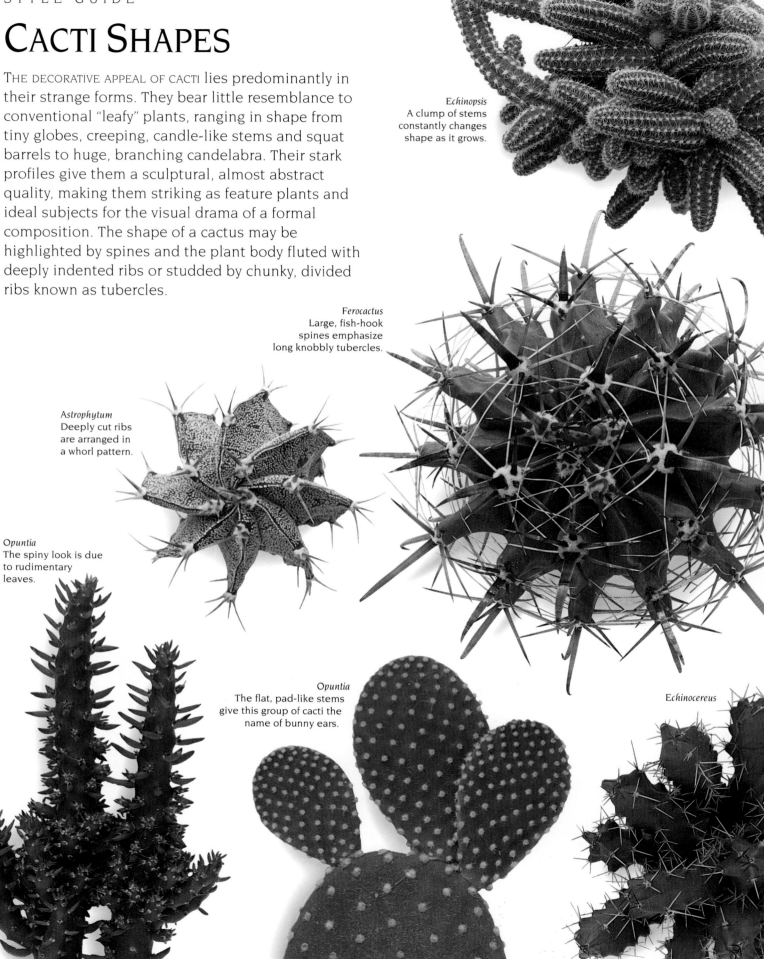

Echinopsis
A clump of stems constantly changes shape as it grows.

Ferocactus
Large, fish-hook spines emphasize long knobbly tubercles.

Astrophytum
Deeply cut ribs are arranged in a whorl pattern.

Opuntia
The spiny look is due to rudimentary leaves.

Opuntia
The flat, pad-like stems give this group of cacti the name of bunny ears.

Echinocereus

Oreocereus
The shape of this cactus is softened by its thick, woolly coat of spines.

Echinopsis
The strong ribs reinforce the linear shape of this cactus.

Echinocactus
Spine cushions, body shape and tubercles all create a bold symmetrical pattern.

Cleistocactus

Cleistocactus
The elegant simplicity of a column is perhaps the most familiar of cacti shapes.

Opuntia
Short jointed stems branch freely to form an irregular shape.

SUCCULENT SHAPES

SUCCULENTS DISPLAY A GREAT DIVERSITY of exotic forms, from simple, cactus-like plants to more complex shrub- or tree-like species that have beautifully shaped leaves and stems as well as attractive outlines. Some plants show the perfect symmetry of the rosette, which may be starkly elegant or softly pretty; others have a more fluid and graceful profile of arching or trailing stems and foliage. There are also some bizarre bulbous or tubular forms. Succulent shapes lend themselves to many differing styles of display and provide a perfect foil for other types of plant in mixed arrangements.

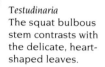

Stem

Testudinaria
The squat bulbous stem contrasts with the delicate, heart-shaped leaves.

Lithops
These are known as living stones because of their smooth rounded shape.

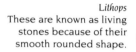

Agave
Long leaves with terminal spines form a spiky rosette.

Echeveria
The symmetrical rosette is a classic succulent shape.

Sedum
Creeping rosettes form leafy mats of foliage.

Echeveria
New offsets echo the shape
of the larger parent plant.

Faucaria
The arrangement of spines
on the leaves gives the
plant the common name,
tiger's jaws.

Crassula
Although bushy in form,
this plant has slender,
lance-shaped leaves.

Kalanchoe
Tiny plantlets adorn the
ends of the tubular leaves.

Cotyledon
The large, spoon-like
leaves are softened
by slightly frilled tips.

STEM AND LEAF SHAPES

SOME CACTUS STEMS look like leaves, some succulent leaves look like stems – and both can vary in form even within a single plant genus. The majority of leaves and stems have strong, fleshy shapes and their visual impact is as powerful as the outline of the plant. Stems and leaves may be deeply serrated, twisted and angular, long and slender, round and fat, scale-like, or delicate and heart-shaped; such a wide array of shapes provides ample scope for effective groups of contrasting and complementary forms.

Crassula
The corrugated appearance of these pendent succulent stems is due to tightly furled leaves.

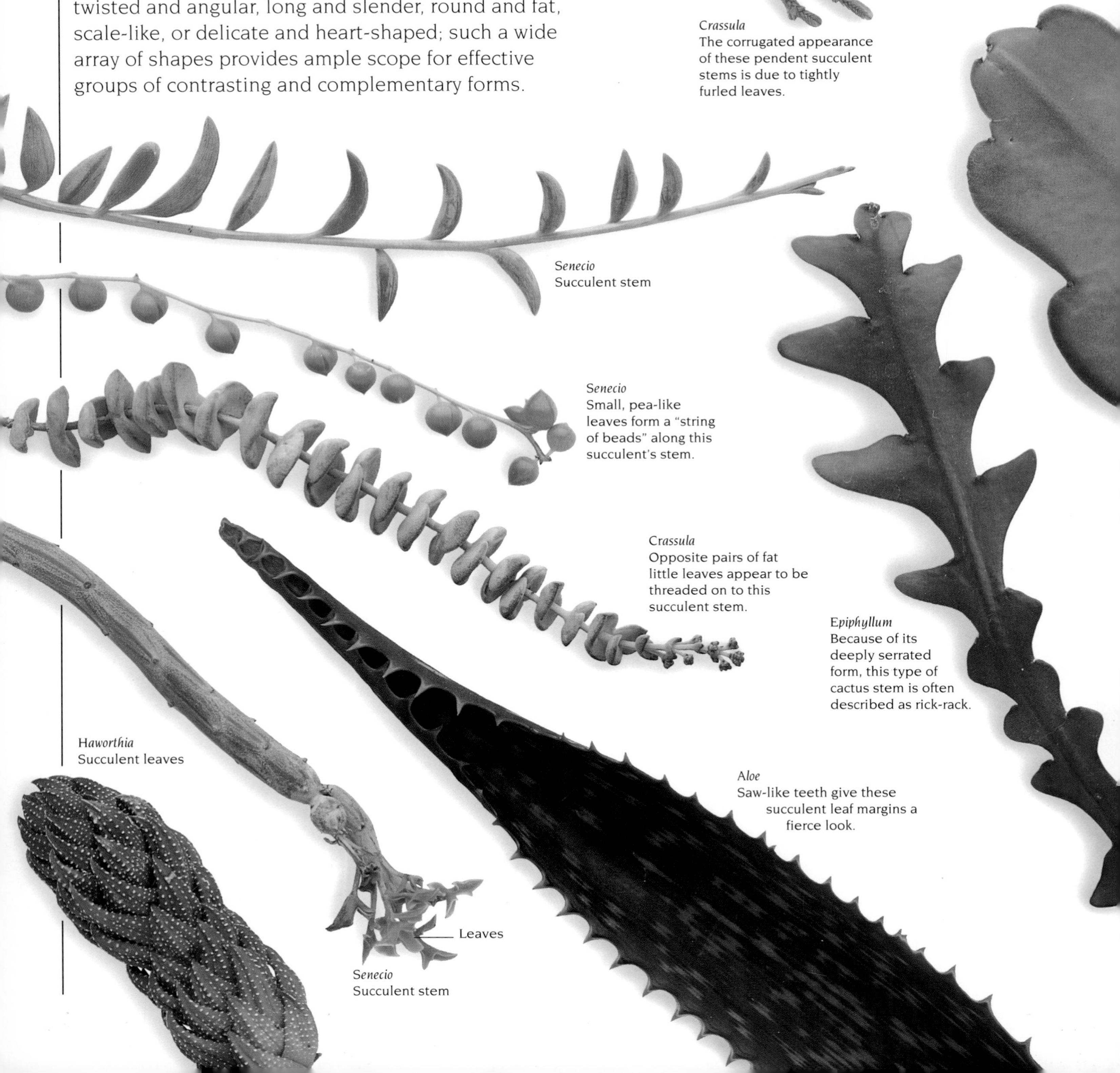

Senecio
Succulent stem

Senecio
Small, pea-like leaves form a "string of beads" along this succulent's stem.

Crassula
Opposite pairs of fat little leaves appear to be threaded on to this succulent stem.

Epiphyllum
Because of its deeply serrated form, this type of cactus stem is often described as rick-rack.

Haworthia
Succulent leaves

Aloe
Saw-like teeth give these succulent leaf margins a fierce look.

Leaves

Senecio
Succulent stem

Heliocereus
This elongated, three-sided cactus stem looks more like a leaf.

Echinopsis
Cactus stem

Senecio
Succulent leaf

Epiphyllum
Cactus stem

Aeonium
Succulent leaf

Testudinaria
Succulent leaf

Crassula
A fleshy oval leaf is common to many succulents.

Crassula
Succulent leaf

Kalanchoe
The elegant line of this arrow-shaped succulent leaf is highlighted by the soft velvety texture.

Epiphyllum
Scalloped edges add a touch of grace to the broad, strap-like cactus stem.

FLOWER COLOURS

WHEN IN BLOOM, both cacti and succulents provide a glorious show: their petals range from pure whites, silvery greys and subtle greens to vibrant reds, hot pinks and dazzling yellows, in a single, vivid wash of colour or blended in strange and exquisite patterns. Commercial hybridizing has added a great many spectacular shades to this palette; only blue still eludes the breeder's skill. The massed petals and sepals of cactus blooms are indistinguishable in hue but succulent flowers usually have green sepals.

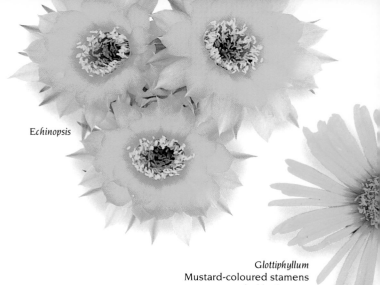

Echinopsis

Glottiphyllum
Mustard-coloured stamens surrounded by butter-yellow petals draw the eye.

Matucana

Aloe
These tubular buds, when fully open, have a tiny fringe of pale petals at the mouth.

Matucana

Rebutia
Bright colours, such as this intense orange, make the flower easily visible to pollinators.

Matucana

Epiphyllum
These blooms open at night and are large and pale so that they are visible to their pollinators in the dusk.

Epiphyllum
Cool white petals contrast in tone with pale green, elongated sepals.

Sempervivum
Subtle hues of maroon, green and silver highlight the daintiness of the flowers.

Epiphyllum
The long crimson sepals fade to apricot as they age.

Echinocereus

Matucana

Rebutia

Stenocactus

Brachystelma
Curved-over petals reveal striking, pale green undersides.

Gymnocalycium

Gymnocalycium
This group of cacti often has unusually coloured flowers.

Harrisia
Purplish green sepals fringe a deep flowercup of pure white petals.

Stapelia
The strange mottling can be deep yellow, purple or brown.

Mammillaria
This brilliantly coloured
posy ring is borne on the
crown of the plant.

Echinopsis

Echinocereus
Striking green
stigmas are common
to the flowers of all
Echinocereus species.

Echinopsis

Epiphyllum
All true *Epiphyllum* species have
pale blooms; this hybrid's vivid
hue was bred in cultivation.

Echeveria
These lilac-pink buds open
to reveal a golden throat.

Echinopsis

Echinopsis
Striped pink petals frame the rich green of the flower's pollen tube.

Echinopsis

Euphorbia
The true flowers are the tiny central cups; the colourful "petals" are leaf bracts.

Senecio
Many small, tubular flowers form a ball of bright colour.

Hoya
This "wax flower" shows a dramatic contrast of pale and deep pink.

Aloe
Stem and flowers are the same coral hue.

Matucana

Pachycormis
Clusters of tiny pink flowers form a haze of colour.

Lewisia
Fine veins accentuate the delicacy of pale pink petals.

Echinocereus

CHOOSING CONTAINERS

FROM RUSTIC WOODEN TUBS to traditional terracotta troughs or ornate stone urns, there are containers to suit every style and setting, whether indoors or out. Cacti and succulents usually thrive in containers and, because most are slow-growing, they do not outgrow their pots quickly. Unless they are very heavy, pots can be moved, like a portable garden, to create new schemes. It is also easy to bring plants indoors for winter, if necessary. A container should complement rather than compete with the planting and its setting, and be in proportion to both. Shape has an impact too: for a unified effect, use several, similarly shaped containers or, to create a striking contrast, choose pots with markedly different forms. Most indoor and all outdoor containers must have drainage holes.

Crassula ovata
Jade plant

Senecio scaposus

Mammillaria pringlei

WOVEN BASKETS
Baskets are available in a variety of textures and shapes, and go well with both spiny and smooth-skinned plants. Place a protective plastic lining or a dish in the bottom of the basket before filling it with compost.

TIMELESS TERRACOTTA
Available in a wide array of shapes and sizes, terracotta containers suit classic and contemporary settings, both indoors and out. Because of its weight, terracotta is ideal for tall plants that might otherwise be top-heavy. Upright pots echo the forms of erect cacti and succulents, while a wide, flared dish flatters low spreading plants. If using deep pots, fill the bottom with broken crocks; most cacti and succulents do not need a great depth of compost.

Euphorbia trigona
'Red Form'

PLANT STANDS
Tall pedestalled stands create an effective display by bringing plants nearer eye level. Like hanging containers, they suit trailing and epiphytic plants. Cuttings may also be planted through the sides to create a fuller effect.

Sedum burrito
Donkey's tail

Agave filifera

Agave victoria-reginae
Queen Victoria century plant

Agave toumeyana

Sphagnum moss lining

Pachypodium lamerei
Madagascar palm

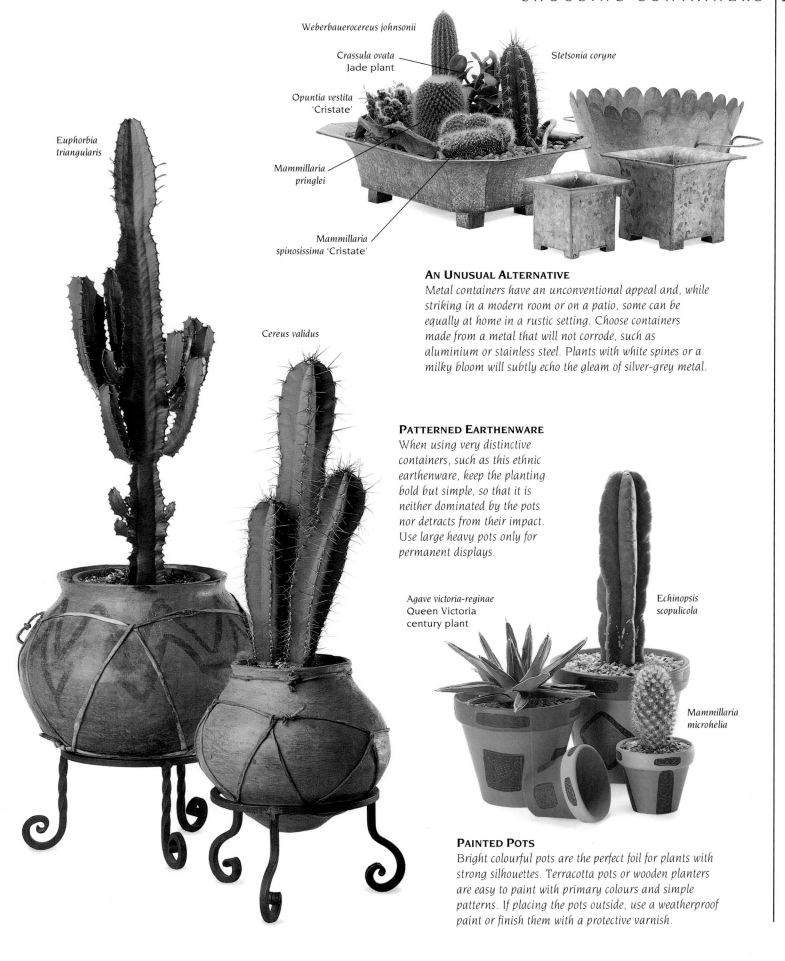

Weberbauerocereus johnsonii

Crassula ovata
Jade plant

Opuntia vestita
'Cristate'

Euphorbia
triangularis

Stetsonia coryne

Mammillaria
pringlei

Mammillaria
spinosissima 'Cristate'

Cereus validus

AN UNUSUAL ALTERNATIVE

Metal containers have an unconventional appeal and, while striking in a modern room or on a patio, some can be equally at home in a rustic setting. Choose containers made from a metal that will not corrode, such as aluminium or stainless steel. Plants with white spines or a milky bloom will subtly echo the gleam of silver-grey metal.

PATTERNED EARTHENWARE

When using very distinctive containers, such as this ethnic earthenware, keep the planting bold but simple, so that it is neither dominated by the pots nor detracts from their impact. Use large heavy pots only for permanent displays.

Agave victoria-reginae
Queen Victoria
century plant

Echinopsis
scopulicola

Mammillaria
microhelia

PAINTED POTS

Bright colourful pots are the perfect foil for plants with strong silhouettes. Terracotta pots or wooden planters are easy to paint with primary colours and simple patterns. If placing the pots outside, use a weatherproof paint or finish them with a protective varnish.

DISPLAY IDEAS

FROM THE MATT, PEBBLE-LIKE leaves of some species to the jointed, trailing stems or ribbed spiny bodies of others, cacti and succulents show great diversity of form, size, texture and colour. The bold architectural outlines of some can be used to create a striking display of arresting shapes; others have waxy or hairy leaves and silky or hooked spines that can be combined for subtle contrasts. The potential for developing imaginative schemes is limitless; the only restriction is to choose plants that need similar conditions if you want to grow them together.

INDOORS

Cacti and succulents make a refreshing change from conventional house plants. Before deciding where to put them, bear in mind their practical needs of light, temperature and humidity (see pp. 150–51). Take the time to assess how plants look in different parts of a room and place them where they will have the most visual impact. Many small succulents, particularly those with rosettes of leaves such as *Aloe* and *Haworthia*, look striking when viewed from above, forming mosaics of colour and texture. By contrast, species with pendent stems look best in hanging containers. Spiny species should be set well away from areas where people might brush against them.

Consider, too, whether an individual plant or a group of plants will be most effective. A large single specimen is most impressive sited against a plain wall. Smaller plants can be placed in formal pairs to frame a window or at either end of a table. Grow groups of plants in a single container, or in individual pots to allow greater flexibility for changing the display through the year.

It is important to match planting arrangements to the decorative style of a room. In a modern setting, for example, with spare clean lines and unfussy decor, a columnar cactus makes a bold yet congruous addition. In a more traditional room with antique furniture, a collection of softly leafy *Crassula*, *Echeveria* or *Kalanchoe* in an ornamental china bowl is more appropriate.

Light can also be used to enhance the plants: cacti with interesting spines or hairs are eye-catching if placed on a sunny windowsill or artificially lit from behind. A strong outline or particularly fine shape can be emphasized by backlighting to reveal its dramatic shadow.

LIVING ART, above
The distinctive form of a single specimen like this Cereus hildmannianus *v.* monstrose *creates a living sculpture that echoes its modern setting.*

FRAMED DISPLAY, left
Small plants placed on glass shelves in front of a window create an ornamental screen, which draws individual plants together into a cohesive design.

A CONTRAST OF MOOD, right
The simple shapes of cacti and succulents in these terracotta pots provide a calm counterpoint to the background of brilliant colours and busy patterns.

PATIOS AND TERRACES

The warm sheltered conditions typically provided by patios and terraces make them an ideal place for growing cacti and succulents, either in raised beds or containers. The strong geometrical shapes of the plants provide a good link between the hard lines and materials of the house and patio and the softer shapes and textures of the garden plants. It is important to choose plants that are in proportion to the style and space available. In a large formal setting, for example, a single feature plant with a dominant stature and shape can make an unusual focal point, or two plants placed sentry-like on either side of a flight of steps can be an unconventional alternative to traditional topiary.

Planting in containers allows greater flexibility for exploiting the plants' display potential, using them as movable design elements. For a strongly patterned effect, plant up several containers with the same species and set the pots in a row on top of a low wall, or at one edge of the patio.

In an informal garden, many succulents, especially small *Sedum*, look effective planted into the crevices of a drystone wall. If space allows, create a succulent bed at one edge or corner of the patio for a luxuriant effect. If space is limited, remove just one or two paving stones, plant one species in the resulting gap and surround the clump with complementary ground cover. If the patio is made of loose gravel or shingle, use the same material to top-dress the bed. Alternatively, try a different material – rounded pebbles if the patio is made of stone slabs, for example – for an interesting contrast of textures. Opt for materials in muted colours, because these enhance the plants without competing with them.

TRADITIONAL DISPLAY, above
For a formal effect, plant a single decorative urn or a handsome terracotta pot with a spiky rosette-shaped succulent such as Agave americana *'Medio-picta alba' and raise the urn on a plinth or pedestal.*

CO-ORDINATED ELEGANCE, left
Make sure the style of the container and its planting blends well with the surrounding plants, as well as the background and setting. A classical trough planted with several plants of Agave attenuata *makes an elegant display on an ornate table. The warm tone of the terracotta container also harmonizes with the colour of the painted wall behind it.*

CONTEMPORARY STYLE, right
In a stark modern setting, keep the planting strong but simple. Use large plants of arresting architectural form, such as this Carnegiea gigantea, *in undecorated containers.*

GARDEN SETTINGS

There is scope to give your imagination free rein in an open garden, especially if there is space to prepare a well-drained bed. Even in cooler climates, a wide variety of plants may be grown outdoors (see pp. 163–6) and tender plants can be sunk into the bed in pots during the summer to give seasonal interest to the display.

When grouping plants, consider scale, shape, texture and colour. If plants are large, shape and form are likely to be most important and have the strongest impact, whereas if smaller plants are featured – perhaps grown in a raised bed to be viewed at close hand – differences in texture and colour are more noticeable.

Combine plants that flower one after the other for succession of colour; if flowering times overlap, ensure that the colours of the blooms complement each other. Also include species with unusual forms and textures to provide year-round interest: for example, the globular form, glossy skin and sparse spines of *Gymnocalycium horstii* can be contrasted with the candle-like stems of *Mammillaria elongata* encased in golden, comb-like spines.

As well as top-dressing the bed with a suitable material, try adding a few large, well-shaped stones to give the planting a sense of substance and permanence. Cacti and succulents may also be grown with other plants, provided that all thrive in the same conditions. For example, the rich burgundy foliage of *Euphorbia amygdaloides* 'Purpurea' makes a splendid foil for the plate-like rosettes of *Aeonium tabuliforme*, or a spreading carpet of evergreen *Juniperus squamata* 'Blue Star' can offset the smooth waxy rosettes of *Sempervivum*.

FORM AND CONTRAST, above
The rounded cushions of golden barrel cacti, Echinocactus grusonii, *form a well-sculpted group that resembles living boulders. A bold contrast is provided by the vertical lines of the majestic columnar cactus.*

SCULPTURAL CENTREPIECE, below
The tentacle-like, undulating leaves of Agave americana *'Marginata' create a focal point in this border, while a soft cascade of bougainvillea provides a colourful backdrop.*

INFORMAL GROUPING
Plant cacti and succulents in informal groups or drifts for a natural effect. Here, deeply ribbed columnar plants add a strongly vertical dimension, echoed by the dark spire of a cypress behind, while low succulents and other plants weave a contrasting tapestry of colour and texture beneath them.

CREATING A DESERT LOOK

MAINLY FROM DRY HABITATS, cacti and succulents offer enormous scope for creating desert-style displays with their diverse range of shapes, colours and textures. Try a few small or slow-growing plants in a miniature desert garden for a long-lasting arrangement that may be placed in a brightly lit position indoors. Most species need very little water (so are convenient if you are often away) and are dormant in winter; ensure that the plants you choose are compatible in these respects (see pp. 56–143). Take care to avoid overwatering the plants if the container has no drainage holes.

Peat

Pebbles

Small washed grit

Thick brown paper

Fine brush

Spoon

23 cm (9 in) diameter terracotta bowl

Trowel

Opuntia species
Prickly pear

Aeonium haworthii
Pinwheel

Mammillaria magnimamma

Echeveria fimbriata

Echeveria elegans

PLANTS, TOOLS AND MATERIALS
As cacti and succulents have shallow roots, the bowl need be only 8 cm (3 in) deep. For this planting, it does not matter if the bowl has drainage holes. The compost is a mixture of peat and grit; the latter makes an arid-looking top-dressing.

PLANTING THE ARRANGEMENT

BOLD EFFECT
To appreciate the plants' sculptural shapes and contrasting textures, do not overcrowd the container.

1 A free-draining compost is essential to keep the plants healthy; to make this, mix two parts peat with one part small washed grit. Then cover the bottom of the bowl with a thick layer of the fresh compost.

2 With the plants still in their pots, try different arrangements, bearing in mind whether the display will be viewed from all sides. Note the arrangement you like best, then remove the plants and loosely fill the bowl with more compost.

3 Starting with the tallest, remove each plant from its pot. With a cactus, wrap a strip of folded brown paper around the stem to form a handle and gently lift the plant from its pot. Tease out the roots of each plant a little. Scoop out a hole in the compost for each plant as you go.

4 Lower the plant into its hole. Check it is sitting at the same depth in the hole as it was in its pot, spread out its roots, and fill in around them with more compost. Once all the plants are in place, lightly firm the compost surface.

5 Gently remove any compost that has lodged between the plants' spines or leaves with a fine, soft brush.

6 Position a few decorative pebbles on the compost and spoon on a layer of grit. Brush the surface and spray it with water to wash the stones clean. Leave it for three to four days, then water lightly.

The tree-like *Aeonium haworthii* gives focus to the planting

Pebbles provide the finishing touch

DESERT DISPLAY
Once planted, a desert garden will survive happily for two to three years. After this time, renew the compost and replace any of the plants that have outgrown the container.

Dainty rosettes of *Echeveria* contrast in shape with the globular spiny *Mammillaria magnimamma*

PLANTING A HANGING BASKET

SOME CACTI AND SUCCULENTS look spectacular in a hanging basket. Try the jungle cacti with slender arching stems and showy pendent flowers or any of the vast array of trailing succulents. One large plant looks elegantly impressive, while a mixed planting can create dramatic contrasts; check that the plants all have the same cultural needs (see pp. 150–51) and growing periods (see the relevant entries in the Plant Catalogue, pp. 56–143). Most species or hybrids that thrive in hanging baskets need some shade from the hot summer sun; hang them from tree branches in the garden or in bright indirect light indoors.

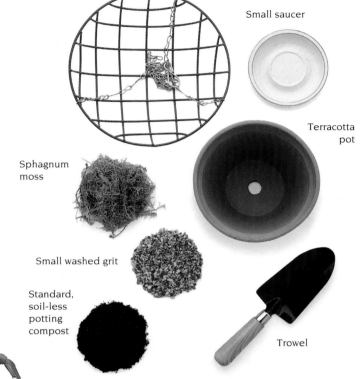

25 cm (10 in) diameter wire-mesh basket with chain

Small saucer

Terracotta pot

Sphagnum moss

Small washed grit

Standard, soil-less potting compost

Trowel

Schlumbergera 'Frida'

PLANTS, TOOLS AND MATERIALS

A wire-mesh hanging basket is both lightweight and free-draining. Choose a green one so that the mesh blends in with the sphagnum-moss lining for a natural look. A saucer is useful for an indoor basket because it prevents drips from spoiling the floor after watering. Use several plants of the same type for a luxuriant effect.

HOW TO PLANT UP THE BASKET

1 Sit the basket in the top of a large pot to steady it while planting it up; make sure that the chains are untangled. Line the basket with sphagnum moss, pressing it down firmly so that it forms a layer at least 5 cm (2 in) thick.

2 To ensure good drainage, add 1 part grit to 2 parts of the soil-less compost. Place the saucer in the bottom of the lined basket and loosely fill the basket with the gritty compost to about two-thirds of its depth.

3 Ease each plant out of its pot by supporting the base of the stems and the root ball in one hand and turning the pot upside-down with the other.

4 Hold the top of the root ball firmly in one hand and gently tease out some of the roots with your fingers, allowing any old loose compost to fall away. Take care not to damage the roots.

5 Position each plant in the basket so that the top of its root ball will be level with the surface of the compost. Space the plants evenly to allow room for future growth: three plants in a triangular formation work well. Once all the plants have been positioned, fill in around them with more compost.

A TERRACOTTA BOWL
As an alternative to a wire-mesh basket, try planting up a hanging container made of terracotta. It provides an attractive foil to the foliage and is convenient indoors because it has no drainage holes so does not drip. Take care not to overwater the compost.

6 Firm the surface of the compost gently, leaving about 1 cm (¹/₂ in) below the rim of the basket to allow for watering. Do not water it for 2–3 days so that any damaged roots have time to heal; otherwise they may rot.

Sturdy chain to support the weight of the planted basket

Masses of flowers create a show of brilliant winter colour

HANGING GARDEN
Hang the basket in a cool place until the cacti produce flowerbuds. Then move it to its final position to enjoy the show of blooms. Planted baskets are heavy, especially just after watering, so use a good-quality support; pulleys are very useful for lowering the basket within easy reach.

WINDOW BOX DISPLAY

THE STRONG, ARCHITECTURAL FORMS and complementary colours of cacti and succulents make them ideally suited for both a semi-permanent or a permanent arrangement in a window box or trough. Choose plants in a variety of contrasting shades, shapes, textures and sizes for a striking display. Remember to check that all the plants prefer similar conditions (see pp. 56–143). In areas that suffer frost, move the trough under cover or indoors for the winter.

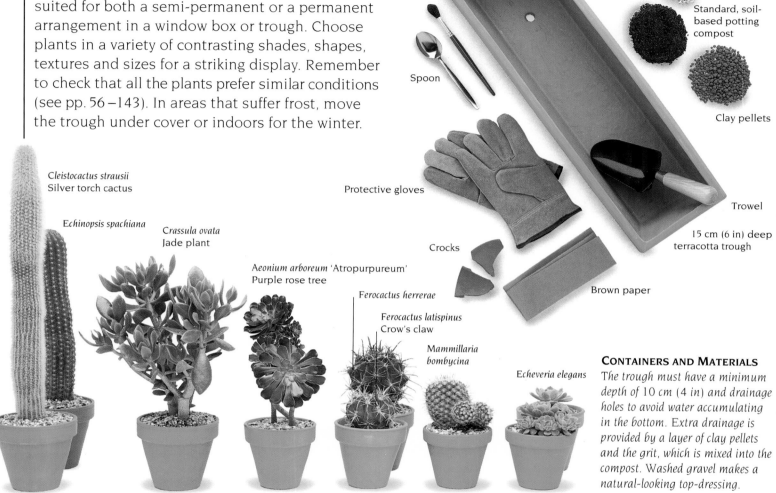

Washed gravel

Small washed grit

Standard, soil-based potting compost

Clay pellets

Fine brush

Spoon

Cleistocactus strausii
Silver torch cactus

Echinopsis spachiana

Crassula ovata
Jade plant

Aeonium arboreum 'Atropurpureum'
Purple rose tree

Ferocactus herrerae

Ferocactus latispinus
Crow's claw

Mammillaria bombycina

Echeveria elegans

Protective gloves

Crocks

Brown paper

Trowel

15 cm (6 in) deep terracotta trough

CONTAINERS AND MATERIALS
The trough must have a minimum depth of 10 cm (4 in) and drainage holes to avoid water accumulating in the bottom. Extra drainage is provided by a layer of clay pellets and the grit, which is mixed into the compost. Washed gravel makes a natural-looking top-dressing.

PLANTING THE ARRANGEMENT

1 Make up a planting mixture with equal parts of grit and compost. Cover each drainage hole with a crock and add a thin layer of clay pellets. Cover these with a double layer of brown paper (or newspaper).

2 Half-fill the container with planting mixture. The paper stops loose compost clogging up the drainage layer and, after the compost has settled down, will eventually disintegrate.

3 Before planting, arrange the plants in their pots. For a pleasing composition, place tall plants at the back and low or trailing ones in front; avoid making the display too symmetrical. Make a note of the best combination.

4 Gently ease each plant out of its pot by supporting the plant in one hand and turning the pot upside-down. Wear gloves when handling spiny plants. Prepare each root ball by breaking it up slightly; this helps the roots to grow out into the new compost.

5 Make a depression in the compost and lower each plant into it so that its root ball is at the same depth as it was in the pot. Insert the largest plants first, spacing them so that they have room to grow. Fill in with compost around the roots and also between the plants as you go. Gently firm the compost surface.

6 Carefully brush off any stray particles of compost from the plants' leaves or from between the spines. Spoon a layer of washed gravel over the compost surface, taking care not to let any fall on the plants. The top-dressing stops the surface drying out and prevents any growth of unsightly green algae. Leave the trough for a few days and then lightly water it; this ensures that the newly planted roots will not rot.

Cleistocactus strausii, a columnar cactus, gives height to the display

Purplish leaf bracts of *Aeonium arboreum* 'Atropurpureum' strike a colourful highnote

THE FINAL ARRANGEMENT

This window box planting will require only very occasional care to keep it healthy and attractive. After three to five years, refresh the display by changing all the compost and replanting. Replace any overgrown or damaged plants with new ones.

Eventually rosettes of *Echeveria elegans* will tumble over the side of the trough

PLANT CATALOGUE

A unique photographic catalogue that features a
wide-ranging selection of cacti and succulents, with
details of their origin, common names, size, shape,
flowers and fruit, spines, growth rate and habit,
special characteristics and cultivation needs. Plants
are arranged alphabetically by genus.

HOW TO USE THIS SECTION

THE PLANT CATALOGUE has been divided into two parts, the first devoted to cacti and the second to other succulents. Within each part, the genera, or plant groups, are arranged in alphabetical order by their Latin or botanical names. The significance of the parts of a plant name is explained below (see box).

Each genus entry features a representative selection of species or forms. Many species of cacti and succulents vary greatly in appearance from plant to plant, whereas other species are fairly uniform. Where the species is variable, the plant shown is usually a common form of the species.

INFORMATION IN THE CATALOGUE

The cacti and succulents in the Plant Catalogue, unless otherwise stated, are easy to grow, dormant in winter, may be grown outdoors or indoors in suitable conditions, and need watering only when in growth. They have unscented flowers and are evergreen perennials.

In comparison to many garden plants, most cacti and succulents grow slowly. The terms "fast-growing" or "slow-growing" and "small" or "large" in genus introductions are used in reference to other succulents or cacti. Many factors, including local conditions, affect how these plants grow; details given here are a general indication. Special propagation tips are also given.

GENUS NAME Botanical or Latin name of the plant group.

GENUS INTRODUCTION Details the place of origin and number of species in the genus, as well as main features and common characteristics of the group, such as body shape and size, spines, flowering, fruits, growth habit and light needs. If applicable, common names, recent name changes or special cultural needs are noted.

HEIGHT AND SPREAD PROFILES A profile for each plant indicates its growth habit, shape and size after five years indoors in a pot (*top*) or ten years in a bed (*bottom*). Five-year profiles show growth achievable by a beginner growing plants in a greenhouse or on a windowsill, although individual plants vary. Experienced collectors may obtain better results. Most plants grow faster in a bed than in a pot. Ten-year profiles show likely growth with low maintenance. The largest scales are deepest green.

LATIN PLANT NAME For succulents, the *Lexicon of Succulent Plants*' classification system has been followed. The authority for cacti is the CITES *Cactaceae Checklist*. Names for forms or varieties are not yet recorded in this work so many visually different plants are included in one species. If featured, such plants are here provisionally given the status of a form (e.g. *Rebutia heliosa* f. *perplexa*).

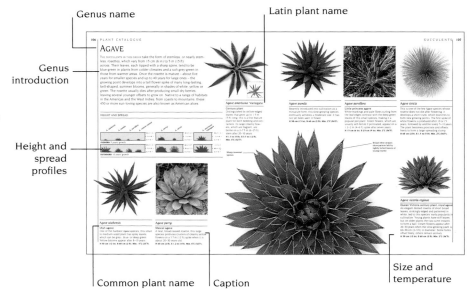

Genus name — Latin plant name

Genus introduction

Height and spread profiles

Common plant name | Caption

Size and temperature

COMMON PLANT NAME If applicable, vernacular names in common use are given.

CAPTION Details include form, growth habit, flower type if not shown, flowering season, unusual features and special cultivation advice. The terms "fast-growing" or "slow-growing" and "small" or "large" highlight growth rates and sizes that are atypical of the genus. Some species vary in appearance; important variations of habit, size, spination or flower colour are noted.

SIZE AND TEMPERATURE Indicates the plant's maximum height (H), or length of trailing or creeping stems (L), and its maximum spread (S). Read with the profiles for an idea of how fast or slowly the plant reaches mature size. Some plants take 100 years, others are full-sized in a few years. Also given is the minimum temperature at which the plant can be cultivated. Latitudes less than 45° North or South often have a lower night temperature which rises significantly by mid-morning. Cacti and succulents can survive such temperatures for short periods, but not frosts.

PLANT NAMES

Genus (first Latin word): group of plants, often of diverse appearance, with common characteristics in the structure of their flowers or seed pods.
Intergeneric hybrid (denoted by x before genus name): natural or cultivated cross between two genera.
Species (second Latin word): naturally occurring plant type in genus with several distinct botanical features.
Variety (denoted by v. before third Latin word): plant with slightly varying botanical structure from a species, often with a distinct variance in look.
Form (denoted by f. before third Latin word): plant differing slightly from the species, for example, in flower colour.
Hybrid or cultivar (denoted by last word/s in quotation marks): a hybrid is a cross between two species of one genus; a cultivar is a hybrid, sport or form, selected or bred in cultivation.

CACTI

This section includes small and globular, barrel-
shaped or tall and columnar desert cacti, as well as
trailing or climbing jungle cacti.

APOROCACTUS

IN THE WILD IN MEXICO, these epiphytic rat's tail cacti (see pp. 10–11) grow on trees and in rocky crevices. They make good plants for hanging baskets. There are now only two true species: both have slender stems, which are studded with short tufts of bristly spines and can creep or trail for a considerable length. Among the first cacti to flower in early spring, they bear a profusion of vividly hued, long-necked blooms on the previous year's growth. Very easy to grow, these plants need a fairly rich compost and a bright situation shaded from hot sun. Water lightly now and then in winter to avoid dieback of the stem tips, and cut out old or discoloured stems at the base to encourage new growth.

Petals and sepals of each flower are arranged in layers

LENGTH AND SPREAD

Aporocactus species and forms

INDOORS:	
1.2 m/4 ft	
60 cm/2 ft	
0 cm/0 in	

INDOORS:
5 years' growth

Aporocactus species and forms

OUTDOORS:	
2.4 m/8 ft	
1.2 m/4 ft	
0 cm/0 in	

OUTDOORS:
10 years' growth

Aporocactus martianus f. conzatianum

Although the flowers of this form are less abundant than those of A. *flagelliformis*, they are larger. The stems, which are most often densely covered with short, golden-brown spines, are also thicker. This cactus rarely produces any berries.
L and S unlimited. Min. 6°C (43°F).

Aporocactus flagelliformis f. flagriformis

A different form of the species A. *flagelliformis*, this cactus has slimmer stems and fewer spines. It is not as common in cultivation and less tolerant of overwatering. Variable in growth habit, its flowers are a deep shade of carmine-pink and the berries are red.
L and S unlimited. Min. 6°C (43°F).

Aporocactus flagelliformis

This cactus bears an abundance of beautiful, double, cerise flowers, 5–8 cm (2–3 in) across, which sometimes produce small red berries. Its pencil-thin stems are densely clothed in short golden spines and, as in other Aporocactus, grow up to 30 cm (12 in) a year. Easier than A. *martianus* to grow, this cactus is also more tolerant of cold.
L and S unlimited. Min. 5°C (41°F).

X APOROPHYLLUM

THIS GROUP IS NOT a true genus but a collection of inter-generic hybrids developed by crossing the *Aporocactus* species with other epiphytic cactus groups, predominantly *Epiphyllum* hybrids. Most of the characteristics of *Aporophyllum* hybrids have been inherited from the *Aporocactus* genus, but the hybrids are distinguished by their larger, open-faced flowers, in brilliant shades of orange, cerise, scarlet and purple as well as white. The stems grow over 2 m (6 ft) long and root into the soil to form large mats. The plants need shade and temperatures no lower than 6°C (43°F), and flower best if fed well each spring and summer. Water them lightly now and then in winter. Propagate from 15 cm (6 in) cuttings to obtain plants that are similar to the parent.

LENGTH AND SPREAD

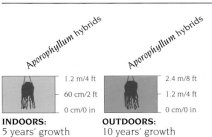

Aporophyllum hybrids	*Aporophyllum* hybrids
1.2 m/4 ft	2.4 m/8 ft
60 cm/2 ft	1.2 m/4 ft
0 cm/0 in	0 cm/0 in
INDOORS: 5 years' growth	**OUTDOORS:** 10 years' growth

X *Aporophyllum* 'Sussex Pink'

X *Aporophyllum* 'Dawn'

X *Aporophyllum* 'Vivide'

X *Aporophyllum* 'Edna Bellamy'

ARIOCARPUS

THESE SIX SPECIES OF living rock, or fossil, cacti from southern Texas and Mexico are endangered in the wild. The small, cone-shaped plants grow very slowly, largely underground, and have pronounced, grey or brown, almost spineless tubercles. They grow in short bursts in late spring and in autumn, when their white, yellow, pink or red, open-faced flowers and fleshy pale berries appear. Especially challenging to grow in cooler areas, these sun-loving cacti need careful watering during their growth period; water once in spring, very occasionally in summer and thoroughly a few times in early autumn. A little ground chalk in the compost benefits the tuberous roots. Mature plants are seldom legally available but seed germinates easily.

Smooth pointed tubercles

Triangular tubercles with a wrinkled surface

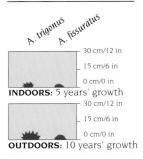

HEIGHT AND SPREAD

A. trigonus
A. fissuratus

30 cm/12 in
15 cm/6 in
0 cm/0 in
INDOORS: 5 years' growth

30 cm/12 in
15 cm/6 in
0 cm/0 in
OUTDOORS: 10 years' growth

Ariocarpus trigonus

Only the rosette of long, curving, leaf-like tubercles is visible on this plant; the flat tuberous body is below the soil. Lemon flowers and small white berries appear in a ring on the crown. A plant of only 25 cm (10 in) diameter may be 100 years old.
H 10 cm (4 in), S 20 cm (8 in). Min. 7°C (45°F).

Ariocarpus fissuratus

Much sought after by collectors, this rare and curious species has fleshy tubercles tightly packed on its crown into flat or slightly domed rosettes. Woolly tufts of spines grow in the centre. Its open-faced pink flowers last for three or four days. This cactus can take 50 years to reach a diameter of 15 cm (6 in). It is very prone to rot if overwatered.
H 5 cm (2 in), S 15 cm (6 in). Min. 5°C (41°F).

ASTROPHYTUM

THERE ARE ONLY FOUR species in this sun-loving genus from Mexico but many different-looking hybrids. Mostly small rotund cacti that are often flecked with white scales, they are quite variable, especially in the type of spine and number of ribs. Many large, bright yellow, daisy-like flowers appear at the plant crown in spring to late summer. Each bloom opens fully in bright light and is long-lasting. The fleshy green seed pods split open to reveal large, helmet-shaped seeds. Slow-growing, the body becomes columnar after many years. Add some ground chalk to the compost to improve the plant's roots and vigour.

HEIGHT AND SPREAD

A. ornatum
A. asterias
A. capricorne
A. myriostigma

30 cm/12 in
15 cm/6 in
0 cm/0 in
INDOORS: 5 years' growth

30 cm/12 in
15 cm/6 in
0 cm/0 in
OUTDOORS: 10 years' growth

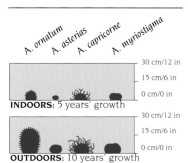

Woolly brown areoles, or spine cushions, line the ridges of the ribs

Astrophytum ornatum

The fastest-growing and largest *Astrophytum*, this variable species bears many large flowers after 5–6 years. The ribs, usually flecked with silver and with mostly pale curving spines, spiral towards the crown.
H 1.2 m (4 ft), S 20 cm (8 in). Min. 7°C (45°F).

Astrophytum asterias

Sea urchin, silver dollar cactus
This small spineless cactus has a grey-green to white-green body. It is a sensitive plant and rots if overwatered, so is best grown grafted. Flowers with deep red throats appear after about five years. In winter, when dry and dormant, the globular or saucer-like body shrinks to a flattish disc.
H 5 cm (2 in), S 13 cm (5 in). Min. 10°C (50°F).

Astrophytum capricorne

Goat's horn cactus
The wiry grey to brown spines that twist around this small cactus are easily broken off if handled. The body, which is usually dark, is sometimes flecked with white. Its flowers often have a wine-red throat.
H 1.2 m (4 ft), S 10 cm (4 in). Min. 5°C (41°F).

Astrophytum myriostigma

Bishop's cap, bishop's mitre, monk's hood
This species is prized for a look that is distinctly uncommon among cacti. Initially squat, it is the size of a small melon when about ten years old. Its bare body may be green, blue or purple, with 4–8 ribs, and eventually becomes slightly columnar. The speckled look is due to innumerable white scales, which are in fact rudimentary spines. Large plants readily bear blooms that are 6 cm (2½ in) across and last 2–3 days.
H 15 cm (6 in), S 20 cm (8 in). Min. 5°C (41°F).

CARNEGIEA GIGANTEA

THIS IS KNOWN AS A monotypic genus because it contains only one species: the giant saguaro cactus. In the wild, in the southwestern U.S.A. and northwest Mexico, this cactus often forms large colonies. It takes about 150 years to reach its full impressive stature of some 12 m (40 ft) and sometimes develops a few branches once it is 3–5 m (10–15 ft) tall. Huge, funnel-shaped, creamy white blooms, followed by red, plum-shaped, edible fruits, first appear on the stem tip in late spring when the plant is 40 years old or more. Mature plants in the wild can produce up to ten million seeds a year but only one seedling in 50 million is usually successful, so a mature cactus may reproduce only once in every five years. Collecting from the wild is now illegal. Fortunately, the seed germinates very readily in cultivation. This sun-loving species is moderately easy to grow at a minimum temperature of 5°C (41°F).

HEIGHT AND SPREAD

INDOORS: 5 years' growth	OUTDOORS: 10 years' growth
30 cm/12 in — 15 cm/6 in — 0 cm/0 in	30 cm/12 in — 15 cm/6 in — 0 cm/0 in

CEPHALOCEREUS

FROM TROPICAL AND SUBTROPICAL Mexican habitats ranging from seashores to mountains, the five sun-loving species in this genus are blue-green, slow-growing, columnar plants. In the wild, they reach about 15.2 m (50 ft) in 200 years; in cultivation, they are usually no taller than 90 cm (3 ft). The spines vary but are sometimes long and silky on the upper stem, forming a pseudocephalium, or "beard". Trumpet-shaped, white, pink or yellow summer flowers briefly appear at night on plants that are at least 20 years old. The round seed pods split open when ripe.

Spines can vary in length

HEIGHT AND SPREAD

C. senilis INDOORS: 5 years' growth	C. senilis OUTDOORS: 10 years' growth
30 cm/12 in — 15 cm/6 in — 0 cm/0 in	30 cm/12 in — 15 cm/6 in — 0 cm/0 in

Cephalocereus senilis

Old man cactus
The long downy spines are thickest at the stem tip, especially on very old plants (see inset), which eventually bear cream to pink nocturnal flowers and rosy seed pods. If the down becomes dirty, wash and comb it gently. The columnar stem seldom branches. Add extra calcium to the compost or soil for healthy growth.
H 15.2 m (50 ft), S 30 cm (12 in). Min. 5°C (41°F).

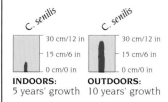

CEREUS

DIVERSE HABITATS in eastern South America and the West Indies are home to the 60 or so species of mostly large, robust, columnar cacti in this genus. Their stems, often blue-green and spiny, grow up to 1.2 m (4 ft) a year and branch freely. Funnel-shaped, pink, white or green flowers appear near the plant's crown, opening mostly at night to fade at dawn in spring or summer. The round or oval edible fruits are green, red or purple. These sun-lovers make good feature or hedging plants.

HEIGHT AND SPREAD

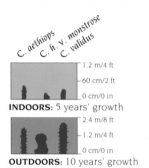

C. aethiops
C. h. v. monstrose
C. validus

1.2 m/4 ft
60 cm/2 ft
0 cm/0 in
INDOORS: 5 years' growth

2.4 m/8 ft
1.2 m/4 ft
0 cm/0 in
OUTDOORS: 10 years' growth

Cereus validus

An attractive feature plant, this variable cactus flowers freely at intervals in summer. Its long thick spines are glossy black on new growth and its fruits are greenish purple. The stem offsets in time to form a clump.
H 7.5 m (25 ft), S 3 m (10 ft). Min. 7°C (45°F).

Flowers are predominantly white with salmon or pink tints

Cactus flowers once stem is 1.2 m (4 ft) tall

Cereus aethiops

Mature plants form stately clumps of tall, slender, blue-green stems studded with distinctive black spines. Once the stem is 90 cm–1.2 m (3–4 ft) tall, it blooms several times at night in summer. Plum-shaped, purple-brown fruits follow.
H 3 m (10 ft), S 1.2 m (4 ft). Min. 7°C (45°F).

Cereus hildmannianus v. monstrose

Curiosity plant
The contorted stem of this variable, white-flowering cactus is caused by deformed growing points. In a small pot, the stem is often more squat than the plant shown here. It has brown fruits.
H 5 m (15 ft), S 3 m (10 ft). Min. 5°C (41°F).

Short spines range from gold to red

Buds open into white or pale pink flowers

CLEISTOCACTUS

DENSE, NEEDLE-LIKE SPINES in hues of white, beige or gold often clothe these branching columnar cacti. The 49 species are widespread in most South American countries, from Argentina to Uruguay. Some have tubular flowers. Others, formerly classified as *Borzicactus*, have more open, lop-sided flowers, tend to have slimmer stems and form arching mounds. Most of these sun-loving plants are quite fast-growing and produce masses of small scarlet, orange, green or golden blooms, usually from the upper part of the stem, between spring and autumn. The round berries are green, yellow or red.

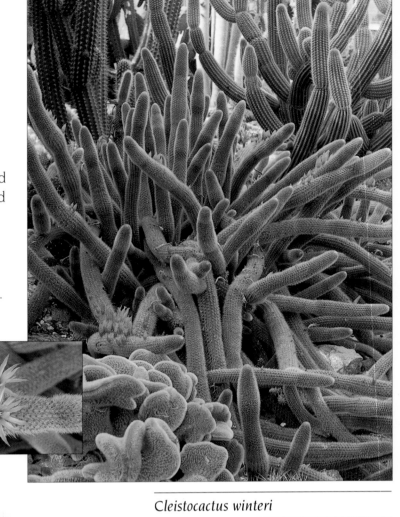

HEIGHT AND SPREAD

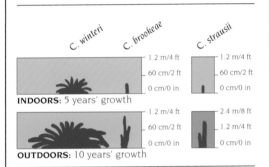

C. winteri   C. brookeae   C. strausii
1.2 m/4 ft   1.2 m/4 ft
60 cm/2 ft   60 cm/2 ft
0 cm/0 in   0 cm/0 in
INDOORS: 5 years' growth

1.2 m/4 ft   2.4 m/8 ft
60 cm/2 ft   1.2 m/4 ft
0 cm/0 in   0 cm/0 in
OUTDOORS: 10 years' growth

Cleistocactus strausii

Silver torch cactus
This variable, fast-growing cactus has eye-catching silvery spines. Solitary when young, the spring-flowering stem branches and clumps as it matures. Its fruits are green. Allow the roots plenty of room.
H 3 m (10 ft), S 2 m (6 ft). Min. 5°C (41°F).

Tubular flowers grow directly from stem

Cleistocactus winteri

Large tangled mounds of long, slender, arching stems covered in short golden spines make this a distinctive bedding plant. The stems may also be cristate, or wavy, in form (see foreground). Mature plants flower almost constantly in spring and summer. The fruits are green. Small plants are ideal for hanging baskets.
H 90 cm (3 ft), S unlimited. Min. 7°C (45°F).

Cleistocactus brookeae

The slender, semi-erect stem of this species, which often becomes prostrate with age, usually has straight, pale gold spines, although in one form the spines are white. In summer, slightly S-shaped flowers appear along the upper part of the stem. Small purple-red berries follow. The cactus slowly spreads into a clump.
H 1.5 m (5 ft), S unlimited. Min. 5°C (41°F).

COPIAPOA

THIS GROUP OF SUN-LOVING Chilean cacti includes about 26 species. Some are globular, with small brown bodies and tiny spines or larger, blue-green bodies and short spines; others are slightly columnar, freely offsetting species with fierce spines. After some years, most develop a powdery or waxy sheen. All have small, open-faced, yellow summer flowers that grow from the woolly plant crown. Small green seed pods develop inside the crown and emerge when ripe. The tuberous-rooted plants usually grow slowly and form large clumps. They need a dry winter and moderate summer watering.

HEIGHT AND SPREAD

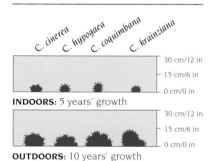

C. cinerea C. hypogaea C. coquimbana C. krainziana

30 cm/12 in
15 cm/6 in
0 cm/0 in

INDOORS: 5 years' growth

30 cm/12 in
15 cm/6 in
0 cm/0 in

OUTDOORS: 10 years' growth

Copiapoa cinerea

This striking cactus is challenging to grow. It varies in shape, type of spine and number of ribs. The large, slow-growing, globular body is solitary at first. Only with great age does it become slightly columnar and begin to produce a few offsets. Pale gold, open-faced flowers appear after about 20 years.
H and S 1.2 m (4 ft). Min. 7°C (45°F).

Light waxy sheen develops after 5–10 years

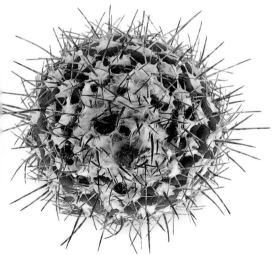

Copiapoa hypogaea

This small, grey-brown, globular cactus flowers freely as soon as it is 5 cm (2 in) in diameter. It has large felty areoles, or spine cushions, and is very variable in shape and in the colour and density of its spines. Protect it from cold to avoid bad scarring.
H 15 cm (6 in), S 38 cm (15 in). Min. 7°C (45°F).

Copiapoa coquimbana

One of the larger-growing *Copiapoa* species, this free-flowering plant is globular at first, then slightly columnar in shape. It readily produces offsets to form a clump. The straight spines vary in colour and density but are usually dark and quite long.
H 46 cm (18 in), S 90 cm (3 ft). Min. 7°C (45°F).

Copiapoa krainziana

Distinguished by long whiskery spines that vary in colour, this small cactus is usually grey to green in hue. Pretty, white-spined forms need to be large before flowering; darker-spined plants grow faster. The globular body freely offsets into a mound.
H 20 cm (8 in), S 30 cm (12 in). Min. 5°C (41°F).

CORYPHANTHA

CHUNKY TUBERCLES GIVE THESE CACTI the common name of beehive cacti. The 60 or so small, sun-loving species from the U.S.A. and Mexico generally have dense spines. A few are columnar but most are globular and slow-growing with a tuberous root. They usually do not flower for several years, then produce large, daisy-like flowers from the plant crown in spring and summer; these are often glossy yellow but some species have pink or red blooms. Green seed pods, which contain large brown seeds, follow.

HEIGHT AND SPREAD

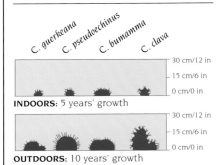

C. guerkeana   C. pseudoechinus   C. bumamma   C. clava

INDOORS: 5 years' growth
30 cm/12 in
15 cm/6 in
0 cm/0 in

OUTDOORS: 10 years' growth
30 cm/12 in
15 cm/6 in
0 cm/0 in

Tubercles vary in size from plant to plant

Coryphantha guerkeana

Pale starry spines and short, curved, often black-tipped central spines encase the body of this species. It is globular or slightly flattened in shape. The plant offsets slowly to form clumps and when it is about five years old, pale yellow flowers appear.
H 10 cm (4 in), S 20 cm (8 in). Min. 5°C (41°F).

Areoles, or spine cushions, are very woolly at the crown

Coryphantha pseudoechinus

The chief attraction of this cactus is its spines, which range from pale or red-brown to black. After five years, small, violet-pink flowers appear. The grey-green body is globular at first, becoming columnar; it is usually solitary but may offset with age.
H 18 cm (7 in), S 30 cm (12 in). Min. 5°C (41°F).

Coryphantha bumamma

Very large, glossy green tubercles make this flattened globular species distinctive. Its stout spines are yellow and, after about five years, golden flowers are produced. This slow-growing cactus is moderately easy to care for and offsets freely. Detach the offsets for use in propagation.
H 13 cm (5 in), S 38 cm (15 in). Min. 5°C (41°F).

Coryphantha clava

This stubbly cactus has yellow to brown spines that fade to off-white. Clumping with age, it bears golden flowers only when mature. The areoles exude a nectar-like secretion on which mould grows; regular spraying with water in summer and autumn and good ventilation help to avoid this.
H 38 cm (15 in), S 60 cm (2 ft). Min. 5°C (41°F).

ECHINOCACTUS

AT ONE TIME, MOST CACTI were called E*chinocactus* but now this genus consists of only six, sun-loving, slow-growing species from the U.S.A. and Mexico. When in flower, they produce a ring of open-faced flowers, which range from golden-yellow to purple-red in hue, on the plant crown. The smaller species are globular and the larger ones are barrel-shaped, resembling the *Ferocactus* (see pp. 74–5). Best-known and easiest to grow is E. *grusonii*; other species are best left to the enthusiast because they need constant care.

HEIGHT AND SPREAD

E. grusonii

30 cm/12 in
15 cm/6 in
0 cm/0 in
INDOORS: 5 years' growth

30 cm/12 in
15 cm/6 in
0 cm/0 in
OUTDOORS: 10 years' growth

Echinocactus grusonii

Golden barrel, mother-in-law's seat
Bright golden spines that emphasize its distinctive barrel shape make this beautiful species ideal as a feature specimen. Pot-grown plants take 30–40 years to reach a flowering size of about 38 cm (15 in) in diameter. Small, funnel-shaped, summer blooms are followed by papery seed pods. Keep the plant warm and dry in winter.
H 1.2 m (4 ft), S 3 m (10 ft). Min. 10°C (50°F).

ECHINOCEREUS

THESE PRETTY, SPINY hedgehog cacti come from the southern U.S.A. and Mexico and vary widely in shape and flower colour; there are about 50 species. Densely spined species flower profusely at an earlier age than those with fewer spines. The flowerbuds form inside the stems, then burst through the skin near the stem tips in late spring and early summer. The large, mostly funnel-shaped flowers with green stigmas open fully only in sun and are long-lasting. The soft, spiny berries range from green to purple. These plants need full sun and summer feeding. Most are hardy – many even tolerate light frost – but they flower best if kept at 10°C (50°F) in winter. Densely spined species may rot if they are watered too early in spring.

HEIGHT AND SPREAD

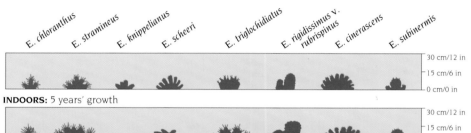

E. chloranthus E. stramineus E. knippelianus E. scheeri E. triglochidiatus E. rigidissimus v. rubrispinus E. cinerascens E. subinermis

30 cm/12 in
15 cm/6 in
0 cm/0 in

INDOORS: 5 years' growth

30 cm/12 in
15 cm/6 in
0 cm/0 in

OUTDOORS: 10 years' growth

Echinocereus chloranthus

Cylinder bells
Strangely coloured flowers are a feature of this small variable species: they are a brownish green and appear freely in spring near the plant crown. The spines range in colour from red or brown to cream, and the small berries are green. This plant slowly forms a clump. It needs a dry winter rest.
H 13 cm (5 in), S 30 cm (12 in). Min. 5°C (41°F).

White areoles, or spine cushions

Needle-like spines

Mature clump of small, slow-growing stems

Echinocereus stramineus

Porcupine hedgehog
When young, this robust cactus is short and columnar. Its flowers – the largest in the genus – open in spring and keep growing to reach 15 cm (6 in) across. The spines vary in colour and the berries are wine-red.
H and S unlimited. Min. 5°C (41°F).

Echinocereus knippelianus

Bold colouring and strength of form
make this a striking cactus. Pink spring flowers and green berries are borne near the stem tip. In the wild, the tuberous root pulls the plant below ground to avoid the hot sun.
H 13 cm (5 in), S 38 cm (15 in). Min. 5°C (41°F).

Echinocereus scheeri

This very variable species has abundant spring flowers that open at dusk and partly close during the day. They appear all along the young, finger-like stems and change colour, usually from pink to vermilion or orange, as they age. Green fruits follow.
H and S unlimited. Min. 5°C (41°F).

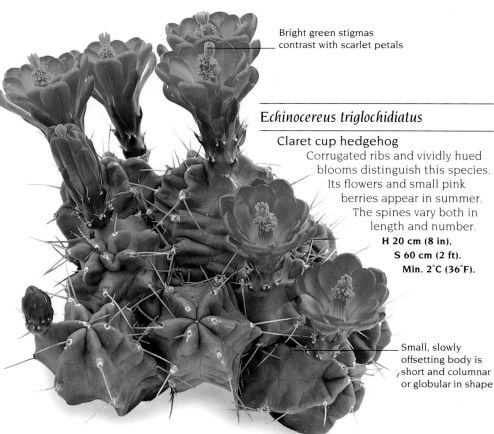

Bright green stigmas contrast with scarlet petals

Echinocereus triglochidiatus

Claret cup hedgehog
Corrugated ribs and vividly hued blooms distinguish this species. Its flowers and small pink berries appear in summer. The spines vary both in length and number.
H 20 cm (8 in), S 60 cm (2 ft). Min. 2°C (36°F).

Small, slowly offsetting body is short and columnar or globular in shape

Echinocereus rigidissimus v. rubrispinus

Rainbow cactus
The short spines often occur in bands of colour, from red to white. Its erect stem slowly forms a clump, but the plant flowers readily when quite small. A ring of pink to magenta, spring flowers with pale throats, then green berries, appear on the crown of each stem. It needs a long, dry, winter rest.
H 23 cm (9 in), S 60 cm (2 ft). Min. 5°C (41°F).

Echinocereus cinerascens

The shape, spines and flower colour of this species vary enormously. It does not flower well until it is about 20–30 cm (8–12 in) in diameter. Its large blooms appear in spring near the stem tips and are followed by green berries that soften when ripe. This cactus forms large spreading mounds of thick prostrate stems.
H and S unlimited. Min. 5°C (41°F).

Echinocereus subinermis

One of the few Echinocereus to have yellow flowers, this small cactus is almost hidden by its clusters of large summer blooms. These are followed by grey-green berries. The small body has few ribs and short, pale, needle-like spines. Moderately easy to care for, the plant grows and offsets slowly.
H 15 cm (6 in), S 38 cm (15 in). Min. 7°C (45°F).

ECHINOPSIS

THE ROBUST SPECIES in this group range in shape from small and globular to tall and columnar, with flowers and spines that differ greatly in size and hue. This diversity is due to the recent amalgamation into one genus of the former genera *Echinopsis*, *Lobivia*, *Pseudolobivia*, *Soehrensia* and *Trichocereus*, which originated in countries such as Chile, Argentina, Ecuador and Peru. The 150 species include night-flowering plants that have several flushes of summer bloom and others that flower more erratically in daytime from spring to summer with displays lasting one or two days. The round berries are often green. The majority of these cacti can withstand neglect and near-freezing winter temperatures.

Long neck

Blooms may be deep red to purple

HEIGHT AND SPREAD

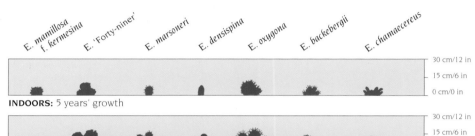

E. mamillosa f. kermesina   E. 'Forty-niner'   E. marsoneri   E. densispina   E. oxygona   E. backebergii   E. chamaecereus

30 cm/12 in
15 cm/6 in
0 cm/0 in

INDOORS: 5 years' growth

30 cm/12 in
15 cm/6 in
0 cm/0 in

OUTDOORS: 10 years' growth

Echinopsis mamillosa f. *kermesina*

When only 8 cm (3 in) in diameter, this small cactus produces flowers that open on summer nights and last for about 24 hours. Protect the plant from cold to avoid unsightly scarring and grow it in full sun.
H 30 cm (12 in), S 23 cm (9 in). Min. 7°C (45°F).

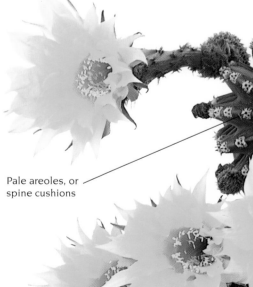

Pale areoles, or spine cushions

Echinopsis 'Forty-niner'

Like all *Echinopsis* hybrids, this pretty cactus was developed to create a more handsome and larger body than that of the species, as well as flowers of a more vivid colour. The dazzling golden blooms open at dusk, at intervals throughout spring and summer, and fade after 24 hours; their necks can be up to 25 cm (10 in) long. This sun-loving, globular plant is very robust.
H 30 cm (12 in), S 1.2 m (4 ft). Min. 2°C (36°F).

Echinopsis marsoneri

Cob cactus

The shape and spines of this small cactus vary. Open, short-necked flowers, which are gold with a red throat, appear on the sides of the stem in summer. This plant is happy in sun or shade, slowly becoming prostrate.
H and S 38 cm (15 in). Min. 5°C (41°F).

Echinopsis densispina

Often labelled with its old name of *Lobivia famatimensis*, this cactus flowers when 2.5–5 cm (1–2 in) tall. In spring or summer, it bears a profusion of fairly large, funnel-shaped flowers with the daisy-like petals that are typical of *Lobivia*; they range from white, yellow and orange to pink, purple or red. The pale spines are bristly. This species prefers light shade or, when in bloom, sun.
H and S 60 cm (2 ft). Min. 5°C (41°F).

Echinopsis oxygona

Widely grown for a century because it is robust and easily propagated, this cactus is a fine flowering plant. The long-necked blooms, some scented, are white to lavender in hue and about 13 cm (5 in) across. They appear intermittently in spring and summer, and open at night for up to 24 hours. The globular body is usually dark green and the spines range from black to white in colour.
H 30 cm (12 in), S 1.2 m (4 ft). Min. 5°C (41°F).

Spiny neck

Flowers open to 13 cm (5 in) across

Echinopsis backebergii

The spines, flower and body colour of this small globular species differ greatly from plant to plant. Its flat-faced summer blooms are often red or purple with a pale throat and are borne freely around the upper stem. The spines may be red, brown, yellow, purple or greyish. This is a good beginner's plant because it flowers and offsets readily. It likes sun or light shade.
H 23 cm (9 in), S 90 cm (3 ft). Min. 5°C (41°F).

Echinopsis chamaecereus

Peanut cactus

This small slender plant has very short white spines, and branches rapidly to form a cluster of creeping candle-like stems. It flowers prolifically, producing funnel-shaped blooms, which open fully only in sun, all along the stem in late spring or early summer. The small berries are spiny. This cactus tolerates neglect and prefers slight shade; it is easily grown from offsets.
H 15 cm (6 in), S unlimited. Min. 0°C (32°F).

ECHINOPSIS

HEIGHT AND SPREAD

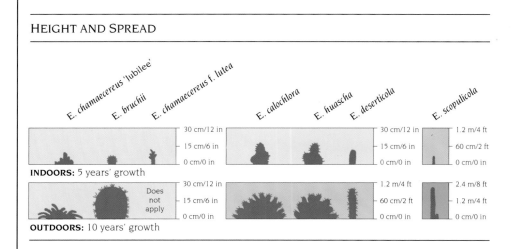

| | E. chamaecereus 'Jubilee' | E. bruchii | E. chamaecereus f. lutea | | E. calochlora | E. huascha | E. deserticola | | E. scopulicola |

INDOORS: 5 years' growth — 30 cm/12 in, 15 cm/6 in, 0 cm/0 in; 30 cm/12 in, 15 cm/6 in, 0 cm/0 in; 1.2 m/4 ft, 60 cm/2 ft, 0 cm/0 in

OUTDOORS: 10 years' growth — 30 cm/12 in, 15 cm/6 in, 0 cm/0 in (Does not apply); 1.2 m/4 ft, 60 cm/2 ft, 0 cm/0 in; 2.4 m/8 ft, 1.2 m/4 ft, 0 cm/0 in

Echinopsis chamaecereus 'Jubilee'

Purple peanut cactus
This hybrid of E. *chamaecereus* (see p. 69) with a differently coloured flower is even more robust than its parent. Its stems are a little shorter and thicker and less fragile.
H 15 cm (6 in), S unlimited. Min. 0°C (32°F).

Thick matt skin

Woolly flowerbud

Flowers open up to 25 cm (10 in) across

Spent bloom

Deep ribs

Echinopsis scopulicola

Easter lily cactus
Huge blooms adorn the thick, almost spineless stem of this impressive columnar cactus in summer. It grows rapidly and, when 1.2 m (4 ft) tall, begins producing flowers, which open at night and fade at dawn. This vigorous sun-loving species makes a good grafting stock.
H 2.4 m (8 ft), S 90 cm (3 ft). Min. 5°C (41°F).

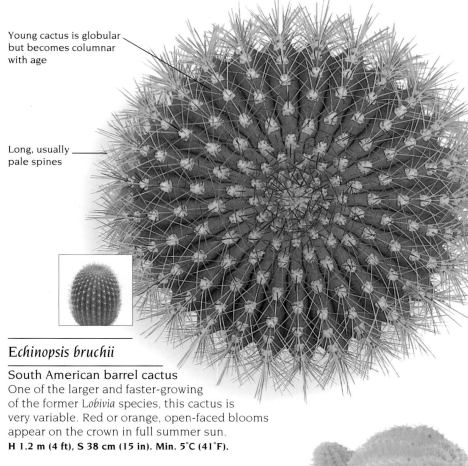

Young cactus is globular but becomes columnar with age

Long, usually pale spines

Echinopsis calochlora

The abundant, funnel-shaped blooms of this striking species may be various shades of red; they open at night in summer and last about two days. Its short spines are yellow or brown. When young, the thick cylindrical body is erect, but it rapidly forms large dense clumps of creeping stems. This is a very robust plant if given full sun.
H 90 cm (3 ft), S unlimited. Min. 5°C (41°F).

Echinopsis bruchii

South American barrel cactus
One of the larger and faster-growing of the former *Lobivia* species, this cactus is very variable. Red or orange, open-faced blooms appear on the crown in full summer sun.
H 1.2 m (4 ft), S 38 cm (15 in). Min. 5°C (41°F).

Echinopsis huascha

When mature, this fast-growing species often forms a dense writhing mound of long, thick, round stems. There are many different forms, some compact, others more prostrate. The spines vary in length and range in hue from red or brown to golden yellow. Once the cactus reaches 30–38 cm (12–15 in), a profusion of red or gold, funnel-shaped flowers appears in summer. This cactus prefers sunny conditions.
H 90 cm (3 ft), S unlimited. Min. 5°C (41°F).

Echinopsis chamaecereus f. lutea

Yellow peanut cactus
A cactus curiosity, this is grown for its banana-like stems because its red flowers rarely appear. It has no chlorophyll so must be grafted on to a green cactus that can supply it with food. The slender elongated stem slowly forms a small clump. Grown only as a pot plant, it needs some care; shade its tender body from summer sun to avoid scorch marks. The grafting stock determines the minimum temperature.
H 13 cm (5 in), S 25 cm (10 in). Av. min.10°C (50°F).

Echinopsis deserticola

Even when small, this fierce-looking cactus often has dark spines up to 10 cm (4 in) long. Its columnar stem is fast-growing and produces erect branches as it matures into a handsome specimen. The body size, the number of ribs and the spines can differ greatly among individual plants. This sun-loving plant eventually forms a clump. Pale pink to white flowers appear in summer.
H 2 m (6 ft), S 1.2 m (4 ft). Min. 7°C (45°F).

EPIPHYLLUM

THESE ARE KNOWN AS ORCHID CACTI for their large spectacular flowers, strap cacti after their broad, leaf-like stems, or phyllocacti because their flowers grow from the stem edges. The 20 species of medium-sized to large, almost spineless epiphytes (see pp. 10–11) grow in the tree canopies of tropical jungles from Mexico to northern South America. The flowers, which are often scented, open at night and last a few hours in warmth but up to a few days in cooler conditions. The plum-like fruits are red or green. *Epiphyllum* are hungry plants, so need regular feeding; they also need warm shade.

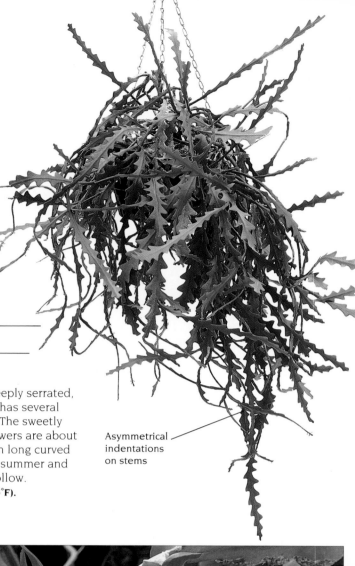

LENGTH AND SPREAD

E. anguliger
E. crenatum v. chichicastenango
E. ackermannii
Epiphyllum hybrids

1.2 m/4 ft
60 cm/2 ft
0 cm/0 in
INDOORS: 5 years' growth

1.2 m/4 ft
60 cm/2 ft
0 cm/0 in
OUTDOORS: 10 years' growth

Epiphyllum anguliger

Rick-rack orchid cactus, fish-bone cactus
So named because of its deeply serrated, trailing stems, this species has several forms with rick-rack stems. The sweetly scented, white or cream flowers are about 8 cm (3 in) in diameter, with long curved necks, and are produced in summer and autumn. Tiny green fruits follow.
L and S unlimited. Min. 7°C (45°F).

Asymmetrical indentations on stems

Epiphyllum crenatum v. *chichicastenango*

If grown in a hanging basket this bushy cactus is fairly compact, but in a pot it becomes tall and spreading. Its curiously asymmetrical, indented, flat stems are erect at first, then form a prostrate trailing clump. Large, sweetly scented flowers and green fruits appear in spring and summer.
L and S unlimited. Min. 7°C (45°F).

Epiphyllum ackermannii

As the only *Epiphyllum* species with vividly coloured, rather than white or cream flowers, this Costa Rican plant's right to inclusion in this genus has long been the subject of debate; it is also confused with an early, red-flowered hybrid of the same name. A clambering cactus that can quickly grow up a tree or a wall, it can also form a trailing or arching mound. Aerial roots are produced from the stems wherever they find moisture. The trumpet-shaped flowers are produced in spring and summer and are followed by green fruits.
L and S unlimited. Min. 5°C (41°F).

Epiphyllum hybrids

Thousands of hybrids have been created by crossing *Epiphyllum* species, often with other mostly epiphytic cacti, to improve the size, longevity and colour range of their blooms. The flowers average 13–20 cm (5–8 in) across but the largest can be 38 cm (15 in); many of them change hue according to local light and temperature. Large-flowered hybrids must be a good size before they produce full-sized blooms. The hybrids' cultivation needs are similar to those of the species but they need warmer temperatures to ensure an extended growing season and a fine display of flowers. Hybrid cuttings 15–20 cm (6–8 in) long, taken in spring, should flower in 1–2 years. Plant several to a pot for a larger plant.
L and S unlimited. Min 7°C (45°F)

Epiphyllum 'Reward'

Epiphyllum 'Lynda Ann'

Epiphyllum 'J. T. Barber'

Epiphyllum 'Fantasy'

Epiphyllum 'Fortuna'

Epiphyllum 'Ignescens'

Epiphyllum 'Jennifer Ann'

Epiphyllum 'Hollywood'

ESPOSTOA

THE LARGE COLUMNAR SPECIES in this variable group are from the Andes of southern Ecuador and northern Peru. Most are swathed in white woolly spines through which longer, needle-like spines protrude. New growth and young stems are most woolly in appearance. After 10–30 years, a pseudocephalium, or especially thick "beard" (see p. 12), of woolly spines develops on one side of the upper stem. From this, tubular flowers, which are mostly pale and sometimes evil-smelling, fleetingly emerge on spring and summer nights – although this happens rarely in cultivation. Red, yellow or green fruits follow. Mostly slow-growing, some of the 16 species achieve tree-like proportions after many years. These plants do best in a very well-drained soil or compost in full sun; avoid overwatering because the roots are prone to rot.

HEIGHT AND SPREAD

E. lanata   *E. melanostele*

30 cm/12 in
15 cm/6 in
0 cm/0 in
INDOORS: 5 years' growth

30 cm/12 in
15 cm/6 in
0 cm/0 in
OUTDOORS: 10 years' growth

Espostoa lanata

Peruvian old-man cactus, snowball cactus
This impressive cactus forms a taller and more slender stem than other species in its genus. Fairly broad, tubular, white flowers with a rather unpleasant scent may open once the plant is 90 cm (3 ft) tall. These are followed by cherry-like, red berries.
H 3.7 m (12 ft), S 90 cm (3 ft). Min. 5°C (41°F).

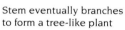

Espostoa melanostele

Often shorter and thicker-stemmed than many *Espostoa* species, this variable plant branches at its base in time. A mature stem may be totally concealed by very long woolly spines. Pale flowers and yellow to red berries appear after 15 years. Do not overwater.
H 2.1 m (7 ft), S 90 cm (3 ft). Min. 5°C (41°F).

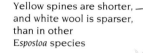

Yellow spines are shorter, and white wool is sparser, than in other *Espostoa* species

Stem eventually branches to form a tree-like plant

FEROCACTUS

KNOWN AS BARREL CACTI after their shape, or as fish-hook cacti because of their spines, these mostly large, sun-loving desert plants come from the southern U.S.A. and Mexico. There are about 35 species. Large, bell- or funnel-shaped, yellow to violet blooms and small, sticky, yellow berries usually appear near the plant crown in summer. The plant body secretes a sugary solution in summer and autumn, thought to attract pollinating ants; wash this off indoor or greenhouse plants to prevent the formation of sooty mould.

Broad, hooked, central spines up to 10 cm (4 in) long

Fine, needle-like spines, 5 cm (2 in) long

HEIGHT AND SPREAD

F. wislizeni F. cylindraceus F. latispinus F. echidne

30 cm/12 in
15 cm/6 in
0 cm/0 in

INDOORS: 5 years' growth

30 cm/12 in
15 cm/6 in
0 cm/0 in

OUTDOORS: 10 years' growth

Ferocactus wislizeni

Candy barrel cactus
Distinctively patterned with white and red or rust-coloured spines, this large cactus bears lemon, orange or red blooms when 30 cm (12 in) in diameter. The plant is tolerant of neglect and eventually becomes columnar in shape.
H 3 m (10 ft), S 90 cm (3 ft). Min. 5°C (41°F).

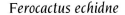

Ferocactus cylindraceus

Fire barrel, compass barrel cactus
The spines, often long, hooked and flame-red at the crown, become denser as this variable species ages. Columnar in the wild, it remains barrel-shaped in cultivation. Its bell-like flowers are orange or yellow.
H 3 m (10 ft), S 90 cm (3 ft). Min. 5°C (41°F).

Ferocactus latispinus

Crow's claw
With age, the red or straw spines of this slow-growing, ball-shaped or flat-topped, globular plant become broad and hooked and lie flat against the body. Cream to purple flowers appear in spring or autumn.
H 25 cm (10 in), S 38 cm (15 in). Min. 5°C (41°F).

Ferocactus echidne

This globular species, which is one of the smaller *Ferocactus*, usually has deeply indented ribs and relatively few, straight, pale yellow spines. It begins to flower when it is about 13 cm (5 in) in diameter.
H and S 30 cm (12 in). Min 5°C (41°F).

GYMNOCALYCIUM

THESE CHIN OR SPIDER CACTI are small and globular, ranging in hue from blue-green to grey or brown. They often have metallic-coloured buds and flower freely when still young. There are 80 species in this extremely variable group. In the wild, in South American countries from Bolivia to Argentina, they grow in the shade of other vegetation, so avoid leaving them in full sun because they may suffer scorch or stunted growth. Most species bear funnel-shaped flowers around the crown at intervals from late spring right through summer; these open fully only in bright light. The plum-shaped fruits may be green, blue or red in colour.

Flowers range from pink to orange and open wide in full sun

HEIGHT AND SPREAD

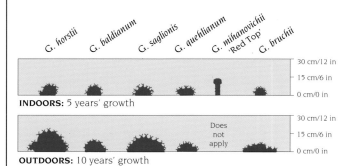
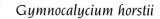

G. horstii   G. baldianum   G. saglionis   G. quehlianum   G. mihanovichii 'Red Top'   G. bruchii

INDOORS: 5 years' growth

OUTDOORS: 10 years' growth

Does not apply

Gymnocalycium horstii

A small number of ribs and areoles give this species a bold, chunky look. Its fruits are waxy and green. Protect it from winter cold to avoid bad scarring.
H 20 cm (8 in), S 60 cm (2 ft). Min. 7°C (45°F).

Gymnocalycium baldianum

One of the few *Gymnocalycium* species with eye-catching, deep red, pink or purple flowers, this plant blooms in early summer when it is only 2.5 cm (1 in) across. Green fruits follow. The flattened body has short, curved, pale brown spines. There are many hybrids with a wide range of flower colours.
H 13 cm (5 in), S 30 cm (12 in). Min. 5°C (41°F).

Gymnocalycium saglionis

Flattened and globular in shape, this is one of the largest cacti in its group. The solitary, silver- or olive-green body contrasts very attractively with black, white or red-brown spines. Pale red, round fruits follow the pink summer flowers. This plant likes sun.
H 25 cm (10 in), S 38 cm (15 in). Min. 9°C (48°F).

Gymnocalycium quehlianum

This species has been cultivated for many years. It has a small grey-green body and steel-coloured buds, which open in summer into long-necked white flowers with a red throat. The straight spines are grey-brown and the berries green. In sun to light shade, this variable plant slowly forms a clump.
H 13 cm (5 in), S 30 cm (12 in). Min. 5°C (41°F).

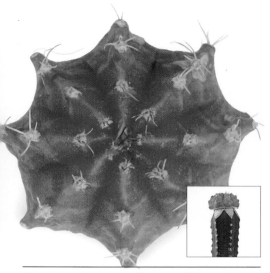

Petal shape and size may vary

Gymnocalycium mihanovichii 'Red Top'

Ruby ball, hibotan
This novel cultivar is called a neon cactus.
To obtain the coloured body it has been
bred without any chlorophyll and grafted on
to a green stock that makes its food. Its pink
summer flowers rarely appear. Other cultivars
have differently coloured bodies. Do not
leave the plant in sun; its tender body may
be scorched and its colour may fade.
H and S 15 cm (6 in). Min. 10–16°C (50–61°F).

Gymnocalycium bruchii

Attractive, bell- or funnel-shaped, spring
flowers are readily produced by this small
flattened cactus, even when it is only 2.5 cm
(1 in) across. Its body is very variable in
shape and is most often green with straight
or curved, white, bristly spines; the fruits
are green. Slow-growing, it eventually forms
a densely packed carpet of stems. This
plant enjoys sun or light shade.
H 13 cm (5 in), S 46 cm (18 in). Min. 5°C (41°F).

LEUCHTENBERGIA PRINCIPIS

THERE IS ONLY ONE SPECIES in this genus: a very slow-growing,
tuberous-rooted species from Mexico that is closely related to
the *Ferocactus* (see p. 75). It has very long, slender tubercles,
which look like a rosette of leaves and are tipped with
fragile papery spines, giving it the name of agave cactus.
After eight years or so, funnel-shaped, yellow flowers
and smooth green fruits appear at the tubercle tips.
The base of the plant becomes increasingly woody with
age. This is a demanding plant to grow, but given full
sun and a minimum temperature of 5°C (41°F), it
produces offsets eventually. Mature plants reach a
height of 20 cm (8 in) and a spread of 60 cm (2 ft).

HEIGHT AND SPREAD

	30 cm/12 in
	15 cm/6 in
	0 cm/0 in

INDOORS:
5 years' growth

	30 cm/12 in
	15 cm/6 in
	0 cm/0 in

OUTDOORS:
10 years' growth

MAMMILLARIA

MOST OF THESE PINCUSHION CACTI flower prolifically, making them good subjects for a collection. Some have finger-like stems, but in the main *Mammillaria* are small, globular and thickly covered with spines. Even when very young, the majority bear rings of beautiful flowers around the crown in spring or early summer with a second and sometimes a third flush of blooms later on. The seed pods are red. These 250 or so sun-loving cacti come from Mexico, Colombia, Guatemala, Honduras, southern U.S.A., Venezuela and the West Indies.

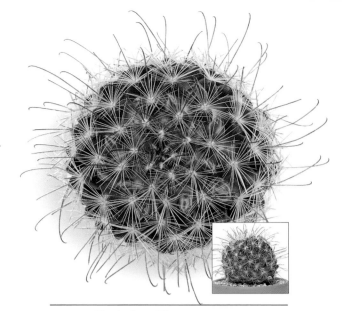

Mammillaria longiflora

This small cactus is well worth growing for its showy, sometimes striped, pink flowers, which are over 2.5 cm (1 in) across and usually the first cactus flowers of spring. The long hooked spines are reddish brown or yellow. The plant needs to be dry when dormant in winter; it rots if overwatered.
H 15 cm (6 in), S 30 cm (12 in). Min. 5°C (41°F).

HEIGHT AND SPREAD

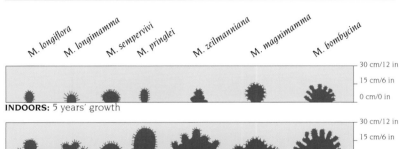

M. longiflora M. longimamma M. sempervivi M. pringlei M. zeilmanniana M. magnimamma M. bombycina

30 cm/12 in
15 cm/6 in
0 cm/0 in
INDOORS: 5 years' growth

30 cm/12 in
15 cm/6 in
0 cm/0 in
OUTDOORS: 10 years' growth

White wool is denser at top of stem

Elongated stems

Mammillaria longimamma

Finger mound
In late spring, this small cactus bears large butter-yellow flowers with relatively broad petals near the plant crown. Its green, unripe fruits look very similar to its long fat tubercles. Like a number of *Mammillaria* species, this plant has a large tuberous root which is prone to rot if overwatered.
H 15 cm (6 in), S 60 cm (2 ft). Min. 5°C (41°F).

Mammillaria sempervivi

This cactus can vary in shape and colour. Its spring flowers are usually cerise, but may be yellow or white, and the very short black spines turn white with time. The flattened globular stem is often solitary until it is 20–30 years old, when it forms offsets. Older plants can become so woolly that they look like white powderpuffs.
H and S 20 cm (8 in). Min. 5°C (41°F).

Mammillaria pringlei

Curved golden spines usually densely cover this species. It bears rings of abundant cerise flowers in spring and often again in autumn. After many years, it forms slightly columnar stems that become prostrate; mature plants often branch at the stem tips.
H 30 cm (12 in), S 1.2 m (4 ft). Min. 5°C (41°F).

Mammillaria zeilmanniana
Rose pincushion

Abundant carmine-pink, spring flowers appear when this species is only about 6 mm (¼ in) in diameter. The purple-black body grows rapidly to form a multi-headed mound. It will not tolerate winter damp.
H 15 cm (6 in), S 60 cm (2 ft). Min. 5°C (41°F).

Mammillaria magnimamma

One of the easiest *Mammillaria* species to grow, this sun-loving cactus has spines of variable length, shape and colour, and pronounced, sometimes angular tubercles. A ring of pale pink to purple flowers appears in spring. The plant offsets freely to form large clumps. It is often seen under different names because of its variability.
H 30 cm (12 in), S 90 cm (3 ft). Min. 5°C (41°F).

Rings of spring flowers

Mammillaria bombycina

Dainty cerise flowers and red, brown or yellow, hooked spines that protrude through a soft white down make this a fine plant. The cactus generally will not flower until it is at least 8 cm (3 in) in diameter. Most often globular in form, this species readily offsets to form a large showy clump.
H 30 cm (12 in), S unlimited. Min. 5°C (41°F).

MAMMILLARIA

HEIGHT AND SPREAD

	M. matudae	*M. candida*	*M. parkinsonii*	*M. hahniana*	*M. wiesingeri*	*M. bocasana v. rubriflora*	*M. saboae f. haudeana*

INDOORS: 5 years' growth

30 cm/12 in
15 cm/6 in
0 cm/0 in

OUTDOORS: 10 years' growth

30 cm/12 in
15 cm/6 in
0 cm/0 in

Spines grow most thickly at the top of the stem

Red seed pods stand out from plant body

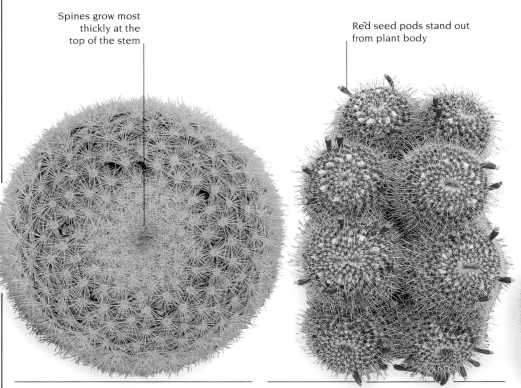

Mammillaria candida

Snowball pincushion
Cloaked in dense white spines, which are often pink-tipped, the body produces rings of spring flowers, usually in succession. These blooms are cream at first, turning pink and then brown as they age. The solitary stem offsets slowly to form a clump. This plant needs extra calcium to flourish: add a teaspoonful of ground chalk to the compost of pot plants.
H 25 cm (10 in), S 60 cm (2 ft). Min. 5°C (41°F).

Mammillaria parkinsonii

Owl's eyes
This species takes many forms but generally has black-tipped white spines. Its usually globular body slowly develops into a large mound by branching into two at each stem tip. The dark-tipped spines on the two new heads look like owl's eyes, giving the cactus its common name. Pink or cream flowers appear around the growing point in spring.
H 15 cm (6 in), S unlimited. Min. 5°C (41°F).

Mammillaria hahniana

Old lady cactus, birthday cake cactus
Cerise flowers are followed in spring by sturdy red pods that stand in a ring on the crown of this cactus, like candles on a cake. The spines are sometimes long, curly, hair-like and white. Solitary at first, the body eventually offsets or branches at the tip.
H 20 cm (8 in), S 60 cm (2 ft). Min. 5°C (41°F).

Mammillaria matudae

Mature specimens often develop into a prostrate mound of long snaking stems that look very effective when planted out in a bed. The stems may also be short and thick. When young, the plant body of this variable species takes the form of a solitary column. Its spines vary in length and density but are usually brown in colour. A plant that is only about four years old and 8–10 cm (3–4 in) tall will flower prolifically in the spring.

H 15 cm (6 in), S 2.1 m (7 ft). Min. 5°C (41°F).

Mammillaria saboae f. haudeana

Fairly new to cultivation, this tiny species produces large, dark-pink to purple summer flowers, which are up to 4 cm (1½ in) across. The fruits develop inside the plant body and appear when the old tubercles wither at the base. Slow-growing, the cactus forms a low dense clump in time. It thrives when grown as a grafted plant (see inset) but may rot in winter damp.

H 5 cm (2 in), S 30 cm (12 in). Min. 5°C (41°F).

Mammillaria wiesingeri

Wine-red or cerise, starry flowers with a yellow throat often appear in two flushes, in spring and again in autumn. They are produced in rings around the upper part of the short columnar stem. The straight spines are brown. Eventually, this solitary cactus offsets to form a clump.

H 20 cm (8 in), S 30 cm (12 in). Min. 5°C (41°F).

Mammillaria bocasana v. rubriflora

Powderpuff cactus, snowball cactus

Less common than the cream-flowered species, this form bears pink or red flowers repeatedly from spring to autumn. Straw-coloured or red spines protrude from long tubercles covered in softer, wispy, white spines. The body may rot if cold and wet.

H 20 cm (8 in), S 60 cm (2 ft). Min. 5°C (41°F).

MATUCANA

THIS GROUP OF PERUVIAN CACTI includes globular or short columnar plants, with spines that can vary in length, colour and density. Globular *Matucana* species flower when still quite small and only 3–5 years old, but the larger cacti must be at least 15 cm (6 in) tall. They flower in spring or summer and sometimes throughout both seasons. The long-necked flowers are often lop-sided and range from yellow to scarlet in colour. Their small, green, round seed pods burst open when ripe to shed their seed. Most of the 20 or so species prefer sun. Keep them at a minimum temperature of 10°C (50°F) to avoid unsightly cold damage and any risk of rot. The former genus *Submatucana* and some *Borzicactus* species are now included in this group.

HEIGHT AND SPREAD

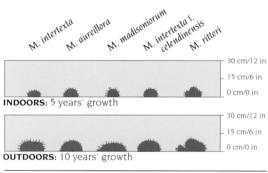

M. intertexta   M. aureiflora   M. madisoniorum   M. intertexta f. celendinensis   M. ritteri

30 cm/12 in
15 cm/6 in
0 cm/0 in
INDOORS: 5 years' growth

30 cm/12 in
15 cm/6 in
0 cm/0 in
OUTDOORS: 10 years' growth

Matucana intertexta

This small variable cactus has pale brown, needle-like spines and red or orange flowers that sometimes appear singly on the plant crown in spring and summer. The plant may develop into a clump when it is mature.
H 10 cm (4 in), S 20 cm (8 in). Min. 10°C (50°F).

Curved golden spines vary in length

Fragile black spines are easily shed

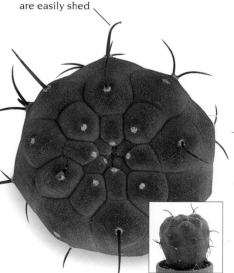

Matucana aureiflora

Rudimentary leaves grow at the tubercle tips on the crown of this small plant. Clusters of golden-yellow flowers appear at intervals throughout spring and summer, even when the plant is young.
H 10 cm (4 in), S 20 cm (8 in). Min. 10°C (50°F).

Matucana madisoniorum

Younger specimens of this smooth and almost spineless, globular, blue-green cactus are the most striking. The few spines are curved or needle-like. Bright red flowers appear on the crown in summer.
H 15 cm (6 in), S 20 cm (8 in). Min. 10°C (50°F).

Matucana intertexta f. *celendinensis*

Formerly *Borzicactus celendinensis*, this is a form of M. *intertexta* and is very similar in appearance. The principal difference between the two is in the flower colour.
H 10 cm (4 in), S 20 cm (8 in). Min. 10°C (50°F).

Matucana ritteri

Vivid vermilion flowers appear in summer
when this cactus is about five years old. It
has needle-like, light brown spines, which
vary in length. The species is closely related
to M. *intertexta* and has a small globular
body that offsets slowly to form a clump.
H 10 cm (4 in), S 20 cm (8 in). Min. 10°C (50°F).

MELOCACTUS

A CEPHALIUM, or densely spined crown,
grows on these bizarre Turk's cap cacti
when each globular body is of mature
flowering size. The main plant body then
stops growing. Small, mostly red to violet,
summer flowers are borne freely but briefly
on the cephalium's centre. Its spines vary
greatly in shape and colour. The 40 or
so variable, challenging species are
slow-growing in pots. They come
from the West Indies, Mexico and
northern South America and are
now endangered in the wild.

Dense, rust-red spines on
unusual double cephalium

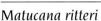

HEIGHT AND SPREAD

M. *matanzanus*
M. *salvadorensis*

- 30 cm/12 in
- 15 cm/6 in
- 0 cm/0 in

INDOORS: 5 years' growth

- 30 cm/12 in
- 15 cm/6 in
- 0 cm/0 in

OUTDOORS: 10 years' growth

Red spines
fade with age

Melocactus matanzanus

A visually arresting species, this has dark
pink to scarlet flowers and large pink seed
pods in summer. It thrives in sun or shade
and grows on Cuban seashores only after
torrential rains wash the soil clean of salt.
H and S 13 cm (5 in). Min. 16°C (61°F).

Melocactus salvadorensis

This small species produces its cephalium
when it is about seven years old. It is
very variable but usually has a green
hemispherical body with reddish, comb-like
spines. Pink to cerise flowers appear in
summer, followed by large red seed pods.
The cactus grows well in sun or shade.
H 13 cm (5 in), S 18 cm (7 in). Min. 16°C (61°F).

NEOPORTERIA

HAVING CONFUSED COLLECTORS for years, this large group of very variable cacti from western South America was recently reclassified into about 30 species. The cacti are mostly small, grey to brown in colour and differ widely in shape. The flowers appear freely in spring, summer or autumn. They are large, open-faced and usually bicoloured in shades of rose and yellow. The barrel-shaped seed pods are red or green. If possible, keep these sun-loving plants above 10°C (50°F) and water them occasionally in winter to guard against unsightly scarring and withered roots.

HEIGHT AND SPREAD

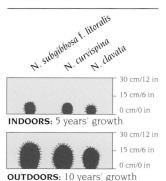

N. subgibbosa f. litoralis
N. curvispina
N. clavata

30 cm/12 in
15 cm/6 in
0 cm/0 in
INDOORS: 5 years' growth

30 cm/12 in
15 cm/6 in
0 cm/0 in
OUTDOORS: 10 years' growth

Neoporteria subgibbosa f. litoralis

This large cactus has white, straw or brown spines and it flowers when quite small, in autumn and sometimes spring. Its globular body becomes columnar and semi-prostrate. The seed pods are red.
H 90 cm (3 ft), S 13 cm (5 in). Min. 7°C (45°F).

Red buds open into pink and yellow flowers

Cactus flowers freely once it is 5–8 cm (2–3 in) in diameter

Neoporteria curvispina

One of the largest growing in its genus, this is globular at first but becomes columnar and creeping in habit. Its spines are red to yellow. Once it is 8–10 cm (3–4 in) tall, it bears flowers and dry red berries in spring and summer. The body scars easily if cold.
H 90 cm (3 ft), S 13 cm (5 in). Min. 7°C (45°F).

Neoporteria clavata

The dark spines of this small cactus provide a dramatic foil for its pink or purple flowers. These appear in spring and often in autumn. With age, the dark body becomes slightly columnar. The seed pods are green or red.
H 30 cm (12 in), S 13 cm (5 in). Min. 7°C (45°F).

OPUNTIA

THIS IS THE LARGEST cactus genus, with over 360 sun-loving species from Canada to Chile and Argentina. Known as prickly pear, cholla, Indian fig or bunny ears, the cacti can be several metres or a few centimetres tall and include some with fleshy pads or branching stems and mat-forming alpine species. Barbed spines and tufts of bristles protect the body. Most species grow very readily; in parts of Australia some are pernicious weeds. The vivid flowers appear in spring to autumn, followed by green, red or purple, often edible, fruit.

HEIGHT AND SPREAD

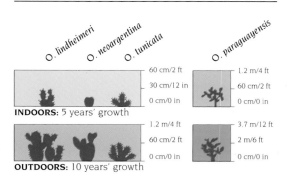

O. lindheimeri	O. neoargentina	O. tunicata	O. paraguayensis

INDOORS: 5 years' growth — 60 cm/2 ft, 30 cm/12 in, 0 cm/0 in; 1.2 m/4 ft, 60 cm/2 ft, 0 cm/0 in

OUTDOORS: 10 years' growth — 1.2 m/4 ft, 60 cm/2 ft, 0 cm/0 in; 3.7 m/12 ft, 2 m/6 ft, 0 cm/0 in

Opuntia lindheimeri

Vivid golden, orange or deep red flowers are produced from the edges of the pads in summer when this spreading bushy species is only two or three pads high. These give way to pear-shaped purple fruits. The pads are studded with dense spine cushions of golden-brown bristles.

H 1.2 m (4 ft), S 3 m (10 ft). Min. 5°C (41°F).

Opuntia neoargentina

Tree opuntia

The pads of this large robust cactus slowly swell in the middle to form a trunk. In dry areas, old pads are deciduous. Cuttings of 15 cm (6 in) flower readily in summer.

H 5 m (15 ft), S 1.2 m (4 ft). Min. 5°C (41°F).

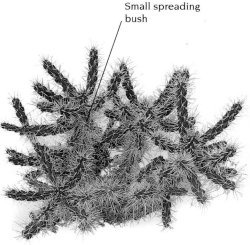

Small spreading bush

Opuntia tunicata

The vicious spines have a silver sheen in bright sunlight and are encased in papery sheaths. Young plants have few spines. In summer, gold to pink, poppy-like flowers and lime-yellow pears adorn the stem tips.

H 90 cm (3 ft), S 2 m (6 ft). Min. 5°C (41°F).

Opuntia paraguayensis

Riverina pear

This fast-growing, tree-like species is banned in Australia but widely grown elsewhere. It flowers abundantly over a long period in summer and has small purple fruits.

H and S 3.7 m (12 ft). Min. 5°C (41°F).

OREOCEREUS

FROM THE HIGH ANDES, these cacti are swathed in a down of long, white, hair-like spines to protect them from the hot sun and mountain cold. In strong light, this down thickens and conceals long, needle-like, central spines, which may be white, red or straw-coloured. The 11 mostly columnar, variable species in this genus take many years to become large and bushy. Only then do they bear crimson summer flowers; these are often lop-sided and arching with a vertical face, and grow near the stem tip. Hollow green berries follow. Keep these sun-loving plants above 10°C (50°F) to avoid scarring or rot.

HEIGHT AND SPREAD

O. trollii
O. celsianus
O. pseudofossulatus

30 cm/12 in
15 cm/6 in
0 cm/0 in

30 cm/12 in
15 cm/6 in
0 cm/0 in

INDOORS: 5 years' growth

60 cm/2 ft
30 cm/12 in
0 cm/0 in

1.2 m/4 ft
60 cm/2 ft
0 cm/0 in

OUTDOORS: 10 years' growth

Oreocereus celsianus

Old man of the mountains
The usually stout woolly stems of this large, very variable species only branch with age. It has pink, lop-sided flowers and straw-coloured or red central spines.
H 3 m (10 ft), S 90 cm (3 ft). Min. 10°C (50°F).

Oreocereus pseudofossulatus

The stems are taller and more slender than most *Oreocereus*, and they branch more readily, often forming a lax bush. Faster-growing than other large *Oreocereus*, this cactus also flowers sooner, producing lop-sided, violet-red flowers after 10–15 years. Its white wool is wispy and the strong central spines are red or yellow.
H 2.7 m (9 ft), S 90 cm (3 ft). Min. 7°C (45°F).

Oreocereus trollii

Old man of the Andes
Only very old specimens of this curiously woolly species flower. The blooms are lop-sided and violet or carmine. The central spines vary greatly in length and can be golden-yellow or red in colour. The plant needs full sun to thrive.
H 90 cm (3 ft), S 60 cm (2 ft). Min. 7°C (45°F).

Sturdy spines protrude through "cotton wool" of fine white spines

Thick solitary stem very slowly forms a small clump

OROYA

ONLY THREE SPECIES OF small, slow-growing, Peruvian cacti make up this sun-loving genus. They are flattened and globular in shape and have comb-like spines that vary widely in density and range from straw or gold to brown in hue. After about five years, summer flowers, which are similar to those of *Neoporteria* (see p. 84), cluster on the plant crown. The small hollow berries are golden-red.

HEIGHT AND SPREAD

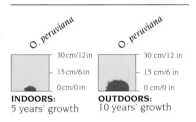

INDOORS:
5 years' growth

OUTDOORS:
10 years' growth

Oroya peruviana

The amalgamation of other former *Oroya* species into this one has created a species with many varied forms. Its spines, once always gold-coloured, now range from yellow to brown. Orange or red buds open into small, yellow-tinged, carmine to crimson flowers. Protect the cactus from cold to prevent unsightly scarring.
H 10 cm (4 in), S 20 cm (8 in). Min. 10°C (50°F).

PACHYCEREUS

THESE HUGE COLUMNAR CACTI make impressive feature plants. Some have solitary stems but many branch readily to form clumps or even trees. Only mature plants that are about 2–5 m (6–15 ft) tall will flower. The nocturnal blooms, which are funnel-shaped and shaded white or pink, are produced on the stem tip in spring to early summer. They are followed by large spiny fruit that are green, yellow or reddish in colour. The 12 sun-loving species are native to parts of the southern U.S.A. and Mexico. Some forms are sensitive to low temperatures.

Pachycereus schottii v. *monstrose*

Totem pole
This slow-growing form rarely flowers. It is prized for its strange knobbly stem; this mutation may be caused by a virus.
H 6 m (20 ft), S 2.4 m (8 ft). Min. 10°C (50°F).

Scar tissue from cold damage

HEIGHT AND SPREAD

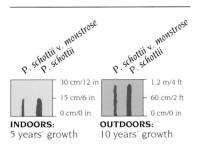

INDOORS:
5 years' growth

OUTDOORS:
10 years' growth

Pachycereus schottii

Senita cereus, whisker cactus
This multi-stemmed cactus bears cream to dark pink flowers and small red berries. When the plant is about 2 m (6 ft) tall, its grey spines become long and curly at the stem tip, making the stem look like a brush.
H 6 m (20 ft), S 2.4 m (8 ft). Min. 10°C (50°F).

PARODIA

ORIGINALLY FROM ARGENTINA, Bolivia, Brazil, Paraguay and Uruguay, these neat, mainly globular cacti flower freely from spring through to early autumn. Their funnel-shaped blooms range in hue from gold to scarlet and are followed by small spiny berries or red pods. Included in the current 100 species are those formerly classed as *Eriocactus*, *Malacocarpus* and *Notocactus*. Most *Parodia* enjoy sun or light shade and a light misting occasionally in winter. They may lose their roots if they dry out, but do not water them if it is cold because they can rot.

Daisy-like flowers with long necks

HEIGHT AND SPREAD

	P. concinna	P. schwebsiana	P. penicillata v. nivosa	P. graessneri	P. mammulosa	P. magnifica	P. herteri

INDOORS: 5 years' growth — 30 cm/12 in, 15 cm/6 in, 0 cm/0 in

OUTDOORS: 10 years' growth — 30 cm/12 in, 15 cm/6 in, 0 cm/0 in

Parodia concinna

Large golden flowers with maroon stigmas appear on the neat globular body of this former *Notocactus* species throughout the spring and summer. The spines are soft and curved and may vary in hue from pale yellow to red. The small, very spiny fruits are dry and papery when ripe. This sun-loving plant offsets after some years to form a clump.
H 13 cm (5 in), S 15 cm (6 in). Min. 5°C (41°F).

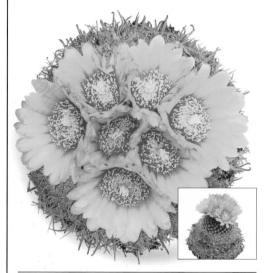

Parodia schwebsiana

Twisted ribs and short, hooked, brown spines give this sun-loving cactus a strange appearance. It produces repeated flushes of orange-yellow, funnel-shaped flowers at the plant crown from spring until autumn. This species gradually develops a columnar shape and offsets to form a small clump.
H 30 cm (12 in), S 10 cm (4 in). Min. 7°C (45°F).

Parodia penicillata v. *nivosa*

The long slender buds of this pretty species open in sun to flame-red, daisy-like flowers in spring and early summer. Given sun and moderate summer watering and feeding, this small, flattened, globular plant grows quite fast and forms a clump with age. The tiny fruits are papery when ripe.
H 18 cm (7 in), S 30 cm (12 in). Min. 7°C (45°F).

Parodia graessneri

Yellowish-green blooms that appear very early in the year and fine, dense, golden spines make this an attractive species. Its small green fruits are papery when ripe. Flattened and globular in shape, the plant grows slowly and is usually solitary, although it may produce a few offsets. It needs full sun to thrive and cannot tolerate winter damp or long, dry periods.
H 15 cm (6 in), S 60 cm (2 ft). Min. 10°C (50°F).

Parodia mammulosa

This robust cactus tolerates some neglect and flowers repeatedly throughout spring and summer. Its large blooms have striking, red to purple stigmas. The species has many forms but is generally flattened and globular, or a solitary column, and is dark green with short, stiff, pale spines. Its hollow cerise-red berries are papery when ripe. This fast-growing plant enjoys full sun.
H 30 cm (12 in), S 13 cm (5 in). Min. 7°C (45°F).

Parodia magnifica

Both main variants of this handsome, sun-loving species make impressive clumps: the form with fewer ribs (above) has a larger, bluer body with shorter, paler spines and offsets far less freely; the other (right) is densely covered with soft golden spines. Open-faced, butter-yellow flowers appear on the plant crown in summer. The small fruits are dry and papery when ripe.
H 30 cm (12 in), S 1.5 m (5 ft). Min. 7°C (45°F).

Parodia herteri

Formerly a *Notocactus*, this cactus is prized for its pink or purple blooms because most flowers of that genus are yellow. The flattened body flowers profusely in summer once it is about the size of a tennis ball. The species has two dominant forms, dark or pale green, which may have white or brown spines. This solitary, sun-loving plant has small, purple-red, papery fruits.
H 20 cm (8 in), S 25 cm (10 in). Min. 7°C (45°F).

PARODIA

HEIGHT AND SPREAD

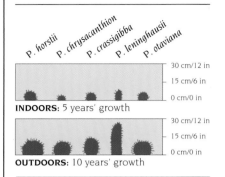

P. horstii P. chrysacanthion P. crassigibba P. leninghausii P. otaviana

30 cm/12 in
15 cm/6 in
0 cm/0 in
INDOORS: 5 years' growth

30 cm/12 in
15 cm/6 in
0 cm/0 in
OUTDOORS: 10 years' growth

Parodia horstii

The summer flowers of this variable cactus display shades of tangerine and orange-red that are atypical of the genus. Its spines are most often long, straight and coloured red and white. One of the larger *Parodia* species, it is globular in shape at first but becomes columnar and prostrate with age. The plant rarely forms offsets.
H 60 cm (2 ft), S 30 cm (12 in). Min. 7°C (45°F).

Parodia chrysacanthion

Golden powder puff
A thick mantle of often bristle-like golden spines and dense white wool on the new growth and crown of mature plants gives this cactus its name. Small yellow flowers appear in spring to summer. This slow-growing and solitary plant prefers sun.
H and S 20 cm (8 in). Min. 5°C (41°F).

Crimson stigmas

Funnel-shaped flowers open wide in sun

Parodia crassigibba

Clusters of large pretty flowers adorn this small cactus when it is only 5–8 cm (2–3 in) in diameter. They can be lemon-yellow or purple in hue and open only in sunshine in spring and early summer. The spines vary from short and bristly to long and curved and range in colour from yellowish grey to rust-brown. This sun-loving plant, formerly a *Notocactus*, has a flattened or globular body with variable but relatively few ribs. When ripe, the fruits are dry and papery.
H 13 cm (5 in), S 15 cm (6 in). Min. 7°C (45°F).

Parodia leninghausii

Goldfinger, golden ball cactus
In the wild, the sloping crown of this cactus faces the sun. Its short, thick, columnar stem is slightly curved at the base and is covered in long, soft, golden spines. Clusters of large, buttercup-yellow, open-faced flowers are produced on the plant crown in summer. The cactus offsets freely when it is about 5–10 years old.
H and S 90 cm (3 ft). Min. 7°C (45°F).

Parodia otaviana

The long, hooked, golden or rust-brown spines of this small cactus contrast dramatically with its scarlet blooms. These are freely produced in spring and summer once the plant body has reached 5–8 cm (2–3 in) in diameter. Tiny papery fruits follow. Slow-growing, the globular green body eventually becomes slightly columnar in shape. This sun-loving plant is one of the easiest *Parodia* species to grow.
H 20 cm (8 in), S 18 cm (7 in). Min. 7°C (45°F).

PERESKIA

SAID TO BE the most primitive of cacti, these 16 sun-loving Barbados gooseberries, or rose cacti, are mostly huge, fast-growing bushes, trees or climbers from the West Indies, and northern South and Central America. They have stout sharp spines, deciduous leaves, and rose-like blooms and small berries in summer to autumn.

Pereskia aculeata

Barbados gooseberry
Masses of large, sharply scented, autumn flowers in shades of white, cream or rose cluster on new growth. Edible, small, spiny, yellow berries follow. When young, the plant resembles any other shrub, but as it develops into a woody climber, its dark thorns become thick and rigid. Prune it in the same way as a grape vine and, if it is grown under cover, repot annually.
H 9 m (30 ft), S unlimited. Min. 4°C (39°F).

HEIGHT AND SPREAD

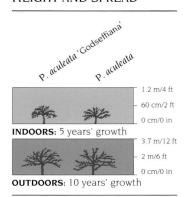

INDOORS: 5 years' growth
OUTDOORS: 10 years' growth

Pereskia aculeata 'Godseffiana'

Grown as a house plant for its pink or bronze young foliage, this cultivar of P. *aculeata* is slightly slower-growing and less free-flowering than the species.
H 9 m (30 ft), S unlimited. Min. 4°C (39°F).

PILOSOCEREUS

WHEN MATURE, THESE LARGE, mostly blue, columnar cacti develop a pseudocephalium (see p. 12) of woolly spines at the crown. Nocturnal, funnel-shaped flowers grow from this "beard" in spring to autumn; they vary in hue, are often foul-smelling and last 24 hours. The large fleshy berries are purple to green. Sun-loving, the 60 species from northern South and Central America and the West Indies need warmth.

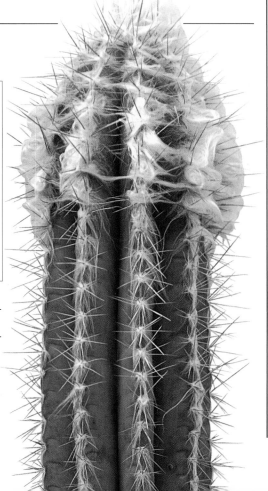

HEIGHT AND SPREAD

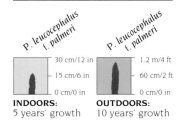

INDOORS: 5 years' growth
OUTDOORS: 10 years' growth

Pilosocereus leucocephalus f. *palmeri*

This impressively large, clumping cactus has grey or beige spines that are yellow on new growth. Its stem can be blue-green and develops a pseudocephalium when 1.2–2 m (4–6 ft) tall. Pale pink to white flowers, which are unpleasantly scented, are followed by large, dark, plum-like fruits.
H 6 m (20 ft), S 1.5 m (5 ft). Min. 10°C (50°F).

REBUTIA

USUALLY AMONG THE FIRST CACTI to bloom each spring, this group of small, mostly globular plants comprises about 40 very free-flowering and colourful species, from Argentina to Bolivia. They differ widely in appearance because they include several hundred forms of the previous genera of *Aylostera*, *Digitorebutia*, *Sulcorebutia* and *Weingartia*. In the wild, many evolve constantly to adapt to the altitude and local conditions. The berries are hardly visible. Most *Rebutia* enjoy sun or light shade; some will tolerate near-freezing temperatures if kept dry. Tinier species make striking specimens when they are grafted.

HEIGHT AND SPREAD

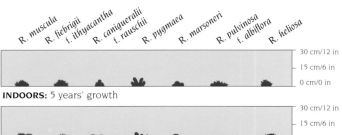

INDOORS: 5 years' growth

OUTDOORS: 10 years' growth

Dense, white, needle-like spines

Rebutia muscula

This handsome, sun-loving cactus flowers profusely in spring and occasionally until autumn; its long-necked blooms need sun to open. The body is usually globular and readily forms pincushion-like clumps.

H 8 cm (3 in), S 30 cm (12 in). Min. 5°C (41°F).

Rebutia fiebrigii f. *ithyacantha*

This pretty species varies hugely in form. It is usually dark green and may become slightly columnar. Abundant flowers are produced from the lower stem in spring. Keep the plant in full sun. When mature, it forms a mound.

H 8 cm (3 in), S 30 cm (12 in). Min. 5°C (41°F).

Rebutia canigueralii f. *rauschii*

Prized for its small button-like stems and dramatic royal-purple flowers, this cactus varies in colour from dark green to purple. The funnel-shaped, spring flowers appear on the lower stems. A sun-lover, the plant is prone to rot and is difficult to grow on its own roots, but thrives when grafted.

H 13 cm (5 in), S 25 cm (10 in). Min. 5°C (41°F).

Short-necked, spring flowers

Deep pollen tube

Rebutia pygmaea

Intensely coloured scarlet, salmon-pink or orange flowers are produced in abundance from the lower stem of this variable cactus. Unusually for *Rebutia*, it forms a clump of short, finger-like stems, which are most often purple-brown and have pale bristly spines. This plant grows best in sun.
H 10 cm (4 in), S 30 cm (12 in). Min. 5°C (41°F).

Rebutia marsoneri

The blooms of this cactus are probably the most brilliant of the yellow-flowered *Rebutia*; their reddish spring buds need bright sun to open fully. The globular, flattened body is solitary or slowly offsetting in habit. It grows best in full sun.
H 8 cm (3 in), S 30 cm (12 in). Min. 5°C (41°F).

Rebutia pulvinosa f. albiflora

One of the few white-flowered species available, this dainty globular plant readily forms a mat of bristly stems. Long-necked, pink-tinged flowers grow from the lower stem and open fully in the spring sun. This is a tolerant plant, but its central stems tend to die off in mature clumps.
H 8 cm (3 in), S unlimited. Min. 5°C (41°F).

Rebutia heliosa

This species readily forms a mound of tiny heads, which are densely covered in short silver-grey spines. A profusion of funnel-shaped, long-necked blooms that open fully only in sun appears on the lower stem in spring. Grafting will produce a healthier, faster-growing and longer-lived plant.
H 8 cm (3 in), S 20 cm (8 in). Min. 5°C (41°F).

REBUTIA

HEIGHT AND SPREAD

R. mentosa f. flavissima	R. steinbachii v. polymorpha	R. steinbachii f. verticillacantha	R. wessneriana	R. heliosa f. perplexa	R. 'Pastel Pink'	R. arenacea	R. steinbachii f. tiraquensis	

INDOORS: 5 years' growth — 30 cm/12 in, 15 cm/6 in, 0 cm/0 in

OUTDOORS: 10 years' growth — 30 cm/12 in, 15 cm/6 in, 0 cm/0 in

Rebutia mentosa f. flavissima

Eye-catching magenta to carmine flowers with short necks cluster around the lower stem; they need sun to open fully. With age, this solitary cactus slowly offsets into a clump. Its spines are pale yellow to gold.
H 10 cm (4 in), S 13 cm (5 in). Min. 4°C (39°F).

Flowerbuds grow from side of plant body

Globular stems form a compact mound

Straight dark spines are sometimes very long

Rebutia steinbachii v. polymorpha

A profusion of flowers, in brilliant, often bicoloured hues of daffodil-yellow, orange, scarlet, pink or purple, are borne on the dark green body in mid- to late spring and again in summer. Very variable in form, the plant often has long spines. It is robust and moderately easy to grow, if given full sun.
H 20 cm (8 in), S 25 cm (10 in). Min. 5°C (41°F).

Rebutia steinbachii f. verticillacantha

Bicoloured flowers, which may be violet or vermilion with gold or orange throats, are produced from mid- to late spring and again in summer. These are often larger than the variable body, which offsets to form a dimpled carpet of many dark green stems. The short spines are pale or dark.
H 13 cm (5 in), S 38 cm (15 in). Min. 5°C (41°F).

Rebutia wessneriana

This flat-topped globular species is prized for its relatively large, orange, red or deep purple flowers, which grow from the base of the stem in spring. The plant most often has dense, soft, white spines. Its very short-spined form, R. *w.* f. *krainziana*, is attractive.
H 8 cm (3 in), S 20 cm (8 in). Min. 5°C (41°F).

Rebutia heliosa f. perplexa

Olive-green, button-like stems form a compact mound, which is covered with dainty blooms from mid- to late spring. These flowers, which have long necks and are delicately shaded rose-pink, grow from the lower stem and open fully only in sun. The short spines are ginger-coloured. This plant grows best in full sun.
H 8 cm (3 in), S 20 cm (8 in). Min. 4°C (39°F).

Rebutia 'Pastel Pink'

With flowers in various shades of pink, this sun-loving hybrid is a good example of the many fine cacti now available in this genus. The spring blooms appear on the lower stem when the plant is only two years old. The globular, pale to dark green body quickly forms a low mound.
H 10 cm (4 in), S 30 cm (12 in). Min. 4°C (39°F).

Spines may be white or brown

Rebutia arenacea

The areoles, or spine cushions, on the spiralling ribs decrease in size towards the plant crown. Their very short, star-like spines encase a brownish green, usually globular body, which offsets slowly into a small clump. In spring, vivid flowers, which are relatively large, are followed by tiny berries. This cactus, recently introduced from Bolivia, grows best in full sun.
H 10 cm (4 in), S 20 cm (8 in). Min. 7°C (45°F).

Rebutia steinbachii f. tiraquensis

This sun-loving cactus is one of the largest in the genus and is very variable. Its spines can be dark red to brown or white to yellow. From mid- to late spring and again in summer, flowers in one of many shades of pink, cherry or purple appear. Flowers of a deeper hue are produced by the larger, red-spined form. The plant offsets slowly.
H 20 cm (8 in), S 25 cm (10 in). Min. 5°C (41°F).

RHIPSALIS

THE GRACEFUL PENDENT STEMS of these variable mistletoe or wickerwork cacti are tubular or leaf-like and are ideal for a hanging basket. Most of these epiphytes (see pp. 10–11) flower in late winter or early spring; small, open-faced blooms, ranging from white to pale pink, are borne along the stems and last for a few days. Bright berries follow, in various colours from white or pink to black. This group of about 40 medium-sized or large, slow- to fast-growing, shade-loving species is widespread in Central and South America.

LENGTH/HEIGHT AND SPREAD

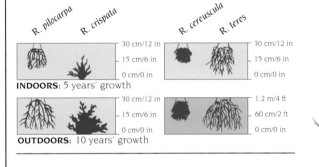

R. pilocarpa   R. crispata   R. cereuscula   R. teres

INDOORS: 5 years' growth

OUTDOORS: 10 years' growth

Rhipsalis pilocarpa

One of the most striking Rhipsalis species, this deep green plant is tinged with purple and flecked with silvery spines. Its slender trailing stems branch into whorls when about 15 cm (6 in) long. Rose-white to cream flowers, which are sweetly scented, appear near the stem tips from autumn to spring. The fruits are pale green with yellow bristles.

L 90 cm (3 ft), S unlimited. Min. 10°C (50°F).

Rhipsalis crispata

The edges of the spineless, leaf-like stems are often crinkled in differing degrees. Slow-growing, the cactus eventually forms a prostrate or pendent bush. Its small cream flowers are produced from spring to early summer and are followed by greenish white berries. This species is more difficult than most Rhipsalis to bring into flower.

H 90 cm (3 ft), S unlimited. Min. 10°C (50°F).

Rhipsalis cereuscula

Coral cactus, rice cactus

When mature, this fern-like species has an abundance of trailing tubular stems, up to 30 cm (12 in) long, which branch at the tip into dense whorls of short shoots. The shoots often produce aerial roots. In winter and spring, small greenish white flowers appear.

L 1.2 m (4 ft), S unlimited. Min. 7°C (45°F).

Rhipsalis teres

This variable cactus often has slightly thicker, stiffer stems than many other fern-like Rhipsalis species and is moderately to fast-growing. Its dark green tubular stems normally form a pendent bush; sometimes they have short pale spines. In spring, small, white to green-white flowers appear, followed by berries of the same colour.

L 3 m (10 ft), S unlimited. Min. 7°C (45°F).

SCHLUMBERGERA

ONLY SIX SMALL TO MEDIUM-SIZED SPECIES comprise this genus from Brazil, but there are many more hybrids. They are very similar in form, with flat jointed stems arching into a small bush. Plants start into growth in late summer and, after a period of short days that have less than 12 hours of light, flower in winter. Too much light, even if it is artificial, can retard or even suppress flowering. Lop-sided, trumpet-shaped, mostly red flowers grow from the truncated tips of new stems and are followed by green or reddish, grape-like fruits. These shade-loving plants are known as Christmas cacti in the Northern Hemisphere or winter-flowering cacti in the Southern Hemisphere. They need regular feeding when in active growth in summer and autumn.

Schlumbergera truncata

Crab cactus, lobster cactus
The truncated stems of this long-cultivated species are much less erect than the newer *Schlumbergera* hybrids. It changes in form as it grows from a small bush to a clambering, prostrate or pendent mat. The small, long-necked flowers are produced later than those of the hybrids.

H 30 cm (12 in), S unlimited. Min. 5°C (41°F).

HEIGHT AND SPREAD

Species and hybrids

- 30 cm/12 in
- 15 cm/6 in
- 0 cm/0 in

INDOORS: 5 years' growth

- 30 cm/12 in
- 15 cm/6 in
- 0 cm/0 in

OUTDOORS: 10 years' growth

Schlumbergera hybrids

Most cultivated *Schlumbergera* are hybrids and make fine pot plants. They are easier to grow than the species, with larger, more shapely flowers. Their diverse flower colours are affected by local light intensity, temperature and the season; blooms that open in autumn are much paler than winter flowers.

H 30 cm (12 in), S unlimited. Min. 5°C (41°F).

Schlumbergera 'Firecracker' and 'Maria'

— Schlumbergera 'Maria'

Schlumbergera 'Firecracker'

Schlumbergera 'Joanne'

Schlumbergera 'Lilac Beauty'

Schlumbergera 'Gold Charm'

SELENICEREUS

PRIZED FOR THEIR BEAUTIFUL pale flowers, which open at night, these large epiphytic climbers (see pp. 10–11) grow mainly in the forests of Mexico and South America. The 20 or so variable species include some that are similar to *Epiphyllum* (see pp. 72–3) but they mostly have slim tubular stems that cling to a host plant by means of aerial roots. The long-necked summer flowers grow near the stem tips, are often strangely scented and produce spiny, plum-like fruits. Most of these shade-loving plants do not flower easily until mature, but they grow quite fast. The stems often make good grafting stocks for other epiphytes, especially *Schlumbergera* (see p. 97) that are trained as standards.

Selenicereus spinulosus

Large summer blooms up to 20 cm (8 in) across appear on plants that are about five years old. The flowers have white inner petals and green to red-brown outer petals. Even on the same plant, the slender clambering stems vary greatly. They may be angular at first, with deep ribs, but later thicken to become smooth and tubular. The spines are pale and bristly. This species makes a good grafting stock for epiphytes.
H and S unlimited. Min. 5°C (41°F).

HEIGHT AND SPREAD

S. pteranthus *S. spinulosus* *S. grandiflorus*

2.4 m/8 ft
1.2 m/4 ft
0 cm/0 in
INDOORS: 5 years' growth

5 m/15 ft
2.2 m/7½ ft
0 cm/0 in
OUTDOORS: 10 years' growth

Selenicereus pteranthus

This climbing species has slender stems that can be deeply ribbed or smooth and tubular. The spines range in colour from pale yellow to brown. White or cream flowers, up to 20 cm (8 in) in diameter, are produced briefly in summer.
H and S unlimited. Min. 5°C (41°F).

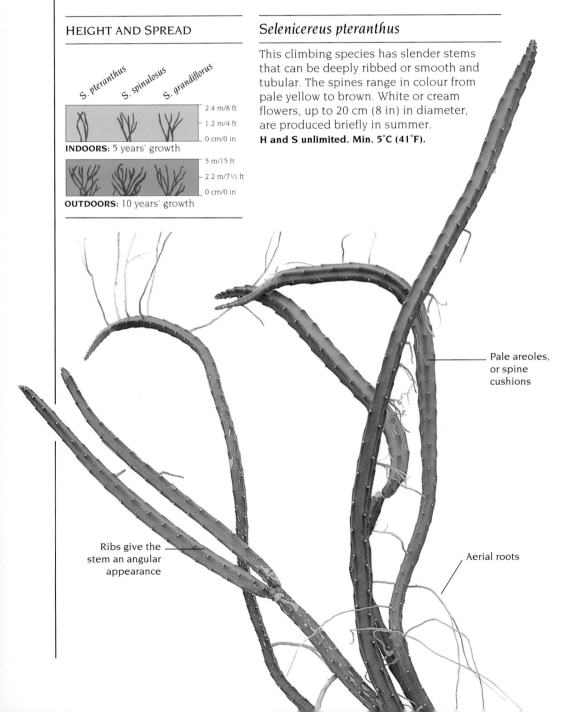

Pale areoles, or spine cushions

Ribs give the stem an angular appearance

Aerial roots

Selenicereus grandiflorus

Queen of the night
Woolly buds open to dramatic, sweetly scented flowers that are up to 30 cm (12 in) across (the largest in the genus). The slim stems are very variable, with deep or shallow ribs and bristly or broad, pale or dark brown spines. In cultivation, the cactus is not very free-flowering.
H and S unlimited. Min. 5°C (41°F).

STENOCACTUS

COMMONLY CALLED WAVE OR BRAIN CACTI because of their crinkly appearance, these can have up to 150 undulating ribs. The 20 or so, mainly solitary, slow-growing species are very variable – no two plants are identical. Many flower in late winter or early spring when only about 5 cm (2 in) across. Funnel-shaped blooms grow from the plant crown between early spring and summer. These are often white, with pink to purple stripes, or yellow. Green seed pods follow. The long spines of these sun-loving Mexican cacti range from straw to brown or black.

HEIGHT AND SPREAD

S. multicostatus
S. multicostatus v. lloydii
S. coptonogonus

30 cm/12 in
15 cm/6 in
0 cm/0 in
INDOORS: 5 years' growth

30 cm/12 in
15 cm/6 in
0 cm/0 in
OUTDOORS: 10 years' growth

Stenocactus multicostatus

A mature plant can have over 100 thin ribs, each less than 1 mm ($1/32$ in) wide, and may possess only a single areole, or spine cushion. The cactus body can be globular or hemispherical in shape. Its pliable spines vary considerably in number and length, with some plants having virtually no spines at all. Their colour ranges from pale yellow to copper-brown. Delicately shaded flowers are borne prolifically in spring and periodically in summer.
H and S 13 cm (5 in). Min. 5°C (41°F).

Stenocactus multicostatus v. *lloydii*

Very similar to S. *multicostatus* in variability of form, spines and growth habit, this cactus has flowers whose petals are a slightly paler shade of pink.
H and S 13 cm (5 in). Min. 5°C (41°F).

Older spines are longer and paler

Stenocactus coptonogonus

Although it is the type species (used to define the genus characteristics), this cactus is closely related to the *Ferocactus* (see pp. 74–5). It is hemispherical to globular and is the only *Stenocactus* species with so few ribs, which are also straight. Its spines vary in length and hue and the white spring flowers are striped magenta.
H 13 cm (5 in), S 15 cm (6 in). Min. 5°C (41°F).

THELOCACTUS

THIS GROUP OF MOSTLY SMALL, sun-loving cacti is originally from southern Texas and Mexico. Recently, the 40 species were amalgamated into 13. The plants are various hues of green or metallic grey and can be flat, squat or conical with dense or sparse spines that are long and curving or straight. An abundance of long-lasting, flat-faced flowers, which range from white or yellow to red or violet, are borne near the crown of mature plants in summer. The small dry seed pods split at the base to scatter the seed. In the main, these cacti grow and produce offsets fairly slowly. Take care not to overwater them because they are prone to rot.

HEIGHT AND SPREAD

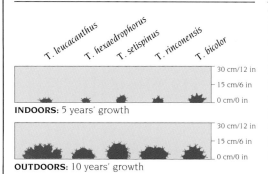

T. leucacanthus *T. hexaedrophorus* *T. setispinus* *T. rinconensis* *T. bicolor*

30 cm/12 in
15 cm/6 in
0 cm/0 in

INDOORS: 5 years' growth

30 cm/12 in
15 cm/6 in
0 cm/0 in

OUTDOORS: 10 years' growth

Thelocactus leucacanthus

The ability of this variable species to offset freely and form large spreading clumps of deep green spiny stems is unusual for this genus. Its long starry spines vary in colour from straw-yellow to grey, and the flowers range from pale yellow to carmine and violet. The young offsets often develop roots while they are attached to the parent stem, so they are easy to divide up and transplant (see p. 157).
H 15 cm (6 in), S 38 cm (15 in). Min. 5°C (41°F)

Thelocactus hexaedrophorus

Ranging from blue- to grey-green, this cactus has relatively few, sturdy, curved spines, which can be grey or banded red. Some older plants develop pronounced, wart-like tubercles with spines that are often banded red and yellow. The flowers of this flattened globular species can be shaded white, cream or mauve.
H 13 cm (5 in), S 18 cm (7 in). Min. 5°C (41°F).

Thelocactus setispinus

If grown from seed, this rewarding cactus produces citrus-scented flowers after only three years, when it is 5 cm (2 in) across. The hooked central spines are yellow or red, fading to grey, and are surrounded by long, star-like spines. This globular species, which is a former *Ferocactus*, offsets slowly.
H 18 cm (7 in), S 25 cm (10 in). Min. 5°C (41°F).

Thelocactus rinconensis

On a young plant, the tubercles of this grey- to blue-green cactus are sometimes very angular. The long slender spines disintegrate and shred into fibres as the plant matures. White, pale gold or pink flowers are produced on the upper part of the flattened globular body.
H 15 cm (6 in), S 30 cm (12 in). Min. 5°C (41°F).

Thelocactus bicolor

Texas pride, glory of Texas
This species, which can be globular or conical, is spiked with dense, sometimes flattened, red and yellow spines. Its feathery blooms appear when it is 5 cm (2 in) across.
H 25 cm (10 in), S 13 cm (5 in). Min. 5°C (41°F).

WEBERBAUEROCEREUS

THE SLENDER SPINY STEMS of these impressive columnar cacti grow very large and may be bushy or tree-like. Some species have ribs with distinctive notches and their spines, which range from white to straw or brown, often turn grey with age. Mature plants flower on summer nights. The blooms are tubular or funnel-shaped, often have long necks, and are sometimes slightly lop-sided. They are shaded white, crimson or sienna and appear near the top of the stem. Red or green, small, scaly berries follow. The eight or so species are native to the Peruvian mountains and need sun to thrive. Like most columnar cacti, they require a good-sized pot.

Indented stem, where new annual growth began, may occur in pot-grown plants

HEIGHT AND SPREAD

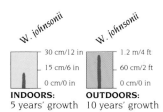

W. johnsonii

- 30 cm/12 in
- 15 cm/6 in
- 0 cm/0 in

INDOORS:
5 years' growth

W. johnsonii

- 1.2 m/4 ft
- 60 cm/2 ft
- 0 cm/0 in

OUTDOORS:
10 years' growth

Weberbauerocereus johnsonii

Golden column
One of the few species in its genus that is densely covered with golden spines, this makes a handsome feature plant, whether it is grown in a large pot or in an open bed. The spines darken with age. Older stems branch to form a tree-like plant and produce long tubular flowers, which are shaded white or pale pink. The berries are green and hairy.
H 6 m (20 ft), S 2 m (6 ft). Min. 7°C (45°F).

SUCCULENTS

A selection of plants ranging in form from tiny
living stones and creeping mats to leafy bushes,
spiralling rosettes and palm-like trees.

ADENIUM

THE EXOTIC BLOOMS of these bushy plants are open-faced and white, pink or crimson in hue; they appear periodically from spring to autumn on young growth. Twin-horned, green seed pods follow. The pithy brown stems are caudiciform, or swollen (see p. 10), with oval leaves. There are only four slow-growing species, which are from east Africa or southern Arabia, but many more vigorous hybrids with a range of flower colours are available. All these sun-loving species prefer dry warmth and can rot if damaged.

Flowers up to 13 cm (5 in) wide

Prominently veined, glossy leaves with pale downy undersides

Stem has poisonous milky sap

HEIGHT AND SPREAD

A. obesum

INDOORS:
5 years' growth
30 cm/12 in
15 cm/6 in
0 cm/0 in

A. obesum

OUTDOORS:
10 years' growth
60 cm/2 ft
30 cm/12 in
0 cm/0 in

Adenium obesum

Desert rose, mock azalea, impala lily
The easiest in its genus to grow, this variable plant flowers readily in 3–4 years from seed. Its pink, white or crimson flowers, which usually have dark outer edges and paler centres, are produced from spring through to autumn.
H 1.2 m (4 ft), S 38 cm (15 in). Min. 16°C (61°F).

ADROMISCHUS

GROWN FOR THEIR DECORATIVE FOLIAGE of varying shapes, colours and textures, these southern African succulents have dainty, mottled, often fleshy leaves that shed easily. Most of the plants form small lax clumps. Tiny pale flower trumpets appear on long stalks in summer. Although from a range of habitats, in cultivation these frost-tender plants need bright shade or diffuse sun. There are about 50 species, some of which grow slowly, but many newly discovered forms.

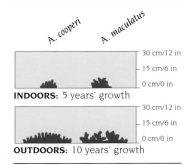

Roots

HEIGHT AND SPREAD

A. cooperi

A. maculatus

INDOORS: 5 years' growth
30 cm/12 in
15 cm/6 in
0 cm/0 in

OUTDOORS: 10 years' growth
30 cm/12 in
15 cm/6 in
0 cm/0 in

Adromischus cooperi

The small, purple-blotched, grey-green leaves are most often spoon-shaped with a flattened wavy edge. The centres of the pale green flowers darken to purple. This succulent is very easily propagated from leaf cuttings.
H 10 cm (4 in), S unlimited. Min. 5°C (41°F).

Adromischus maculatus

Calico hearts, clam plant
With age, the caudex, or swollen stem (see p. 10), becomes very bulbous. The leaves are pale to dark grey-green and often heart-shaped with a wavy margin, waxy tips and purple flecks. This usually low carpeting succulent has white or purple flowers.
H 10 cm (4 in), S unlimited. Min. 5°C (41°F).

AEONIUM

THE FAST-GROWING, ROSETTE-SHAPED SUCCULENTS in this diverse group can be stemless or shrub-like, small or medium-sized, sun- or shade-loving. The growing point in the centre of a mature rosette develops into a stem with clusters of small, long-lasting, starry blooms that are white, yellow, pink or red. After flowering, the rosette, and in some species the entire plant, dies. The tiny seed pods are papery when ripe. Most of the 30 species of pinwheel plants are dormant in summer and start growing in autumn. Largely from the Canary Islands and the Mediterranean region, they tolerate dry cold but can rot in cold damp conditions.

HEIGHT AND SPREAD

A. arboreum 'Atropurpureum'	A. tabuliforme	A. arboreum	A. haworthii	A. arboreum 'Albovariegatum'	A. arboreum 'Schwartzkopf'	
Does not apply						1.2 m/4 ft — 60 cm/2 ft — 0 cm/0 in

INDOORS: 5 years' growth

Does not apply						1.2 m/4 ft — 60 cm/2 ft — 0 cm/0 in

OUTDOORS: 10 years' growth

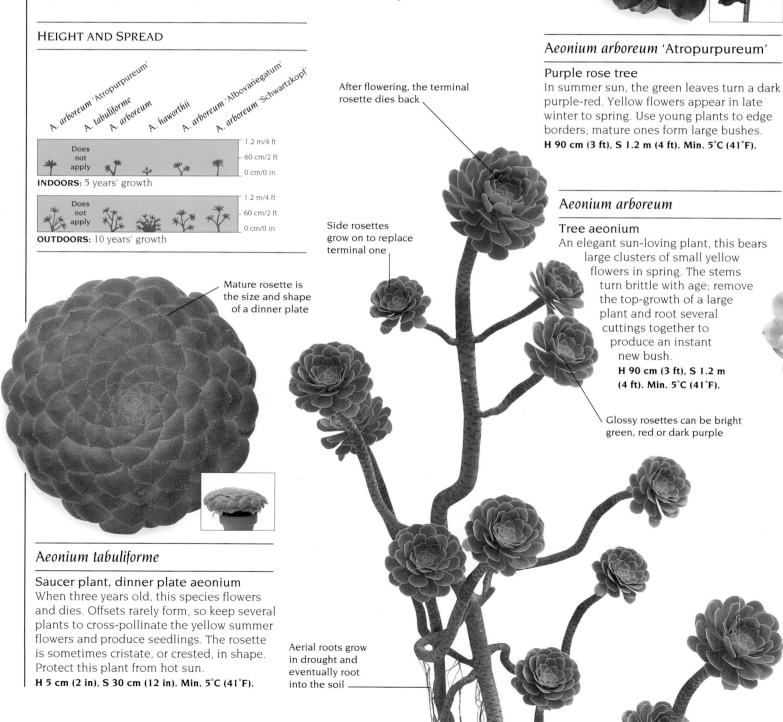

Mature rosette is the size and shape of a dinner plate

After flowering, the terminal rosette dies back

Side rosettes grow on to replace terminal one

Aeonium tabuliforme

Saucer plant, dinner plate aeonium
When three years old, this species flowers and dies. Offsets rarely form, so keep several plants to cross-pollinate the yellow summer flowers and produce seedlings. The rosette is sometimes cristate, or crested, in shape. Protect this plant from hot sun.
H 5 cm (2 in), S 30 cm (12 in). Min. 5°C (41°F).

Aerial roots grow in drought and eventually root into the soil

Aeonium arboreum 'Atropurpureum'

Purple rose tree
In summer sun, the green leaves turn a dark purple-red. Yellow flowers appear in late winter to spring. Use young plants to edge borders; mature ones form large bushes.
H 90 cm (3 ft), S 1.2 m (4 ft). Min. 5°C (41°F).

Aeonium arboreum

Tree aeonium
An elegant sun-loving plant, this bears large clusters of small yellow flowers in spring. The stems turn brittle with age; remove the top-growth of a large plant and root several cuttings together to produce an instant new bush.
H 90 cm (3 ft), S 1.2 m (4 ft). Min. 5°C (41°F).

Glossy rosettes can be bright green, red or dark purple

Rosettes of fleshy leaves look like large flowers

Growing point in centre of rosette

Aeonium haworthii

Pinwheel

This sun-loving plant offsets freely to form a lush domed mound and is good for miniature gardens when young. Some of the older heads flower each spring, bearing short spikes of creamy yellow blooms.

H 60 cm (2 ft), S 1.2 m (4 ft). Min. 2°C (36°F).

Aeonium arboreum 'Albovariegatum'

The rosettes of this large bushy cultivar are at their best in summer, when they become variegated and often flushed with pink. The variegation may disappear in winter temporarily. The plant grows a little more slowly than the green-leaved species, A. *arboreum*, but is otherwise similar.

H 90 cm (3 ft), S 1.2 m (4 ft). Min. 5°C (41°F).

Woody stem branches to form a sparse bush

Aeonium arboreum 'Schwartzkopf'

Black aeonium

So dark a purple that it appears almost black, this cultivar retains its dramatic colour throughout the winter if placed in a bright position. A striking edging for summer borders, it has larger rosettes than A. *arboreum* and is more robust.

H 90 cm (3 ft), S 1.2 m (4 ft). Min. 5°C (41°F).

AGAVE

THE SUCCULENTS IN THIS GROUP take the form of stemless, or nearly stemless, rosettes, which vary from 15 cm (6 in) to 5 m (15 ft) across. Their leaves, each tipped with a sharp spine, tend to be blue-green in plants from colder climates and a soft grey-green in those from warmer areas. Once the rosette is mature – about five years for smaller species and up to 40 years for large ones – the growing point develops into a tall flower spike of many long-lasting, bell-shaped, summer blooms, generally in shades of white, yellow or green. The rosette usually dies after producing small dry berries, leaving several younger offsets to grow on. Native to a range of habitats in the Americas and the West Indies, from coasts to mountains, these 450 or more sun-loving species are also known as American aloes.

Agave americana 'Variegata'

Century plant
Distinguished by yellow-edged leaves that grow up to 1.5 m (5 ft) long, this is a fine feature plant for both bedding and containers. Its large creamy flowers, which are fragrant, are borne on a 2–7.5 m (6–25 ft) stem after 20–30 years.
H 1.5 m (5 ft), S 3.7 m (12 ft). Min. 0°C (32°F).

HEIGHT AND SPREAD

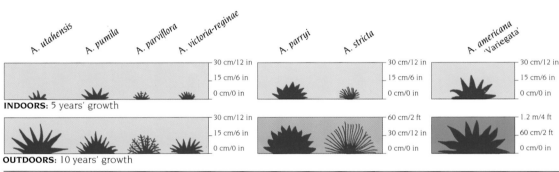

A. utahensis	*A. pumila*	*A. parviflora*	*A. victoria-reginae*	*A. parryi*	*A. stricta*	*A. americana 'Variegata'*	

INDOORS: 5 years' growth — 30 cm/12 in, 15 cm/6 in, 0 cm/0 in

OUTDOORS: 10 years' growth — 30 cm/12 in, 15 cm/6 in, 0 cm/0 in; 60 cm/2 ft, 30 cm/12 in, 0 cm/0 in; 1.2 m/4 ft, 60 cm/2 ft, 0 cm/0 in

Sharp terminal spine

Agave utahensis

Utah agave
One of the hardiest *Agave* species, this small to medium-sized plant has spiky leaves, which can be grey-, blue- or deep green. Yellow blooms appear after 8–10 years.
H 30 cm (12 in), S 60 cm (2 ft). Min. -5°C (23°F).

Agave parryi

Mescal agave
A neat, broad-leaved rosette, this large species produces clusters of creamy yellow flowers on a 3.7 m (12 ft) spike when it is about 20–30 years old.
H 60 cm (2 ft), S 1.2 m (4 ft). Min. 0°C (32°F).

Agave pumila

Recently introduced into cultivation as a miniature form, this slow-growing species eventually achieves a moderate size. It has not yet been seen in flower.
H 38 cm (15 in), S 60 cm (2 ft). Min. 2°C (36°F).

Agave parviflora

Little princess agave
White markings and pale fibres curling from the leaf edges contrast with the deep green leaves of this small species, making it a popular pot plant. Green flowers, which are usually self-fertile if pollinated, appear on a 1.2–2 m (4–6 ft) spike after seven years.
H 15 cm (6 in), S 23 cm (9 in). Min. 2°C (36°F).

Agave stricta

This is one of the few *Agave* species whose rosette does not die after flowering: it develops a short trunk, which branches to form new growing points. The first spike of white flowers is produced after 10 or 15 years, followed by another every 5–10 years. The plant becomes prostrate and offsets freely to form a large spreading clump.
H 60 cm (2 ft), S 1.5 m (5 ft). Min. 2°C (36°F).

Broad white stripes show pattern left by tightly furled leaves of young rosette

Agave victoria-reginae

Queen Victoria century plant, royal agave
An elegant domed rosette of short broad leaves, strikingly edged and patterned in white, led to this species' early popularity in cultivation. Young plants have stiff leaves, but on older plants the tips curve inwards to form a ball. Cream flowers appear after 20–30 years when the slow-growing plant is 60–90 cm (2–3 ft) in diameter. Some forms offset freely; others remain solitary.
H 30 cm (12 in), S 60 cm (2 ft). Min. 2°C (36°F).

ALOE

WIDESPREAD FROM ARABIA TO South Africa, *Aloe* species range from a 2.5 cm (1 in) stemless rosette to a 9 m (30 ft) tree. The 300 or so species in this genus are often confused with the *Agave* (see pp. 106–7) but they differ in several ways. The *Aloe*, unlike the *Agave*, flowers annually and its rosette is formed by leaves that grow out, rather than unfurl, from the centre. Long flower stems bearing clusters of small, long-lasting, tubular blooms, which can be red, orange, green or sometimes yellow, are produced mostly in winter and spring. The small oval berries are green. Larger species thrive in sun, whereas smaller ones need shade; a few are dormant in summer.

Saw-like teeth on edge of narrow leaves can be sparse or numerous

Aloe kedongensis

Branching and offsetting freely to make large, dense, bushy clumps, this fast-growing, sun-loving species is easy to propagate, even from cuttings as long as 2 m (6 ft). Its leaves may vary in breadth and length. The plant flowers freely, when still quite small, over a long period during the warmer months and produces well-spaced blooms on solitary stems.
H and S 3.7 m (12 ft). Min. 7°C (45°F).

HEIGHT AND SPREAD

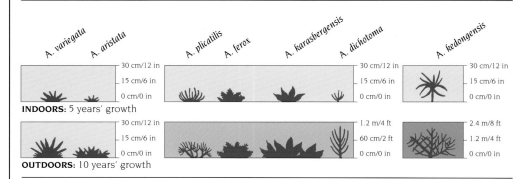

A. variegata   A. aristata   A. plicatilis   A. ferox   A. karasbergensis   A. dichotoma   A. kedongensis

INDOORS: 5 years' growth

- 30 cm/12 in
- 15 cm/6 in
- 0 cm/0 in

OUTDOORS: 10 years' growth

- 30 cm/12 in / 1.2 m/4 ft / 2.4 m/8 ft
- 15 cm/6 in / 60 cm/2 ft / 1.2 m/4 ft
- 0 cm/0 in

Leaves arranged in one plane, like a fan

Aloe plicatilis

Fan aloe
This sun-lover eventually forms a large, unusually shaped bush or tree, which is dormant in summer. Its sparse orange or red flowers appear from spring to summer.
H and S 3 m (10 ft). Min. 7°C (45°F).

Aloe ferox

Older plants of this very variable, large, single-stemmed *Aloe* usually have fewer spiny leaves. In spring, a branched flower spike of dense, orange-red blooms appears. This sun-lover tolerates dry cold.
H 5 m (15 ft), S 2 m (6 ft). Min. 2°C (36°F).

Aloe variegata

Partridge-breasted aloe, tiger aloe, kanniedood aloe
The spring blooms can be salmon to scarlet. The small rosette, when young, is slow to produce offsets; it spirals with age.
H 23 cm (9 in), S 60 cm (2 ft). Min. 7°C (45°F).

Aloe karasbergensis

The leaves of this stemless clumping plant vary from a pale greenish white to mauve and are patterned with lighter stripes or rows of spots. Once about 46 cm (18 in) in diameter, the plant bears well-spaced, pale pink to strawberry-red flowers on tall stems in summer. It grows best in sun.
H and S 3.7 m (12 ft). Min. 7°C (45°F).

Aloe aristata

Lace aloe

Long, soft, slender thorns on the leaf edges give this freely clumping species its lacy appearance. When the plant is dry or dormant, its rough leaves curve inwards into a small ball. Orange-red flowers are borne on a 90 cm (3 ft) stem in spring to early summer. The plant is happy in sun or shade and tolerates a light frost if kept dry.
H 15 cm (6 in), S 90 cm (3 ft). Min. 2°C (36°F).

Narrow, blue-green leaves are rigid

Each rosette of leaves is arranged in one plane

Aloe dichotoma

Tree aloe

Branching slowly into a large, often densely headed tree, this sun-loving *Aloe* brightens up winter with spikes of massed yellow flowers. It may rot if it is cold and damp.
H 9 m (30 ft), S 6 m (20 ft). Min. 7°C (45°F).

BRACHYSTELMA

THESE SUCCULENTS HAVE small to large underground tubers and deciduous climbing foliage that dies back in dry periods. They bear small, oddly shaped flowers and horned seed pods. There are about 100 variable species, mostly from southern Africa and India, but new ones are still being discovered, since they are visible in the wild only briefly each year while in growth. These challenging, slow-growing plants, which are sensitive to damp cold and dry heat, thrive in a gritty compost if the tuber is planted flush with the surface.

Long curved petals are united at the tips

HEIGHT AND SPREAD

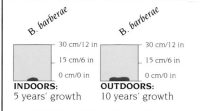

B. barberae
30 cm/12 in
15 cm/6 in
0 cm/0 in
INDOORS:
5 years' growth

B. barberae
30 cm/12 in
15 cm/6 in
0 cm/0 in
OUTDOORS:
10 years' growth

Brachystelma barberae

The appeal of this plant lies in its bizarre appearance. Clusters of carrion-scented, maroon to chocolate-coloured flowers appear on the large tuber's new growth between spring and early summer. The short bushy stems have tiny oval leaves. While in active growth, this plant prefers full sun.
H 2.5 cm (1 in), S 20 cm (8 in). Min. 10°C (50°F).

CARALLUMA

THE STRANGE FLESHY FLOWERS of this group of about 100 variable species are mostly star-shaped and often patterned, ranging from purple, black or yellow to red. They open in summer or autumn, usually at the plant base. The angular stems have rudimentary leaves, which resemble spines. In the wild, in Africa and India, the clump grows like a mushroom ring, spreading outward as the centre dies. In cultivation, this process afflicts the whole plant if it is cold and damp, so renew plants from cuttings each year or plant in hanging baskets for better air circulation.

Erect ridged stems

Favourable conditions produce blood-red flowers on new growth

HEIGHT AND SPREAD

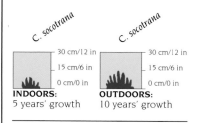

C. socotrana
30 cm/12 in
15 cm/6 in
0 cm/0 in
INDOORS:
5 years' growth

C. socotrana
30 cm/12 in
15 cm/6 in
0 cm/0 in
OUTDOORS:
10 years' growth

Caralluma socotrana

Sculptural, coral-like stems give this small succulent a strange look. The short stems branch and become prostrate; they sometimes turn brown and appear dehydrated. The plant enjoys sun or shade and produces twin-horned, papery seed pods.
H 15 cm (6 in), S 60 cm (2 ft). Min. 10°C (50°F).

CEROPEGIA

WIDESPREAD IN THE WILD from Africa to the Far
East, this variable genus of over 150 species,
which are mostly small and shade-loving, is
constantly being expanded. Many have stems that
can clamber up other plants. The tuberous-rooted
species are deciduous; others may die back partly in
drought or a dry winter. They often need warmth to
grow well and flower over long periods, producing a
large number of strangely shaped, mottled blooms.
Twin-horned seed pods follow.

LENGTH AND SPREAD

	C. woodii		*C. rendallii*	*C. sandersonii*	

| INDOORS: 5 years' growth | 30 cm/12 in / 15 cm/6 in / 0 cm/0 in | | | 2.4 m/8 ft / 1.2 m/4 ft / 0 cm/0 in |
| OUTDOORS: 10 years' growth | 1.2 m/4 ft / 60 cm/2 ft / 0 cm/0 in | | | 2.4 m/8 ft / 1.2 m/4 ft / 0 cm/0 in |

Brown to green creeping or trailing stems

Small fleshy leaves

Flower shape and colour can vary

Tubular flowers with a bulbous base and united petals

Slender trailing or creeping stems

Ceropegia rendallii

This variable species has deciduous twining
stems that bear lasting summer flowers and
small seed pods. The underground tuber
slowly forms a clump. It likes diffuse sun or
shade but rots in cold damp conditions.
**Tuber: S 5 cm (2 in), stems: L 1.1 m (3¹/₂ ft).
Min. 10°C (50°F).**

Ceropegia sandersonii

Fountain flower, parachute plant
A few times each summer, this fleshy-
rooted species bears a profusion of large,
mostly cone-shaped flowers, with parachute-
like green canopies. They appear all along
the rough stems and last for a few days.
L and S unlimited. Min. 10°C (50°F).

Ceropegia woodii

Heart vine, rosary vine
The leaves are very variable in shape and
colour, ranging from grey-green to purplish
brown. Heart-shaped pairs are the prettiest
and the most common. Mauve-pink hairy
flowers appear in summer.
L and S unlimited. Min. 5°C (41°F).

CONOPHYTUM

THESE TINY CARPETING PLANTS are composed of a pair of swollen leaves; each leaf is partly joined to form two ears or fully united to look like a pea. In early summer, the leaves become dormant, withering into a papery sheath that protects a newly developing leaf pair. The new leaves burst through in autumn and variously hued daisies later emerge from the leaf fissure. This unusual growth cycle demands careful watering. These sun-loving, slow-growing succulents from South Africa and Namibia take 20–30 years to reach 15 cm (6 in) across. Recently, the 400 or more species were amalgamated into about 100 species.

Daisy-like flowers range from white to purple

Leaf heads are slightly domed or flat at the top

HEIGHT AND SPREAD

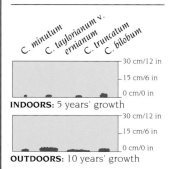

C. minutum
C. taylorianum v. ernianum
C. truncatum
C. bilobum

30 cm/12 in
15 cm/6 in
0 cm/0 in
INDOORS: 5 years' growth

30 cm/12 in
15 cm/6 in
0 cm/0 in
OUTDOORS: 10 years' growth

Conophytum minutum

Dainty, freckled green heads cluster into a neat, ball-shaped mound. This very variable species usually has cone-shaped leaf heads and can take up to 20 years to fill an 8 cm (3 in) pot.
H 2.5 cm (1 in), S 10 cm (4 in). Min. 6° C (43°F).

Conophytum taylorianum v. ernianum

The grey-green leaf heads, which are usually almost square with two short ears, spread to form a relatively large dimpled mat. This succulent flowers well, producing small, pink to mauve blooms.
H 8 cm (3 in), S 38 cm (15 in). Min. 6°C (43°F).

Conophytum truncatum

Usually green with darker spots, the leaf heads of this variable species are flattened on top and have a sunken fissure. The flowers open in the evening and have spidery petals in shades of salmon, straw or ivory.
H 2.5 cm (1 in), S 18 cm (7 in). Min. 6°C (43°F).

Conophytum bilobum

This species is very variable and has many synonyms. One of the largest in its genus, it has rabbit-eared leaf heads that may be up to 5 cm (2 in) tall. Rarely dormant in summer, the plant bears abundant, yellow or copper-coloured flowers.
H 8 cm (3 in), S 18 cm (7 in). Min. 6°C (43°F).

COTYLEDON

EXTREMELY DIVERSE IN FORM, this slow- to moderately fast-growing group of African succulents includes tiny knobbly plants and large bushes. The sometimes hairy foliage can be white or silvery to greenish yellow or brown. These plants flower well, producing spikes of long-lasting, bell-shaped blooms, which range from white or pale yellow to burnt orange and crimson in colour. The dust-like seed is contained in dry papery capsules. Some of the 60 or so species prefer sun; others thrive in shade.

Withered flower stems

Cotyledon buchholziana

Brown stems, which are slim, tubular and upright, make this small, sun-loving plant distinctive. The leaves appear only briefly after the autumn flowers, which are solitary, long-lasting and rust or purple. This slow-growing species is prone to rot if too damp.
H 15 cm (6 in), S 38 cm (15 in). Min. 6°C (43°F).

HEIGHT AND SPREAD

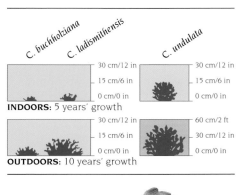

C. buchholziana *C. ladismithensis* *C. undulata*

30 cm/12 in		30 cm/12 in
15 cm/6 in		15 cm/6 in
0 cm/0 in		0 cm/0 in

INDOORS: 5 years' growth

30 cm/12 in		60 cm/2 ft
15 cm/6 in		30 cm/12 in
0 cm/0 in		0 cm/0 in

OUTDOORS: 10 years' growth

Leaf shape and size can vary

Young upright stems

Cotyledon undulata

Silver ruffles, silver crown
These handsome leaves have a delicate silvery bloom and are sometimes edged with scarlet. Orange to red flowers are borne on long stems. If the plant is grown outdoors, the leaves blush purple under their silvery bloom in summer. After a few years, this sun-loving bush tends to sprawl untidily, so renew it from cuttings.
H 60 cm (2 ft), S 1.2 m (4 ft). Min. 7°C (45°F).

Leaves crinkled on upper edges

Cotyledon ladismithensis

Cub's paws, bear claws
The fleshy leaves have three or more teeth at the tip, are often hairy and can be tan-coloured. In summer, mustard to greenish brown flowers cluster on the short stems. This small bush can be semi-prostrate.
H 30 cm (12 in), S 60 cm (2 ft). Min. 6°C (43°F).

CRASSULA

WITHIN THIS LARGE GENUS from Madagascar and Africa are many commonly cultivated, fleshy-leaved succulents. The 350 or so species are very diverse; some are only 2.5 cm (1 in) tall when fully grown, whereas others become 5 m (15 ft) trees. The plants can be slow- or fast-growing, solitary or clumping, sun- or shade-loving, and easy or difficult to care for. They are often dormant in summer, bearing clusters of small starry flowers on the stem tips from late autumn to early spring. These mostly white, pink or red blooms are long-lasting and provide good winter colour. The seed pods are minute.

Glossy green leaves may be round or lance-shaped and are sometimes edged in red

HEIGHT AND SPREAD

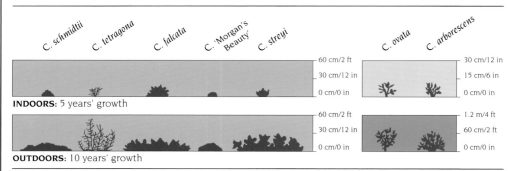

C. schmidtii   C. tetragona   C. falcata   C. 'Morgan's Beauty'   C. streyi   C. ovata   C. arborescens

INDOORS: 5 years' growth

OUTDOORS: 10 years' growth

Crassula ovata

Money plant, jade plant, Chinese rubber plant
If well fed and watered in summer, this large bush or small tree produces dense clusters of white flowers from late autumn to mid-winter. An evergreen succulent, it sheds its old leaves in spring, when it benefits from pruning to keep it in shape.
H 5 m (15 ft), S 1.5 m (5 ft). Min. 5°C (41°F).

Crassula arborescens

Silver dollar plant
In sun, the round blue leaves of this large species have red margins. They are also thick and waxy; prune the bush regularly to prevent them weighing down the brown stems. Pink flowers appear in late autumn.
H 3 m (10 ft), S 1.2 m (4 ft). Min. 5°C (41°F).

Crassula schmidtii

Ideal as a winter-flowering pot plant, this small variable species has tiny, sometimes red-spotted leaves and bright pink to red flowers. It quickly forms a mat; clip it after flowering to keep it tidy. This *Crassula* prefers light shade but dislikes winter damp.
H 10 cm (4 in), S unlimited. Min. 5°C (41°F).

Crassula tetragona

When young, this small, upright, sun-loving bush with glossy, needle-like leaves looks like a conifer and is a good choice for miniature displays. Small clusters of white flowers appear in autumn. Prune after flowering to keep its spreading form neat.
H 60 cm (2 ft), S unlimited. Min. 5°C (41°F).

Sweetly scented flowers open in late summer

Silver-grey, propeller-shaped leaves

Crassula falcata

Propeller plant, scarlet paintbrush
Frothy masses of small red flowers sit atop the long stems of this sun-loving species. The stems form a spreading, eventually prostrate, clump. New shoots then grow from the plant base and the stem tips; use these shoots as cuttings and discard old plants.
H 23 cm (9 in), S 3 m (10 ft). Min. 5°C (41°F).

Crassula 'Morgan's Beauty'

The winter flowers of this slow-growing hybrid are some of the prettiest in the genus, contrasting well with its small mound of dense silver foliage. In winter, water the plant sparingly and split up large clumps to avoid rot. It likes sun or shade.
H 13 cm (5 in), S 90 cm (3 ft). Min. 10°C (50°F).

Crassula streyi

The dramatic contrast of its differently coloured leaf surfaces make this a beautiful feature plant. When it is grown in shade, its glossy leaves become a rich deep green on the upper surfaces and wine-red on the undersides. In sun, the foliage becomes dull and muted in colour. Clusters of small white flowers appear in autumn. The prostrate stems slowly form a low clump.
H 30 cm (12 in), S 2 m (6 ft). Min. 10°C (50°F).

CYPHOSTEMMA

SOME SPECIES IN THIS GENUS have been cultivated in Germany for more than 400 years. The medium-sized to large succulents have a woody caudex, or swollen trunk (see p. 10), from which a leafy stem grows each summer, sometimes quite late in the season. After 10–20 years, clusters of long-lasting, tiny, greenish yellow flowers are borne on stalks that emerge at the stem tip. These African relatives of the vine then produce inedible, grape-like fruits. Many of the 20 or so slow-growing, sun-loving species exude white latex droplets, which are often mistaken for an insect infestation, from the undersides of the leaves.

HEIGHT AND SPREAD

C. juttae *C. bainesii*

30 cm/12 in
15 cm/6 in
0 cm/0 in
INDOORS: 5 years' growth

60 cm/2 ft
30 cm/12 in
0 cm/0 in
OUTDOORS: 10 years' growth

Cabbage-like leaves

Deeply serrated leaf edges

Cyphostemma juttae

One of the larger species, this succulent normally has a thick tubular trunk. With great age, it develops a few branches near the crown and eventually forms a large bush. It is fairly common in cultivation but can be difficult to grow as it dislikes cold and high humidity. The fruits become red when ripe.
H 2 m (6 ft), S 30 cm (12 in). Min. 10°C (50°F).

Cyphostemma bainesii

The conical, almost bottle-like trunk usually becomes fat and bulbous in old age. It has fleshy leaves that are divided into three leaflets. When young, these are silvery green. This plant can be challenging to grow because it is prone to rot in damp conditions. Its green fruits ripen to red.
H 76 cm (30 in), S 60 cm (2 ft). Min. 10°C (50°F).

Papery peeling bark

Trunk branches only rarely

DUDLEYA

THE LEAVES OF THESE mainly small rosettes often have a silvery bloom, which is more pronounced in winter. In summer, small, long-lasting, starry flowers, which are mostly yellow, appear on long, sometimes prostrate stems. These sun-loving plants are best kept dry during winter. The 40 or so solitary or clump-forming species are very variable and will hybridize freely in the wild, in the U.S.A. and Mexico.

Silvery white leaves are usually narrow and tapering

HEIGHT AND SPREAD

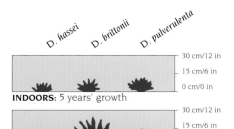

D. hassei   D. brittonii   D. pulverulenta

30 cm/12 in
15 cm/6 in
0 cm/0 in
INDOORS: 5 years' growth

30 cm/12 in
15 cm/6 in
0 cm/0 in
OUTDOORS: 10 years' growth

Dudleya hassei

This spiky rosette reaches up to 13 cm (5 in) in diameter and branches freely to form large, coral-like clumps. Its white flowers are borne on 30 cm (12 in) stems, which grow from the sides of the rosette. The plant's open habit makes it less prone to rot than many other *Dudleya* species.
H 23 cm (9 in), S 90 cm (3 ft). Min. 7°C (45°F).

Dudleya brittonii

Silver dollar plant
Generally a startling silver-white, this solitary rosette resembles a flower. Masses of pale yellow flowers are borne on 90 cm (3 ft) stems.
H 38 cm (15 in), S 76 cm (30 in). Min. 10°C (50°F).

Relatively slow-growing rosette carried on a short stem

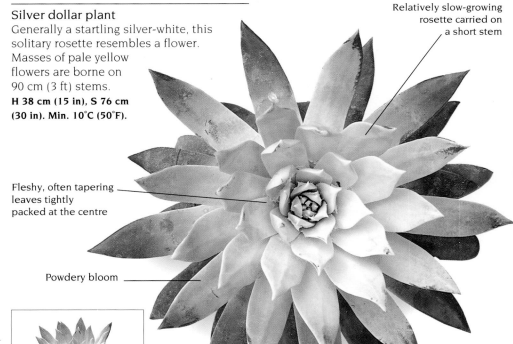

Fleshy, often tapering leaves tightly packed at the centre

Powdery bloom

Dudleya pulverulenta

The tightly packed rosette of this small species may be shaded silver-grey to pure white. It branches slowly to form a relatively dense clump of prostrate stems. Unusually for this genus, the succulent bears scarlet flowers on flower stems that can be up to 1.5 m (5 ft) long. Protect the plant from winter cold and high humidity to guard against the risk of rot.
H 18 cm (7 in), S 76 cm (30 in). Min. 10°C (50°F).

ECHEVERIA

MOST OF THE ROSETTE-SHAPED SUCCULENTS in this large group are from Mexico. The 150 or so species vary in shape and size and are green to blue, red, purple or pink. They are greener when in active growth in spring or summer and become richly coloured during dormancy. Some have tall stems, others are stemless. Tall spikes of small, long-lasting, bell-shaped flowers, which are often bicoloured in hues of gold, orange and red, are produced from the rosette. Small dry berries follow. In each season of the year, there are some *Echeveria* in flower. A few species are very challenging, but the thousands of hybrids are often beautiful and easy to grow. Generally sun-loving, *Echeveria* are more compact and intensely coloured when grown outdoors, but they also make good house plants for a bright position. Many species tolerate dry cold, but may rot if it is damp.

Echeveria fimbriata

The late summer flowers of this erect bushy plant are red and orange or red and yellow. Its foliage is usually purplish green.
H 60 cm (2 ft), S 90 cm (3 ft). Min. 5°C (41°F).

HEIGHT AND SPREAD

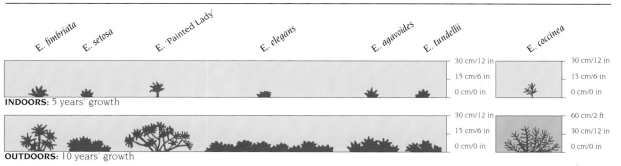
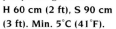

E. fimbriata	E. setosa	E. 'Painted Lady'	E. elegans	E. agavoides	E. tundellii	E. coccinea	

INDOORS: 5 years' growth

OUTDOORS: 10 years' growth

Echeveria setosa

Mexican firecracker
The summer flowers of this small, variable, clumping plant are bright yellow and red. Prone to rot and scorch, it needs dry shade.
H 13 cm (5 in), S 90 cm (3 ft). Min. 7°C (45°F).

Echeveria 'Painted Lady'

This spreading bushy hybrid has red flowers in summer and often pronounced leaf markings. It forms a prostrate clump with age and should be divided every few years.
H 38 cm (15 in), S unlimited. Min. 5°C (41°F).

Echeveria coccinea

The abundant, reddish yellow, spring flowers of this bushy, narrow-leaved species last well when cut. Upright at first, its stems become prostrate and root into the soil to form a spreading mound.

H 60 cm (2 ft), S 90 cm (3 ft). Min. 5°C (41°F).

Echeveria elegans

This species is a good choice for formal summer bedding. It acquires a pink hue in full sun and pale yellow flowers appear in summer. The usually small but fast-growing parent offsets to form a mat of rosettes.

H 8 cm (3 in), S unlimited. Min. 5°C (41°F).

Echeveria agavoides

Wax agave, moulded-wax agave
Grown for its variable but pretty foliage, this large stemless rosette offsets readily to form impressive clumps. In full sun, the usually pale grey-green leaves blush red. Its reddish summer flowers are tiny.

H 25 cm (10 in), S 90 cm (3 ft). Min. 5°C (41°F).

Downy hairs are more pronounced on young rosettes and stems

Echeveria tundellii

The downy, soft blue rosette offsets and develops into a small mound, which in summer provides a foil to arching stems of brilliant flame-red and yellow flowers. Rosettes begin to flower when they are only 2.5 cm (1 in) in diameter.

H 13 cm (5 in), S 60 cm (2 ft). Min. 5°C (41°F).

Flower colour is typical of *Echeveria* species

EUPHORBIA

THIS HUGE GROUP OF SHRUBS and perennials includes about 1,200 slow- to fast-growing succulent species, mainly from tropical and subtropical areas. They range from small, cactus-like plants to bushy or tree-like ones and are mostly sun-loving. Their tiny flowers lack petals and sepals but are often enclosed by brightly hued, long-lasting leaf bracts. Both male and female plants are needed to produce the green seed pods. *Euphorbia*, known as spurge or milkweed, must be handled with gloves because they have a milky sap that irritates skin and can cause blindness. To stop the flow of sap from a "bleeding" plant, immerse it in water.

HEIGHT AND SPREAD

Squat globular body

Euphorbia obesa

Basketball euphorbia, gingham golf ball, Hottentot's hut
Smooth-bodied, spineless and usually olive-green, this succulent has pale green or mauve markings. The small, slow-growing body becomes slightly columnar with age. Tiny leaf bracts appear at the crown in summer. The plant, which enjoys sun or shade, needs a dry winter dormancy.
H 20 cm (8 in), S 13 cm (5 in).
Min. 10°C (50°F).

E. obesa | E. francoisii | E. decaryi | E. horrida | E. grandialata | E. neohumbertii | E. milii

	30 cm/12 in
	15 cm/6 in
	0 cm/0 in
INDOORS: 5 years' growth

	60 cm/2 ft
	30 cm/12 in
	0 cm/0 in

	30 cm/12 in
	15 cm/6 in
	0 cm/0 in
OUTDOORS: 10 years' growth

	1.2 m/4 ft
	60 cm/2 ft
	0 cm/0 in

Leaf bract

Thorns look like cactus spines

Euphorbia francoisii

The leaves may be dark green, white or red, and can vary greatly in shape. Yellow-green, kidney-shaped leaf bracts appear on the tips of the short prostrate stems in summer. This small succulent has a long tap root and spreads slowly by means of its underground stems.
H 13 cm (5 in), S 38 cm (15 in). Min. 10°C (50°F).

Euphorbia grandialata

The thorny angular stems, which are banded with pale green markings, are upright at first but branch at the base to form a large spreading bush relatively quickly. Tiny, petal-less flowers and coral-red leaf bracts are produced in summer. This species grows best in sun.
H 2 m (6 ft), S 2.4 m (8 ft). Min. 10°C (50°F).

Euphorbia neohumbertii

The erect stem has a handsome rosette of variable deciduous leaves. New growth from the banded, normally light brown stem is bright green. Leaf bracts, small and green with red tips, appear in spring while the stems are still-bare. This succulent is happy in sun or shade, but not in cold.
H and S 60 cm (2 ft). Min. 10°C (50°F).

Euphorbia milii

Crown of thorns
Tiny white, gold, red, rose or orange leaf bracts open periodically on new growth all year if the plant is kept moist and warm. In warmer climates, the thorny, fast-growing bush makes a good hedging plant. This variable species grows well in sun or shade.
H 2 m (6 ft), S 1.5 m (5 ft). Min. 13°C (55°F).

Euphorbia decaryi

Short upright stems with rosettes of variable leaves at their tips grow from slowly spreading underground stems. In summer, yellow-green and red leaf bracts appear at the stem tips. Protect this small shade-lover from cold and from high humidity to guard against rot.
H 15 cm (6 in), S 60 cm (2 ft). Min. 10°C (50°F).

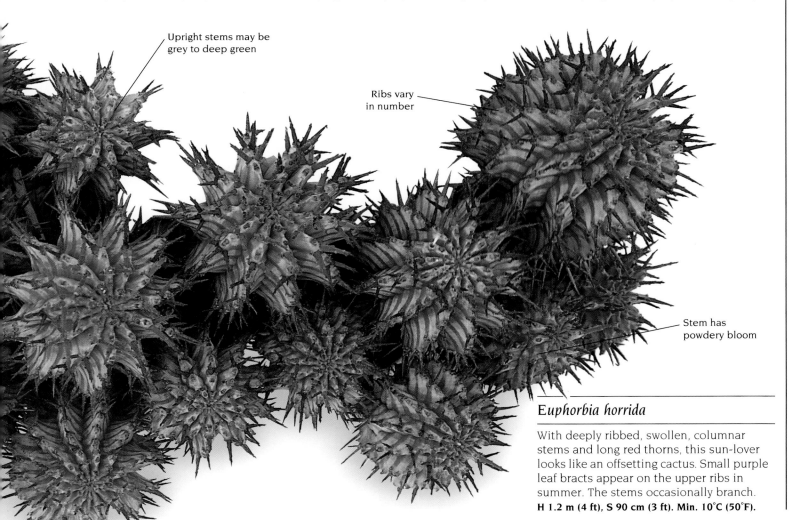

Upright stems may be grey to deep green

Ribs vary in number

Stem has powdery bloom

Euphorbia horrida

With deeply ribbed, swollen, columnar stems and long red thorns, this sun-lover looks like an offsetting cactus. Small purple leaf bracts appear on the upper ribs in summer. The stems occasionally branch.
H 1.2 m (4 ft), S 90 cm (3 ft). Min. 10°C (50°F).

FAUCARIA

THE FLESHY, BRIGHT GREEN LEAVES of these southern African plants are semi-cylindrical or triangular in shape and nearly all are tipped with soft short teeth, giving rise to their common name of tiger's jaws. The 30 or so sun-loving species often form small prostrate clumps. After only two years, large, stemless, bright yellow, daisy-like flowers grow from the centre of each rosette in autumn and open in full sun. The plants start growing in late spring or in early summer and fall dormant after flowering. The green seed pods are woody when ripe. To avoid risk of rot, take care not to overwater plants early in the year.

Stemless flowers

HEIGHT AND SPREAD

F. tuberculosa		F. tuberculosa	
	30 cm/12 in		30 cm/12 in
	15 cm/6 in		15 cm/6 in
	0 cm/0 in		0 cm/0 in
INDOORS: 5 years' growth		**OUTDOORS:** 10 years' growth	

Faucaria tuberculosa

Warty tiger's jaws
Strange "warts" – tiny white tubercles – stud the upper surfaces of the leaves, which are usually thick, short and roughly triangular. The number of warts and teeth can vary considerably from plant to plant. The flowers are about 5 cm (2 in) wide.
H 10 cm (4 in), S 60 cm (2 ft). Min. 5°C (41°F).

FRITHIA PULCHRA

KNOWN AS PINK BABY'S TOES, the sole species in this genus forms a compact stemless rosette of fleshy leaves with flat translucent tips. When mature, the succulent is usually no more than 2.5 cm (1 in) tall and 13 cm (5 in) across. Masses of small, crimson to pink, daisy-like flowers with white bases open in sun from late spring through until autumn. Tiny brown fruits follow. This succulent usually lives for only five years or so but will slowly develop offsets that can be used to propagate new plants. Frost-tender, it needs sunny conditions and a minimum temperature of 5°C (41°F) to thrive.

HEIGHT AND SPREAD

	30 cm/12 in	Does not live ten years	30 cm/12 in
	15 cm/6 in		15 cm/6 in
	0 cm/0 in		0 cm/0 in
INDOORS: 5 years' growth		**OUTDOORS:** 10 years' growth	

Fleshy, toe-like leaves with a rough grey skin

Leaf tips have "windows" to diffuse harsh sunlight

GASTERIA

THESE COMPACT SUCCULENTS, known as ox tongues, form a distichous fan (two facing rows of upright fleshy leaves) when young, and some spiral into a rosette as they age. They usually have dark green leaves that are variously spotted, striped or stippled white. Related to the *Aloe* (see pp. 108–9), they also have long-lasting, tubular flowers borne sparsely on long stems. Blooms that are mostly orange or red with yellow-green tips appear in spring. Mature plants flower until winter. Their green seed pods ripen to brown. The 75 or so species, from southern and southwestern Africa, grow in sun or shade.

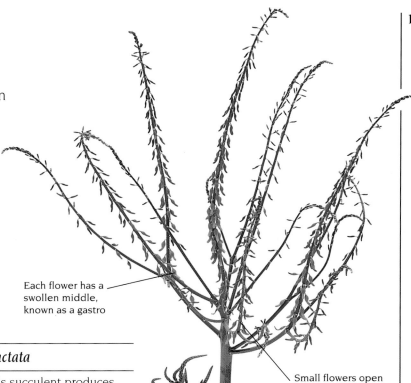

Each flower has a swollen middle, known as a gastro

Small flowers open in succession from the base of the stems

HEIGHT AND SPREAD

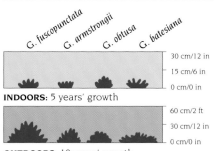

G. fuscopunctata *G. armstrongii* *G. obtusa* *G. batesiana*

30 cm/12 in
15 cm/6 in
0 cm/0 in
INDOORS: 5 years' growth

60 cm/2 ft
30 cm/12 in
0 cm/0 in
OUTDOORS: 10 years' growth

Gasteria fuscopunctata

When it flowers, this succulent produces elegant arching sprays of dainty pendent flowers. The pointed leaves grow to 30 cm (12 in) or more, making this species one of the largest in its genus, so it is most suitable for a large collection or a spacious position. The spiky rosette, which is dark green and patterned with sparse brownish spots, is slow-growing and eventually develops into a clump.
H 60 cm (2 ft), S 90 cm (3 ft). Min. 5°C (41°F).

Flower spikes grow from near the centre of the rosette

Leaves have rough skin

Gasteria armstrongii

Each small fan is formed of a few thick leaves, which are normally rough and tongue-shaped. The leaves vary considerably in size and shade of green from plant to plant. This succulent forms a low clump.
H 23 cm (9 in), S 60 cm (2 ft). Min. 5°C (41°F).

Gasteria obtusa

When still young, the small, fan-shaped plant offsets freely to form large clumps. The leaves vary widely; they can be spotted grey or green and, occasionally, variegated with bands of yellow, cream or white.
H 20 cm (8 in), S 90 cm (3 ft). Min. 5°C (41°F).

Gasteria batesiana

Generally dark green with lighter bands or spots, the leaves of this species are also rough, dagger-shaped and concave on their upper surfaces. They are arranged in a tight rosette, which offsets fairly readily in cultivation to form large clumps.
H 15 cm (6 in), S 90 cm (3 ft). Min. 5°C (41°F).

GIBBAEUM

THE FLESHY LEAVES OF THESE compact carpeting plants from the South African Cape range from pea-shaped to long and finger-like. They are often arranged in pairs of unequal length, with the longer leaf being slightly hooked at the tip. White to violet-red, daisy-like flowers are produced near the stem tips in spring and sometimes in autumn. Their small green seed pods are woody when ripe. The 20 or so species grow best in sun. Water them well in autumn for a good show of flowers; at other times water sparingly.

HEIGHT AND SPREAD

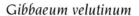

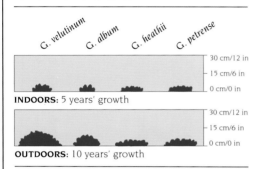

INDOORS: 5 years' growth

OUTDOORS: 10 years' growth

5 cm (2 in) wide flowers

Some leaves have hooked tips

Gibbaeum velutinum

Asymmetrical paired leaves provide a foil for relatively large flowers that vary from white to lavender or red. These are borne readily from spring through to autumn.
H 13 cm (5 in), S 90 cm (3 ft). Min. 5°C (41°F).

Gibbaeum album

Each pair of downy white leaves on this neat, slow-growing species forms a swollen, almost globular head. The heads divide after flowering and eventually spread to create a low knobbly mound. Not as free-flowering as other species in the genus, this succulent bears white blooms. The plant is prone to rot if it is overwatered.
H 10 cm (4 in), S 23 cm (9 in). Min. 5°C (41°F).

Gibbaeum heathii

In cultivation, this species forms dense mounds of soft, pea-like heads. These proliferate into low carpets that are comparatively large for the genus. The flowers, in various shades of cream and rose, usually appear only in favourable outdoor situations. Although this succulent is moderately easy to grow, it requires protection from prolonged wet or damp conditions in order to guard against rot. G. *heathii* is quite widespread in the wild.
H 5 cm (2 in), S 90 cm (3 ft). Min. 5°C (41°F).

Gibbaeum petrense

Although it has very small heads, which are composed of pairs of thick triangular leaves only 1 cm (½ in) long, this species spreads into large, pale grey-green carpets that can trail prettily over banks or walls. The flowers are produced more readily than in many other *Gibbaeum* species and can be pink to reddish violet in colour.
H 5 cm (2 in), S 90 cm (3 ft). Min. 5°C (41°F).

GRAPTOPETALUM

FROM ARIZONA AND MEXICO, these small green, blue or grey, sometimes speckled rosettes are related to *Echeveria* (see pp. 118–19). Their small, upward-facing, starry flowers are long-lasting, fairly large and shaded white to red. They are produced on mostly long stems from spring to winter. Tiny seed pods follow. All 12 species in this group prefer bright light, but some can suffer scorch in hot sun.

Leaves are often slate-grey and can vary in shape

HEIGHT AND SPREAD

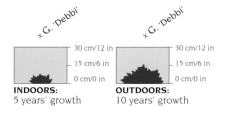

G. bellum
30 cm/12 in
15 cm/6 in
0 cm/0 in
INDOORS:
5 years' growth

G. bellum
30 cm/12 in
15 cm/6 in
0 cm/0 in
OUTDOORS:
10 years' growth

Graptopetalum bellum

Outstanding for its long-lasting, clear red, spring flowers borne on short stems, this species makes a good house plant. With age, it offsets to form clumps. Although it needs moderate summer watering, it rots in cold and damp or very wet conditions.
H 10 cm (4 in), S 76 cm (30 in). Min. 10°C (50°F).

X GRAPTOVERIA

THESE SUCCULENTS are intergeneric hybrids, or crosses between the genera of *Graptopetalum* (see above) and *Echeveria* (see pp.118–19). In the wild, the species from both genera vary hugely according to the habitat, so the many hybrids and cultivars bred from them are difficult to identify correctly. They do, however, retain the basic characteristics common to both parent groups. Cuttings taken from the same plant but grown under different conditions produce dissimilar plants.

Rosettes of pink-tinged leaves offset to form a clump

Small, bell-shaped flowers

HEIGHT AND SPREAD

x G. 'Debbi'
30 cm/12 in
15 cm/6 in
0 cm/0 in
INDOORS:
5 years' growth

x G. 'Debbi'
30 cm/12 in
15 cm/6 in
0 cm/0 in
OUTDOORS:
10 years' growth

x *Graptoveria* 'Debbi'

This colourful hybrid has long flower spikes, which bear orange-red blooms in late summer. It likes shade or sun.
H 15 cm (6 in), S 60 cm (2 ft). Min. 5°C (41°F).

HAWORTHIA

THIS GENUS OF SOUTHERN AFRICAN rosette-shaped succulents currently includes up to 80 small species. They are hugely variable in form, resulting in a confusing number of names. Leaf shapes and markings vary, but a pattern of raised white spots is common. Many species take on red to orange hues while dormant in hot weather, then regain their green colour in cooler weather when they start to grow. The long-lasting clusters of small white flowers appear from spring to autumn on long thin stalks and are followed by green berries. These plants prefer diffuse sun or shade and offset freely into spreading clumps.

HEIGHT AND SPREAD

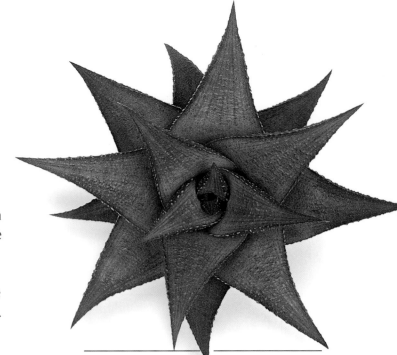

H. venosa　H. attenuata v. clariperla　H. cymbiformis　H. truncata　H. coarctata v. adelaidensis　H. pumila

	30 cm/12 in
	15 cm/6 in
	0 cm/0 in

INDOORS: 5 years' growth

	30 cm/12 in
	15 cm/6 in
	0 cm/0 in

OUTDOORS: 10 years' growth

Haworthia venosa

A particularly variable species, this plant displays a range of fine foliage. The broad, triangular, sometimes stippled leaves can be olive-green to purple-brown and their upper surfaces are often criss-crossed with transparent markings. Both short-stemmed and stemless forms readily produce underground stems, which form new plants some distance from the parent.
H 10 cm (4 in), S 30 cm (12 in). Min. 5°C (41°F).

Haworthia attenuata v. *clariperla*

Zebra plant
The numerous raised white dots on the leaves of this plant, often wrongly named H. *fasciata*, sometimes merge into stripes.
H 8 cm (3 in), S 90 cm (3 ft). Min. 5°C (41°F).

Haworthia cymbiformis

In full sun, the soft, semi-transparent leaves of this robust and variable succulent turn slightly orange. The rosette offsets rapidly in shade to form a low spreading mat.
H 8 cm (3 in), S 90 cm (3 ft). Min. 5°C (41°F).

Haworthia truncata

Cut window plant
These fat leaves resemble stepping stones. They are variable, slow-growing and have opaque "windows" at the tips (see p. 11).
H 5 cm (2 in), S 38 cm (15 in). Min 5°C (41°F).

Large white dots emboss
incurving leaves

Haworthia coarctata v. adelaidensis

This plant is one of the few species in its
genus to form such striking clumps of tough,
leafy columns. Normally dark green,
it turns a rich purple-red in full
sun. The leaves are often
stippled with bands of
white spots.
**H 15 cm (6 in), S 38 cm (15 in).
Min 5°C (41°F).**

Stem surrounded
by tightly packed,
usually scale-like leaves

Haworthia pumila

Pearly dots
Although *pumila* means small and this plant
was once thought to be a small A*loe* (see
pp. 108–9), in fact it has the largest rosette
of the *Haworthia* genus as well as a sturdy
flower stem. The rosette offsets with age.
H 15 cm (6 in), S 30 cm (12 in). Min. 5°C (41°F).

Leaves curve in
towards stem tip

Compact upright clump
formed by stem
branching at base

HOODIA

THESE SMALL SPINY SUCCULENTS are from southern Africa and are known as African hats. The 20 or so species form clumps of short, upright, sometimes branching stems in muted greens. Bizarre flowers, which are large, flat and saucer-like, and mottled dark yellow, brown or red, appear freely near the stem tips in summer. Twin-horned seed pods follow. Cultivating these slow-growing plants can be difficult; they need temperatures of at least 10–16°C (50–61°F) in sun or shade and tend to rot in winter damp or shrivel if too dry.

HEIGHT AND SPREAD

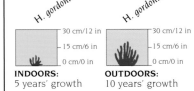

INDOORS: 5 years' growth

OUTDOORS: 10 years' growth

Hoodia gordonii

If kept warm and correctly watered, this is one of the least difficult *Hoodia* species to grow. It has pale green to purple, branching stems with short woody tubercles that are sometimes pointed. This succulent readily forms a clump. The flesh-coloured to brown flowers can vary in shape.
H and S 30 cm (12 in). Min. 13°C (55°F).

HUERNIA

THE UPRIGHT BRANCHING STEMS of these mostly small plants slowly spread into large mats. The 60 or so species from southern and eastern Africa often have flowers that look like carrion to attract pollinating insects. The long-lasting, star-shaped blooms, with deep cups and twin-horned seed pods, cluster at the bases of new stems from summer to autumn. Challenging to grow, the plants like sun or shade.

Huernia striata

Striking flowers, with characteristic star-shaped petals, nestle at the base of the angular mottled stems. These blooms are pale green to yellow-brown, with dark purple stripes and often a small, black, central cup. This small *Huernia* species has short, blue-green, slightly toothed stems that spread slowly to form a carpet.
H 15 cm (6 in), S 38 cm (15 in). Min. 7°C (45°F).

HEIGHT AND SPREAD

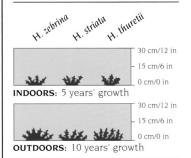

INDOORS: 5 years' growth

OUTDOORS: 10 years' growth

Huernia zebrina

Lifebuoy flower, owl's eyes
This is one of the few *Huernia* species with an annulus, or distinct raised ring, on the flower, which can be greenish to sulphur-yellow with maroon markings.
H 15 cm (6 in), S 38 cm (15 in). Min. 10°C (50°F).

Sharp, evenly spaced teeth

Huernia thuretii

The flowers of this small succulent can differ greatly but they are most often buff-coloured with blood-red spots or stripes. Initially angular, the upright stems sometimes branch so that the plant's compact clump gradually spreads to form a low mat. The stems vary in colour from a dull green to reddish purple.

H 15 cm (6 in), S 38 cm (15 in). Min. 10°C (50°F).

JATROPHA

IN THIS LARGE GROUP of about 175 species, there are only about 20 succulents, which are very diverse in form, ranging from leafy, nettle-like plants to swollen-trunked trees. These succulents can be slow- or fast-growing and are found throughout the world, mostly in tropical regions in sun or shade. They usually tolerate a minimum temperature of 10°C (50°F), and can be easy or difficult to cultivate. Related to the *Euphorbia*, or spurge (see pp. 120–21), they have similar flowers; these are usually tiny, grouped in threes, and enclosed by cup-shaped, coloured leaf bracts. The green fruits can be pea- to walnut-sized.

HEIGHT AND SPREAD

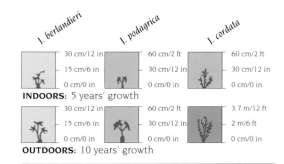

J. berlandieri

| 30 cm/12 in |
| 15 cm/6 in |
| 0 cm/0 in |

J. podagrica

| 60 cm/2 ft |
| 30 cm/12 in |
| 0 cm/0 in |

J. cordata

| 60 cm/2 ft |
| 30 cm/12 in |
| 0 cm/0 in |

INDOORS: 5 years' growth

J. berlandieri

| 30 cm/12 in |
| 15 cm/6 in |
| 0 cm/0 in |

J. podagrica

| 60 cm/2 ft |
| 30 cm/12 in |
| 0 cm/0 in |

J. cordata

| 3.7 m/12 ft |
| 2 m/6 ft |
| 0 cm/0 in |

OUTDOORS: 10 years' growth

Large, bright green leaves have 3 lobes

Peeling bark can be light brown to grey-green

Swollen stem

Short annual stems with blue-green foliage

Jatropha berlandieri

The small, round caudex, or swollen trunk, produces many long-lasting spikes of poppy-red flowers from the tips of its short stems in summer. Green, pea-like berries follow. This slow-growing plant likes sun or shade and can rot if it is cold and damp.

H 15 cm (6 in), S 20 cm (8 in). Min. 10°C (50°F).

Jatropha cordata

Tree jatropha
This sun-loving succulent forms a bush or a swollen-trunked tree and is fairly easy to cultivate. Its five-lobed leaves and small, long-lasting, summer flowers appear near the ends of the smooth shiny branches.

H 9 m (30 ft), S 3.7 m (12 ft). Min. 10°C (50°F).

Jatropha podagrica

Interesting as a pot plant because of its swollen stem, this species slowly becomes a large branching tree. Given warmth and sun, it grows easily and blooms almost constantly in summer and autumn, bearing clusters of scarlet flowers at the stem tips.

H 1.5 m (5 ft), S 60 cm (2 ft). Min. 13°C (55°F).

KALANCHOE

WIDESPREAD IN SUBTROPICAL and tropical countries throughout the world, the 200 species in this genus vary greatly, from small leafy succulents to huge, tree-like plants. Species and hybrids are equally suitable as house plants; many are grown for their decorative, often hairy foliage and some of the trailing species are excellent in hanging baskets. The mostly bell-shaped, long-lasting flowers vary in colour from white, yellow or orange to brown, red or purple. They appear at the stem tips mainly in early spring, but also occasionally in autumn. Small, brown, dry seed pods appear after flowering. These succulents are sometimes fast-growing and many are easy to cultivate in sun or shade, but several species cannot tolerate low temperatures.

Kalanchoe beharensis

Felt bush, elephant's ears
Large, olive- to grey-green leaves with velvety bronze hairs give this sun-loving plant its common names. The slender stems quickly grow into a large bush or tree. Minute, yellow-green flowers appear in spring on mature plants only. Plantlets, which form on the stalks of cut leaves (see p. 155), grow readily into new plants.
H 3.7 m (12 ft), S 2.1 m (7 ft). Min. 7°C (45°F).

HEIGHT AND SPREAD

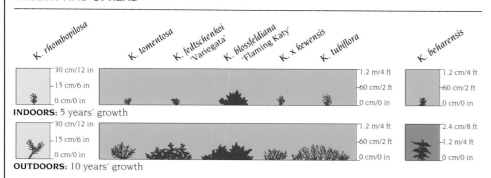

K. rhombopilosa   *K. tomentosa*   *K. fedtschenkoi* 'Variegata'   *K. blossfeldiana* 'Flaming Katy'   *K. x kewensis*   *K. tubiflora*   *K. beharensis*

INDOORS: 5 years' growth

OUTDOORS: 10 years' growth

Leaves usually spotted dark red

Kalanchoe rhombopilosa

Flat whorls of grey-green to white leaves adorn short upright stems that, with age, form a small prostrate bush. It bears tiny, lime-yellow spring flowers. A hard knock can defoliate this fragile plant, but its leaves root easily. Plant in sun or shade.
H 15 cm (6 in), S 38 cm (15 in). Min. 7°C (45°F).

Leaves are generally pale blue-green

Darker leaf tips vary from reddish to dark or golden-brown

Kalanchoe tomentosa

Panda plant, plush plant, pussy ears
Grown for its soft felty leaves rather than its tiny summer flowers, this bushy species is an ideal house plant when young. It thrives in sun or shade. Grow new neater plants from cuttings after three years or so.
H 60 cm (2 ft), S 1.2 m (4 ft). Min. 7°C (45°F).

Leaf edges are tinged red in bright shade

Aerial roots

Kalanchoe fedtschenkoi 'Variegata'

South American air plant, aurora borealis
This fast-growing, spreading bush has variegated leaves and clusters of dusty pink spring flowers. It grows best in shade.
H 60 cm (2 ft), S unlimited. Min. 7°C (45°F).

Kalanchoe blossfeldiana 'Flaming Katy'

In open ground, this dwarf hybrid eventually forms a dense spreading bush of often red-edged, glossy leaves. Small flowers appear in winter or early spring if there is less than 12 hours of daylight. This shade-loving plant is often forced and sold in flower as a house plant all year round.
H and S unlimited. Min. 10°C (50°F).

Kalanchoe x kewensis

When young, this elegant hybrid forms a bush of upright stems. In spring, vivid pink flowers appear, which contrast well with the deep green, antler-like leaves. Like many other bushy *Kalanchoe*, it becomes untidy with age and is best grown anew from cuttings. It thrives in sun or shade.
H 60 cm (2 ft), S 90 cm (3 ft). Min. 7°C (45°F).

Plantlets grow at the leaf tips and are easily shed to form new plants

Leaves can be blotched pink, purple, grey or greenish brown

Hairless central stem branches after flowering, eventually becoming prostrate

Kalanchoe tubiflora

Mother of thousands
A starburst of long tubular leaves, each with a frill of plantlets, grows from the central upright stem. The numerous plantlets are very robust, whether in sun or shade, and will even take root in carpets or fabric. Once the plant reaches its mature size, dense clusters of orange-red to purple flowers are produced in early spring.
H 60 cm (2 ft), S unlimited. Min. 5°C (41°F).

LAMPRANTHUS

MASSES OF VIVIDLY HUED, daisy-like blooms in almost any colour but blue make these ice plants, or Livingstone daisies, excellent ground cover in frost-free areas. There are more than 60 mostly South African species. Whether bushy, creeping or trailing, they readily adapt to and stabilize arid soil. Some flower over long periods between spring and autumn; others have a short flowering season. The blooms grow near the stem tips and need sun to open. Fleshy fruits, which are woody when ripe, follow. There are countless hybrids and forms of this fast-growing succulent. Although some species tolerate light frost, they can rot if it is cold and damp.

HEIGHT AND SPREAD

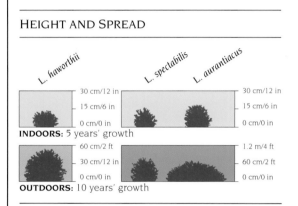

L. haworthii   L. spectabilis   L. aurantiacus

30 cm/12 in
15 cm/6 in
0 cm/0 in
INDOORS: 5 years' growth

30 cm/12 in
15 cm/6 in
0 cm/0 in

60 cm/2 ft
30 cm/12 in
0 cm/0 in
OUTDOORS: 10 years' growth

1.2 m/4 ft
60 cm/2 ft
0 cm/0 in

Lampranthus spectabilis

Well worth growing for its long flowering season, this sun-loving, prostrate bush produces brilliant, white to purple flowers, which are about 5 cm (2 in) across, throughout spring. The succulent's narrow tubular leaves are grey-green.
H 60 cm (2 ft), S unlimited. Min. 2°C (36°F).

Lampranthus haworthii

In spring, this spectacular succulent is entirely smothered by large, bright pink, magenta or purple flowers, which are about 5 cm (2 in) across. More blooms appear occasionally during the summer. Its candelabra-like leaves are blue-green. This plant does best in sun and is a good choice for frost-free gardens or for tubs. It quickly spreads sideways, forming a domed bush.
H 60 cm (2 ft), S unlimited. Min. 2°C (36°F).

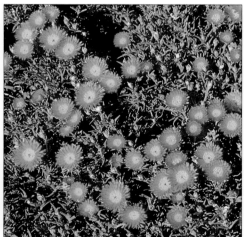

Lampranthus aurantiacus

The vivid orange flowers are about 5 cm (2 in) in diameter and are produced in profusion in spring. This sun-loving bush has upright, then prostrate, stems and blue-green tapering leaves.
H 60 cm (2 ft), S unlimited. Min. 5°C (41°F).

LITHOPS

THE TINY SUCCULENTS that belong to this fascinating South African genus consist of united pairs of swollen leaves and are known as living stones or pebble plants. Most of the 60 species vary widely in colour and in intensity of patterning. In the heat of summer, they become semi-dormant. Then in early autumn, white or yellow, daisy-like flowers grow from the leaf fissure. Small fleshy seed pods follow. After a winter rest, *Lithops* burst into growth in late spring. These slow-growing sun-lovers do not tolerate incorrect watering or poor light.

HEIGHT AND SPREAD

L. salicola   L. pseudotruncatella v. pulmonuncula   L. aucampiae   L. karasmontana

30 cm/12 in
15 cm/6 in
0 cm/0 in
INDOORS: 5 years' growth

30 cm/12 in
15 cm/6 in
0 cm/0 in
OUTDOORS: 10 years' growth

Pure white daisies open in afternoon sun

Pairs of leaves form a small clump

Lithops salicola

Only one other *Lithops* species has mostly slate-grey leaf heads with grey patterning. This variable succulent is one of the taller *Lithops* and its leaf heads, atypically for the genus, stand proud of the soil surface.
H 5 cm (2 in), S 23 cm (9 in). Min. 2°C (36°F).

Flowerbud

Lithops pseudotruncatella v. pulmonuncula

Young plants have a shallow slit across the finely marked, round or oval leaves. Uneven in size and mostly flat-topped, the grey or brown leaves sit almost flush with the soil.
H 2.5 cm (1 in), S 23 cm (9 in). Min. 2°C (36°F).

Lithops aucampiae

The grey-brown leaf heads, up to 5 cm (2 in) across, are large for *Lithops* and flat-topped, with one leaf in the pair usually smaller than the other. The variable plant slowly forms a small clump. Its flowers open in sun.
H 2.5 cm (1 in), S 23 cm (9 in). Min. 2°C (36°F).

Lithops karasmontana

This species is very variable: the leaf heads may be blue-grey to brown and many have muted markings. The flat-topped leaf heads often have one leaf smaller than the other. The flowers are white.
H 2.5 cm (1 in), S 23 cm (9 in). Min. 2°C (36°F).

MONADENIUM

ORIGINALLY, THIS GROUP came mostly from eastern and southern tropical Africa. Like *Euphorbia* (see pp. 120–21), the plants have tiny true flowers, surrounded by small leaf bracts. The bracts are often hooded, are shaded white, cream, pink or red, and appear in spring, summer or autumn on young growth. Small green berries follow. Some of the 50 slow- to fast-growing species have underground tubers and annual leafy growth; others form small bushes and several are large and tree-like. With a few exceptions, *Monadenium* species are challenging to grow; most require high temperatures in sun or shade.

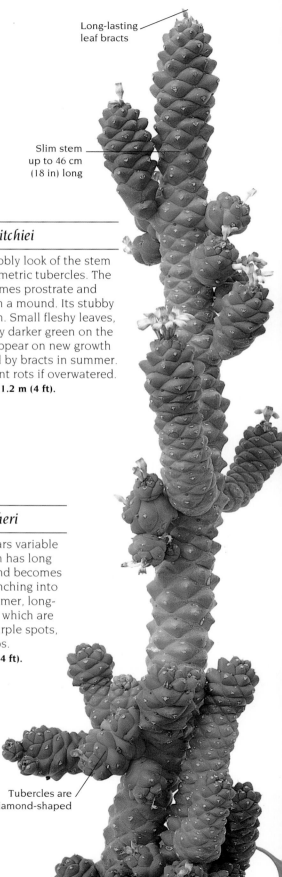

Long-lasting leaf bracts

Slim stem up to 46 cm (18 in) long

Tubercles are diamond-shaped

HEIGHT AND SPREAD

M. ritchiei M. guentheri M. rhizophorum v. stoloniferum M. magnificum M. lugardae

INDOORS: 5 years' growth

30 cm/12 in
15 cm/6 in
0 cm/0 in

30 cm/12 in
15 cm/6 in
0 cm/0 in

OUTDOORS: 10 years' growth

30 cm/12 in
15 cm/6 in
0 cm/0 in

1.2 m/4 ft
60 cm/2 ft
0 cm/0 in

Monadenium ritchiei

The strange knobbly look of the stem is due to its geometric tubercles. The stem often becomes prostrate and branches to form a mound. Its stubby spines are brown. Small fleshy leaves, which are usually darker green on the upper surface, appear on new growth and are followed by bracts in summer. This difficult plant rots if overwatered.
H 30 cm (12 in), S 1.2 m (4 ft).
Min. 13°C (55°F).

Rosettes of small leaves on stem tips

Monadenium guentheri

New growth briefly bears variable fleshy leaves. The stem has long hexagonal tubercles and becomes prostrate in habit, branching into a dense clump. In summer, long-lasting hooded bracts, which are greenish white with purple spots, appear on the stem tips.
H 30 cm (12 in), S 1.2 m (4 ft).
Min. 10°C (50°F).

Monadenium rhizophorum v. stoloniferum

This plant forms small sparse clumps from underground stems; its top-growth also roots in the soil. Pale green summer bracts, spotted green or red, grow at the stem tips. This shade-lover needs a dry dormancy.
H 8 cm (3 in), S unlimited. Min. 10°C (50°F).

Stem branches at base

Glossy leaves are
usually large and up
to 10 cm (4 in) long

Monadenium magnificum

The variable foliage of this fast-growing tree
or bush is borne on an angular stem with a
caudex, or swollen base (see p. 10). Red-
brown spine clusters grow on the stem.
Small, bright scarlet, long-lasting bracts are
produced near the stem tips in summer.
H 2.1 m (7 ft), S1.2 m (4 ft). Min. 10°C (50°F).

Monadenium lugardae

The succulent stems bear rosettes of foliage
and form fine clumps. In summer, hooded
pale green bracts grow near the stem tips.
The plant rots in cold damp conditions.
H 60 cm (2 ft), S 90 cm (3 ft). Min. 10°C (50°F).

Thickness
of stem
can vary

PACHYPHYTUM

THESE MEXICAN SUCCULENTS have small
to medium-sized, sometimes
stemless rosettes of fleshy leaves,
in shades of green, blue, orange,
red or purple. Related to *Echeveria*
(see pp. 118–19), the 12 or so
species produce arching spikes
of long-lasting, pendent
flowers enclosed by bell-
shaped sepals. Tiny seed pods
follow the flowers in spring,
summer or autumn. *Pachyphytum*
species are sometimes slow-growing
and may prefer sun or shade.

HEIGHT AND SPREAD

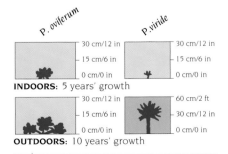

Pachyphytum viride

Rosettes of green, purple-red or orange
leaves are carried on a slow-growing
upright stem that is relatively tall. The plant
eventually forms a clump and grows well in
sun or shade. Greenish white flowers with
wine-red petals are borne on arching spikes
in spring and early summer.
H and S 60 cm (2 ft). Min. 7°C (45°F).

Pachyphytum oviferum

Sugar almond plant, pearly moonstones
The powdery, often pinkish blue rosettes of
leaves resemble sugared almonds. They
grow along short clumping stems. Arching
spikes of flowers with powdery, grey-green
sepals and red petals appear in spring and
early summer. The succulent prefers sun.
H 15 cm (6 in), S unlimited. Min. 6°C (43°F).

PACHYPODIUM

THESE WIDELY VARIABLE succulents are closely related to *Adenium* (see p. 103). They usually have swollen bases or trunks, which are grey to brown and spiny. Some of the 12 species from southern Africa and Madagascar take 25 years to reach 13 cm (5 in) in diameter, while others quickly soar to 9 m (30 ft). All but the tree-like species are deciduous. Trumpet-shaped flowers, which are white, red or yellow appear at the stem tips in different seasons. Twin-horned seed pods follow. Challenging to grow, these frost-tender sun-lovers are very prone to rot. The rarer, slow-growing species are often grafted on to P. *lamerei*.

HEIGHT AND SPREAD

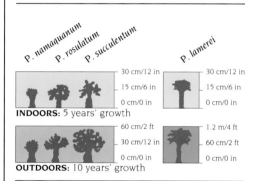

P. *namaquanum* P. *rosulatum* P. *succulentum* P. *lamerei*

30 cm/12 in
15 cm/6 in
0 cm/0 in
30 cm/12 in
15 cm/6 in
0 cm/0 in
INDOORS: 5 years' growth

60 cm/2 ft
30 cm/12 in
0 cm/0 in
1.2 m/4 ft
60 cm/2 ft
0 cm/0 in
OUTDOORS: 10 years' growth

Pachypodium namaquanum

Half-man, ghost-man

Rare in the wild, this palm-like plant is now available in cultivation. Its solitary, erect, brown stem with long pointed spines tilts its head toward the sun. In warm climates, the large but slow-growing stem produces flowers after 10–15 years. Small, red-brown blooms appear on the plant crown in spring. In colder climates, flowers rarely emerge and the plant needs cosseting to survive the winter without rotting.

H 1.5 m (5 ft), S 23 cm (9 in). Min. 10°C (50°F).

Spines are reddish brown

Pachypodium rosulatum

Both the leaves and the large greyish trunk vary in shape. The trunk is swollen from an early age and slowly forms a head of slim branches. Open-faced, canary-yellow flowers appear in late winter and early spring, before the plant comes into leaf.

H 1.5 m (5 ft), S 90 cm (3 ft). Min. 13°C (55°F)

Pachypodium lamerei

Madagascar palm

If given warmth and care, this tree-like species reaches a flowering size of 1.2 m (4 ft) in ten years. In summer, it bears fragrant flowers, which are white with a gold throat. After flowering, the stems branch. The spines are long, grey and pointed.

H 6 m (20 ft), S 2 m (6 ft). Min. 10°C (50°F).

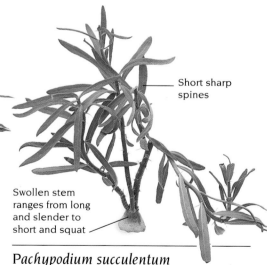

Short sharp spines

Swollen stem ranges from long and slender to short and squat

Pachypodium succulentum

This variable species usually has a swollen, half-buried stem topped with slender but bushy branches. Small, trumpet-shaped, white, crimson or pink flowers are produced quite freely toward the stem tips during spring and summer. The succulent is relatively easy to grow.

H 1.5 m (5 ft), S 2 m (6 ft). Min. 7°C (45°F).

PEDILANTHUS

ALTHOUGH WIDESPREAD IN THE CARIBBEAN and from the southern U.S.A. to northern South America, *Pedilanthus* succulents are seldom cultivated, apart from P. *tithymaloides* and its forms. The 12 bushy species, known as rick-rack plants, are closely related to *Euphorbia* (see pp. 120–21). They differ mainly in their flowers, which are enclosed by small leaf bracts shaped like a bird's head and are green, red or brown in colour.

HEIGHT AND SPREAD

P. *tithymaloides* 'Variegata'	P. *tithymaloides* 'Variegata'
30 cm/12 in	2.4 m/8 ft
15 cm/6 in	1.2 m/4 ft
0 cm/0 in	0 cm/0 in
INDOORS: 5 years' growth	**OUTDOORS:** 10 years' growth

Pedilanthus tithymaloides 'Variegata'

Redbird flower
With its zig-zagging stems and white or pink variegated foliage, this cultivar makes a fine pot plant. Tiny greenish flowers and red to yellow bracts appear near the stem tips from summer to autumn. The small fruits are green. The plant dislikes harsh sun and cold, damp conditions.
H 2.7 m (9 ft), S 1.5 m (5 ft). Min. 13°C (55°F).

SANSEVIERIA

THESE BOWSTRING HEMP PLANTS from tropical Africa are very variable. Their rosettes of usually dark green, fleshy leaves differ in size and shape and are often variegated. Like the *Agave* (see pp. 106–7), each rosette dies after flowering. Spikes of pale, often scented flowers and white to orange berries appear from spring to autumn. The 60 species are happy in sun or shade, if sparingly watered. Fine border plants in warm areas, they are also good in wire-mesh hanging baskets, where their underground stems push through to form a cascade of rosettes.

Sword-shaped leaves usually have silvery bands and a broad yellow or cream border

HEIGHT AND SPREAD

S. *trifasciata* 'Golden Hahnii'	S. *trifasciata* 'Laurentii'
30 cm/12 in	1.2 m/4 ft
15 cm/6 in	60 cm/2 ft
0 cm/0 in	0 cm/0 in
INDOORS: 5 years' growth	
30 cm/12 in	1.2 m/4 ft
15 cm/6 in	60 cm/2 ft
0 cm/0 in	0 cm/0 in
OUTDOORS: 10 years' growth	

Sansevieria trifasciata 'Golden Hahnii'

Golden bird's nest
Each rosette is no more than 30 cm (12 in) across, but it offsets to make large clumps. Protect its variegated leaves from hot sun.
H 15 cm (6 in), S unlimited. Min. 13°C (55°F).

Sansevieria trifasciata 'Laurentii'

Mother-in-law's tongue, snake plant
In good summer light, tall spikes of pale green flowers and orange berries appear. This plant grows best in a small pot.
H 1.2 m (4 ft), S unlimited. Min. 13°C (55°F).

SEDUM

THE SEVERAL HUNDRED stonecrop plants include slow-
to fast-growing succulents from all over the world.
Most hardy species are small bushes or carpeting
plants and make good, albeit invasive, ground cover.
The tender species are more fleshy and diverse,
ranging from small rosettes to large bushes. Free-
flowering, *Sedum* mostly bear flat-topped clusters of
starry, long-lasting, white, gold or red flowers and
tiny seed pods at the stem tips. Tender species
bloom in spring; hardy ones in summer and autumn.
These pale to blue-green plants like sun or shade.

Stems may shed
their leaves in
dry conditions

LENGTH/HEIGHT AND SPREAD

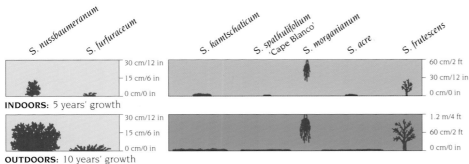

S. nussbaumeranum *S. furfuraceum* *S. kamtschaticum* *S. spathulifolium* 'Cape Blanco' *S. morganianum* *S. acre* *S. frutescens*

INDOORS: 5 years' growth
30 cm/12 in
15 cm/6 in
0 cm/0 in
60 cm/2 ft
30 cm/12 in
0 cm/0 in

OUTDOORS: 10 years' growth
30 cm/12 in
15 cm/6 in
0 cm/0 in
1.2 m/4 ft
60 cm/2 ft
0 cm/0 in

Tiny red flowers

Sedum kamtschaticum

In winter, this mat-forming succulent sheds
most of its abundant, slightly toothed
leaves. A skeleton of bare stems with only
small rosettes of leaves at the tips remains.
The golden or orange flowers are produced
in summer and autumn, in sun or shade.
H 8 cm (3 in), S unlimited. Min. -35°C (-30°F).

Sedum spathulifolium 'Cape Blanco'

Although it is quite happy in shade, this
small carpeting plant has leaves of a darker
purple and silver hue in full sun. It is good
for growing in rock gardens and in wall
crevices and has yellow summer flowers.
H 5 cm (2 in), S unlimited. Min. -15°C (5°F).

Sedum morganianum

Burro's tail, donkey's tail
Pale, powdery green leaves clothe the long
pendent stems so that they appear plaited.
Light pink to scarlet flowers cluster at the
stem tips in spring. This shade-loving plant
needs careful watering to guard against rot.
L 2.7 m (9 ft), S unlimited. Min. 7°C (45°F).

Sedum nussbaumeranum

Golden sedum
In shade, the leaves at the stem tips are pale lime-yellow but in sun they are rust in colour. The spring flowers are bright white.
H 23 cm (9 in), S unlimited. Min. 5°C (41°F).

Sedum furfuraceum

Tight clusters of variable, dark green to purple leaves grow at the tips of the creeping stems. They are very dark if grown in the full sun that this small, slow-growing plant prefers. Its spring flowers are pale pink.
H 8 cm (3 in), S 90 cm (3 ft). Min. 5°C (41°F).

Sedum acre

Biting stonecrop, common stonecrop
Ideal for planting in crevices or in paths, this dwarf creeping plant flowers freely in summer, producing innumerable, short-stemmed heads of tiny golden flowers. Its leaves vary in shape and size. The plant is very easy to grow in sun or shade, but can become invasive if not checked.
H 2.5 cm (1 in), S unlimited. Min. -40°C (-40°F).

Very small leaves are shed in periods of drought

Sedum frutescens

Tree sedum
A good natural bonsai, this bush sheds its lower branches when dormant. It bears clusters of tiny white flowers in late spring.
H 1.5 m (5 ft), S 90 cm (3 ft). Min. 7°C (45°F).

Swollen trunk

Peeling skin

SEMPERVIVUM

THESE SMALL HARDY ALPINES, or houseleeks, from northern Africa and Europe make fine rock-garden and pot plants. Their neat rosettes of leaves offset freely in spring to form a spreading carpet. In free-draining and exposed conditions, many turn red or violet in mid-summer while semi-dormant. Each rosette, when a few years old, bears a tall, long-lasting spike of starry, pink, summer flowers and tiny dry seed pods, then dies. The 35 species of this sun-loving succulent hybridize prolifically, so it is difficult to identify unnamed plants.

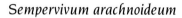

White filaments

HEIGHT AND SPREAD

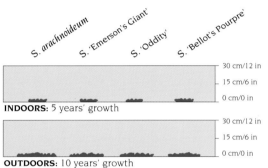

| S. arachnoideum | S. 'Emerson's Giant' | S. 'Oddity' | S. 'Bellot's Pourpre' |

30 cm/12 in
15 cm/6 in
0 cm/0 in
INDOORS: 5 years' growth

30 cm/12 in
15 cm/6 in
0 cm/0 in
OUTDOORS: 10 years' growth

Compact rosettes are 2.5 cm (1 in) or less in diameter

Sempervivum arachnoideum

Cobweb houseleek
The only species with "cobwebs", which stretch from the leaf tips over the crown, this succulent is very common and variable in the wild. Most marked in summer, the cobweb filaments may disappear in winter.
H 2.5 cm (1 in), S 60 cm (2 ft). Min. -15°C (5°F).

Sempervivum 'Emerson's Giant'

In summer, the pointed, scale-like leaves of this symmetrical rosette turn from green to a reddish purple colour.
H 2.5 cm (1 in), S 60 cm (2 ft). Min. -15°C (5°F).

Sempervivum 'Oddity'

Grown from a chance seedling in the U.S.A., this hybrid is valued for its unusual, quill-like leaves, tipped violet in summer, which make it look like an *Echeveria* (see pp. 118–19). It is not known to have flowered.
H 2.5 cm (1 in), S 60 cm (2 ft). Min. -15°C (5°F).

Sempervivum 'Bellot's Pourpre'

The tightly furled leaves of this hybrid become suffused with red that turns a rich purple in the hot summer sun. Like all *Sempervivum* with hairy or downy leaves, it needs protection from winter damp.
H 2.5 cm (1 in), S 60 cm (2 ft). Min. -15°C (5°F).

SENECIO

THIS HUGE GENUS OF OVER 1,000 species includes about 100 very slow- to fast-growing succulents, which are mainly from Africa and India. Grown for their decorative foliage, they are very diverse and range from small, stick-like plants to large bushes. The flowers, borne on long stems in spring, summer or autumn, resemble white or red brushes or golden daisies. They are usually long-lasting. Most succulent *Senecio* species are fairly easy to grow although some from Madagascar need warmth.

Cocoon-shaped leaves thickly covered with silvery white hairs

LENGTH/HEIGHT AND SPREAD

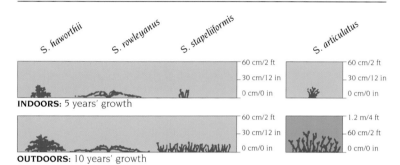

S. haworthii   S. rowleyanus   S. stapeliiformis   S. articulatus

INDOORS: 5 years' growth — 60 cm/2 ft, 30 cm/12 in, 0 cm/0 in

OUTDOORS: 10 years' growth — 60 cm/2 ft, 30 cm/12 in, 0 cm/0 in; 1.2 m/4 ft, 60 cm/2 ft, 0 cm/0 in

Senecio haworthii

Cocoon plant
There are several forms of this sun-loving species. Mature plants eventually form a large sprawling bush. They also lose their lower leaves, so are best renewed every few years from 8 cm (3 in) stem cuttings (see p. 156). Cultivated plants seldom bear the yellow, daisy-like flowers.
H 30 cm (12 in), S 90 cm (3 ft). Min. 5°C (41°F).

Senecio articulatus

Candle plant
If watered freely its jointed stems grow very fast and long, but this species is best grown in poor dry soil to form a compact knobbly plant. The summer-dormant succulent bears tiny, long-lasting, foul-smelling, cream flowers in autumn. It likes sun or shade.
H 90 cm (3 ft), S unlimited. Min. 5°C (41°F).

Senecio rowleyanus

String of beads
Fine trailing stems, studded with pea-like, often bluish leaves, make this fast-growing shade-lover a good choice for hanging baskets. Long-lasting, cup-shaped heads of tiny white flowers, scented like hyacinths, appear near the stem tips in autumn.
L and S unlimited. Min. 5°C (41°F).

Senecio stapeliiformis

Belisha beacon plant
The variable stems grow from underground creeping stems, and are mottled green with spine-like leaves on the ribs. Long-lasting scarlet flowers appear on short stalks in summer. This plant, which likes sun or shade, can become invasive.
H 15 cm (6 in), S unlimited. Min. 5°C (41°F).

STAPELIA

FLESHY, FIVE-PETALLED, FOUL-SMELLING blooms give these African succulents the name of starfish flowers or carrion plants. Sometimes huge, and mustard to maroon in hue, the summer flowers usually appear at the base of new stems; twin-horned seed pods follow. Most of the 100 slow- to fast-growing species form clumps of short, green or brown, angular stems, which briefly bear vestigial leaves along the ribs. After a few years, the older stems in the centre of the clump die back. In cooler climates, rot then sets in, so the plant should be renewed from cuttings from time to time. *Stapelia* like sun or light shade and thrive in hanging baskets, but cannot tolerate prolonged drought or cold, damp conditions.

HEIGHT AND SPREAD

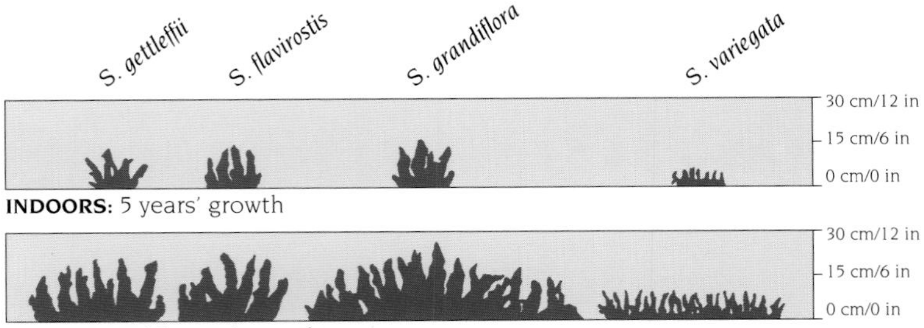

S. gettleffii *S. flavirostis* *S. grandiflora* *S. variegata*

			30 cm/12 in
			15 cm/6 in
			0 cm/0 in

INDOORS: 5 years' growth

			30 cm/12 in
			15 cm/6 in
			0 cm/0 in

OUTDOORS: 10 years' growth

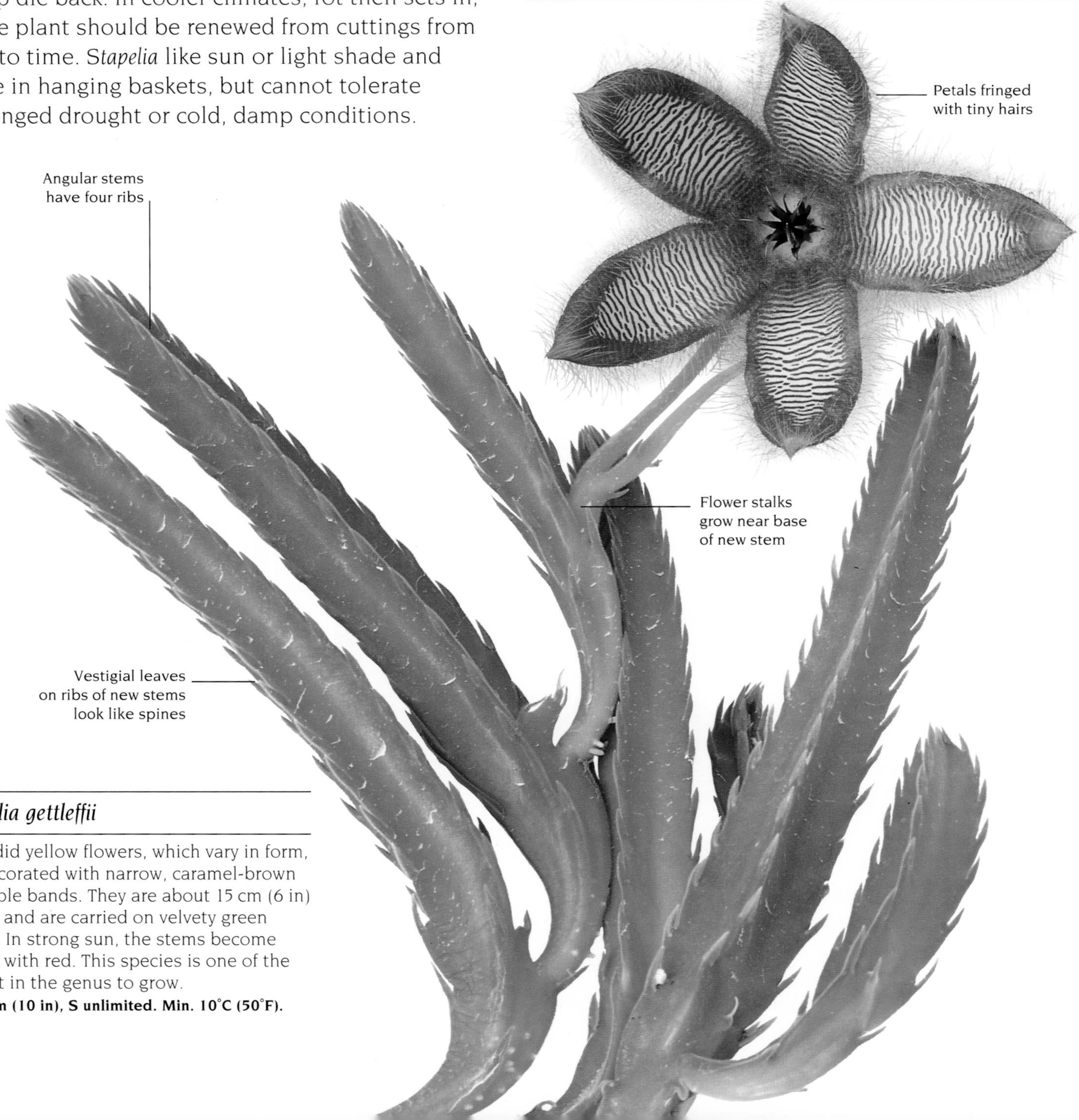

Petals fringed with tiny hairs

Angular stems have four ribs

Flower stalks grow near base of new stem

Vestigial leaves on ribs of new stems look like spines

Stapelia gettleffii

Splendid yellow flowers, which vary in form, are decorated with narrow, caramel-brown to purple bands. They are about 15 cm (6 in) across and are carried on velvety green stems. In strong sun, the stems become tinged with red. This species is one of the easiest in the genus to grow.

H 25 cm (10 in), S unlimited. Min. 10°C (50°F).

Stapelia flavirostis

This species, which is closely related to
S. *grandiflora*, has longer hairs at the petal
edges and variable stems. The flowers can
be up to 10 cm (4 in) wide and are coloured
rust to pale purple with ochre bands.
H 25 cm (10 in), S unlimited. Min. 10°C (50°F).

Stapelia grandiflora

Giant toad plant
Purple-brown or pale yellow flowers, up to
25 cm (10 in) across, appear on chunky
erect stems, which have tiny hairs. The stems
make good grafting stocks (see pp. 158–9).
H 30 cm (12 in), S 1.5 m (5 ft). Min. 10°C (50°F).

Stapelia variegata

Mostly spotted or striped purple, the
flowers are 8 cm (3 in) wide. The short,
slender, robust stems of this widely grown
species are green or blue-green and
become tinged red in sun or drought.
H 10 cm (4 in), S 90 cm (3 ft). Min. 7°C (45°F).

TESTUDINARIA

THE FIVE DECIDUOUS SPECIES in this genus are from southern Africa and
Mexico. Each plant has a slow-growing woody caudex (see p. 10), or
tuber, which sits below or on the soil surface in sun or shade. Dormant
for half the year, it produces fast-
growing, climbing or twining
stems with fine leaves. At the
season's end, this top-growth dies
back. Tiny yellow flowers appear
along the upper stems of older
plants. The group's status as a
distinct genus is in dispute.

Hemispherical
caudex

Foliage normally grows
from autumn until
spring

HEIGHT AND SPREAD

T. elephantipes   T. macrostachya

30 cm/12 in
15 cm/6 in
0 cm/0 in
INDOORS: 5 years' growth

30 cm/12 in
15 cm/6 in
0 cm/0 in
OUTDOORS: 10 years' growth

Testudinaria elephantipes

Plant this "elephant's foot" with its base
below the soil to avoid dehydration, and
water it well in spring to break its dormancy.
**Tuber: H 60 cm (2 ft), S 90 cm (3 ft),
foliage: L 5 m (15 ft). Min. 10°C (50°F).**

Testudinaria macrostachya

Tortoise plant
Almost identical to T. *elephantipes*, this plant
has slightly larger leaves and a flatter tuber.
**Tuber: H 60 cm (2 ft), S 90 cm (3 ft),
foliage: L 5 m (15 ft). Min. 10°C (50°F).**

CARE
&
CULTIVATION

A practical guide to every aspect of choosing,
planting and caring for cacti and succulents
successfully, whether growing them indoors, in a
greenhouse or in the garden. It also demonstrates
the best ways to propagate the plants and how to
diagnose and remedy cultivation problems.

EQUIPMENT AND MATERIALS

MOST GENERAL GARDENING EQUIPMENT is perfectly adequate for growing cacti and succulents, but there are a few items, which are shown here, that are especially useful. Gritty composts and soils, as well as top-dressings, provide the free drainage in which these plants thrive. When propagating new plants, a few pots or seed trays on a windowsill are sufficient for most purposes. If you have a conservatory or greenhouse, install a circulatory or extractor fan or an automatic vent-opener to keep it well ventilated. In temperate or cool climates, some form of greenhouse heating is necessary for the winter.

CULTIVATION TOOLS

Good-quality tools are always worth the extra initial expense because they are durable and easy to work with. A few items are invaluable for handling spiny cacti, particularly those with very fine or barbed spines. Use thick gloves, a paper collar, a cloth wad or barbecue tongs to guard against becoming "attached" to a cactus. Remove any spines that do become embedded with tweezers. Pat the skin with adhesive tape to strip out bristles or soak the affected part in hot soapy water.

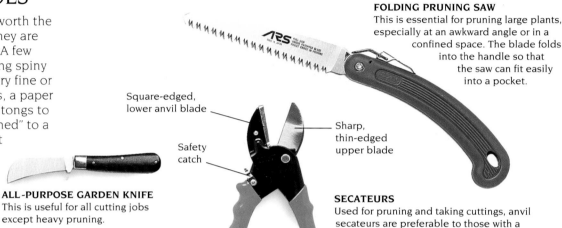

FOLDING PRUNING SAW
This is essential for pruning large plants, especially at an awkward angle or in a confined space. The blade folds into the handle so that the saw can fit easily into a pocket.

Square-edged, lower anvil blade

Sharp, thin-edged upper blade

Safety catch

SECATEURS
Used for pruning and taking cuttings, anvil secateurs are preferable to those with a by-pass, or scissor, action, which may not always make a clean cut, especially on woody stems. Left-handed people may find anvil secateurs easier to handle than by-pass ones.

ALL-PURPOSE GARDEN KNIFE
This is useful for all cutting jobs except heavy pruning.

RETRACTABLE-BLADE KNIFE
With its thin sharp blade, this is a good alternative for grafting to the all-purpose knife.

GLOVES
Suede or leather gloves provide protection when handling spiny or thorny plants. Heavy-duty vinyl gloves are more flexible, but they can be uncomfortable in hot weather.

NARROW-BLADED TROWEL
The narrow blade makes this trowel convenient when digging between plants or in confined spaces.

DIBBER
Use this to make holes in compost when inserting seedlings or cuttings.

WIDGER
If lifting seedlings and cuttings or potting up small plants, use this to avoid damaging their roots.

WIDE-BLADED TROWEL
Use this to dig in open or raised beds, plant up large containers or window boxes, and when mixing up potting composts.

HAND HOE
This type of hoe is useful for weeding in small areas and between closely spaced plants.

SPOON
A large spoon makes a good mini-trowel for use in small spaces.

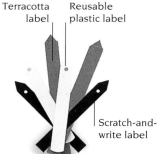

MINIMUM-MAXIMUM THERMOMETER
By recording the highest and lowest temperatures, this type of thermometer can help to find the most suitable site for a plant. It also may indicate why a plant has suffered some types of damage.

MOISTURE METER
The only accurate way to measure moisture content throughout a container or bed is with a meter. Water only when the meter indicates that the soil is dry. A meter is essential whenever watering should be kept to a minimum.

SEED TRAY
Used for growing seedlings or rooting cuttings, this should be 4–6 cm (1½–2½ in) deep to stop the compost from drying out too quickly.

Terracotta label

Reusable plastic label

Scratch-and-write label

Pot is deeper than it is wide

Pan is wider than it is deep

BRUSHES
A very fine paintbrush is essential for pollination. A larger soft brush is useful for removing grit, dirt and cobwebs from spiny plants without damaging them.

PLANT LABELS
Use labels to identify plants. This is very important when propagating.

POT AND PAN WITH SAUCERS
Small, full-depth pots or larger shallow pans are suitable for most cacti and succulents. Plastic pots are more robust than terracotta ones and plants in them need less watering. Drip saucers are useful indoors.

COMPOSTS AND TOP-DRESSINGS

Soil-less compost

Proprietary cactus potting compost

Pea-sized pebbles

Soil-based compost

Peat

Small gravel

Crushed stone

Many composts are recommended for use with cacti and succulents but only a few basic types are really necessary. Special proprietary cactus composts are available but it is easy and less costly to make your own. For indoor plants, seedlings or cuttings, mix two parts commercial soil-less compost with one part 6 mm (¼ in) washed grit. For outdoor containers and raised beds, make a soil-less compost from three parts peat, coconut fibre or wood bark and one part 6 mm (¼ in)

washed grit; use equal parts of peat and grit for small containers that do not drain easily. Add a balanced base fertilizer according to the supplier's instructions. Do not use sand as it clogs compost and hinders drainage.

Soil- or loam-based composts are suitable for both indoor and outdoor use, but they can compact if allowed to dry out. A good mix is three parts of John Innes No. 2 or No. 3 compost to one part 6 mm (¼ in) washed grit, enriched with balanced base fertilizer.

Any display is enhanced by a top-dressing that completely covers the soil. Top-dressings also reduce water splashmarks on the plants and soil erosion, conserve moisture and suppress weeds. Use a top-dressing in a size and colour appropriate to the container or bed. Local stone is often the best, although pumice, perlite or pea-sized beach pebbles may also be suitable. The top-dressing must be inert, so do not use crushed limestone, which increases the soil's alkalinity.

BUYING AND PLANTING

AS WITH OTHER PLANTS, the first steps in growing cacti and succulents successfully are to choose healthy plants and then to establish them in a position that suits their cultural needs (see pp. 150–51). For an indoor display of cacti and succulents, a position near a sunny window is fine. The greenhouse or conservatory, however, is the best place to house a large collection because it offers bright, even light and an easily regulated temperature and humidity.

Plants in containers can be placed outdoors in summer once the temperature averages 21°C (70°F). A permanent outdoor planting is possible in areas that are virtually frost-free and hardy succulents can be planted outdoors in temperate climates.

Epiphytes and other shade-loving plants, which need special growing conditions, do well in natural shade in warm areas. Wherever the plants are sited, give them a good start by planting them correctly.

BUYING PLANTS

Supermarkets, florists and garden centres generally stock cacti and succulents that are easy to grow. They do, however, offer only a limited choice. A specialist cactus nursery or a local cactus show will have a much larger and a more interesting variety of plants on sale.

Some cactus nurseries and botanic gardens have permanent collections and it is worth visiting one or two of these in order to see what mature specimens of cacti and succulents look like and how to display them effectively.

Even distribution of brightly coloured, undamaged spines

Plump, well-shaped stem

Regular overall shape

Waxy, evenly coloured skin

Deformed leaf indicates insect damage or disease

Compost is old, weed-ridden and too low in the pot

UNHEALTHY SUCCULENT
Symptoms of poor growth are often more visible in succulents than in cacti. Avoid plants that show signs of disease or pests, that have few or pale leaves and spindly growth, or that are pot-bound or in poor compost.

Uneven growth indicates poor care

Plant is lop-sided because of poor root system

HEALTHY PLANTS
Choose unblemished plants that display signs of new growth. A well-presented plant in fresh, weed-free compost shows that the grower has looked after it well.

CACTUS IN POOR CONDITION
Do not buy cacti that show signs of pests, diseases or uneven growth. Check that the skin is not dull and the spines are not damaged.

Planting into Containers

Mostly shallow-rooted, succulents and cacti do not require a great depth of compost. Plants less than 15 cm (6 in) across are best grown in pots that are about 2.5 cm (1 in) wider than the plant's diameter; larger plants require a pot 5–10 cm (2–4 in) wider than their diameter. For pots up to 9 cm (3½ in) diameter or for very tall plants, full-depth pots are best. Otherwise, use half pots, known as pans, which are 8–15 cm (3–6 in) deep.

When planting into individual pots, follow the process shown (right). For details on how to plant into different types of container, see pp. 46–51. Make sure that outdoor containers have drainage holes and line the bottom with material such as clay pellets or gravel.

When growing plants together in one container, choose plants with similar cultural needs and growing seasons. Many slow-growing succulents do well when planted with desert cacti, but can be swamped by fast-growing succulents. Plant *Lithops* on their own because their watering needs and growth cycle (see p. 133) differ from those of other plants.

1 If necessary, wrap a paper collar around the plant or wear gloves as protection against the spines. Gently ease the plant out of its pot and tease out the roots.

2 Line a clean, suitably sized pot with fresh cactus potting compost. Position the plant so that the top of its root ball is about 1 cm (½ in) below the pot's rim.

3 Fill in with more compost to within 1 cm (½ in) of the pot's rim, while supporting the cactus with the paper collar. Then gently firm in the plant, with a widger if needed.

4 Using a spoon, carefully cover the compost with a top-dressing such as 6 mm (¼ in) small washed grit. Let the plant settle and water lightly after 3–4 days.

Planting in a Bed

In frost-free areas, cacti and succulents can be planted in any sunny location, as long as the soil is very free-draining and not too alkaline or acidic, and there is shelter from strong winds. In climates that occasionally suffer near-freezing temperatures, plant next to a sunny wall to provide extra protection. To ensure good drainage in a greenhouse or a region where the annual rainfall exceeds 635 mm (25 in), build a raised bed or a raised sloping mound with a suitable soil or compost (see p. 151). Applying a top-dressing to the bed (see p. 147) also improves drainage and hinders erosion.

When planting, allow enough space between the plants for future growth. Harden off indoor plants for a few days in the shade before planting outdoors. For a summer planting, prepare a bed or a gravel-filled trough and plunge plants in terracotta pots in it up to the pots' rims.

Planting in Wall Crevices

Some small creeping succulents native to rocky habitats, such as certain *Sedum* species, shrubby *Mesembryanthemum* or *Crassula*, grow well even in the shallow soil of a wall crevice. Seedlings and rooted cuttings are easiest to plant into crevices and quickly establish.

With the aid of a widger, scrape out some soil from the crevice. While supporting the plant with one hand, gently ease in the plant's roots. Fill in with a little new compost with the widger and firm the plant in position.

1 Clear the top-dressing from the planting area. Dig a hole big enough for the root ball. Ease the plant from its pot, wearing gloves if needs be, and tease out the roots.

2 Place the plant in the hole at the same depth as it was in its pot. Spread out the roots. Fill in and firm the soil; replace the top-dressing. Water after 3–4 days.

PLANT NEEDS

IT IS OFTEN ASSUMED that cacti and succulents need little or no care because they come from deserts. In fact, their basic cultural needs are similar to those of other plants, except that cacti and succulents require less water and are sensitive to cold. Although they can tolerate a great deal of neglect, they are likely to retreat into dormancy and look unattractive. If given appropriate levels of light, water, warmth and nutrients, however, as well as a suitable growing medium, these plants will grow well and, since most flower on new growth, should bloom every year.

Cacti and succulents are broadly divisible into desert plants, which like dry sun, and jungle plants, which prefer moist shade. All need a free-draining soil, feeding during their growing season and warmth. For details of individual plant needs, refer to the relevant entries in the Plant Catalogue (pp. 56–143) and the Plant Selection Lists (pp. 165–6).

LIGHT

When mature, most cacti and succulents need full sun, so they are best cultivated outdoors in warmer climates with a minimum temperature of 16°C (61°F), in a sunny position such as a windowsill or in a greenhouse. In summer, the greenhouse may need some shading to prevent plants being scorched. Cover young plants moved outdoors in strong sun with shading fabric for a few days until they have become acclimatized. Greenhouses receive most light if their roof ridge runs from east to west, less if the ridge runs north to south.

Jungle plants prefer the bright shade found beneath a tree, under a greenhouse bench or by a shady window. In warm climates, a permanent shade house, with a slatted, solid or net roof,

and open or adjustable sides, reduces the light by up to 50 per cent.

When cacti and succulents are dormant, which is usually in winter, they tolerate lower light levels. Where winter sun is weak, however, place even the shade-loving plants in a bright position. Natural daylight can be supplemented by artificial lights that have wavelengths adjusted to plant needs. The distance between a plant and the lights is often critical, so follow the manufacturer's instructions. Indoors, position a mirror behind a plant to provide an even light.

A few cacti, such as *Schlumbergera*, and some succulents, for example *Crassula*, are so light-sensitive that they do not flower unless the days are shorter than 12 hours. Artificial light can suppress flowering, so keep the plants in a little-used room until they come into bud.

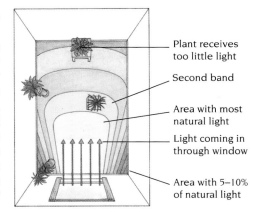

Plant receives too little light

Second band

Area with most natural light

Light coming in through window

Area with 5–10% of natural light

LIGHT DISTRIBUTION IN A ROOM
Light levels diminish rapidly away from the window. In the second band (above), it may be only half as bright as in front of the window and too dark for most cacti and succulents. The darkest areas are beside the window and at the back of the room.

TEMPERATURES

Most cactus species and some succulents are sensitive to temperature as well as light. They are generally dormant in winter and are in active growth in the summer, but extreme heat or cold can also induce dormancy at any time of the year. The plants will then remain dormant until the temperature returns to an appropriate range for growth.

In the wild, cacti and succulents survive a wide variety of temperature ranges. *Sempervivum* may be covered in snow in winter; plants from the Andes, such as *Oreocereus*, tolerate fierce sun and night frosts; others, like *Epiphyllum*, live in constantly hot, steamy jungles. In

cultivation, most cacti and succulents do well indoors, although they will appreciate being moved outdoors into the fresh air in summer. In winter, in a centrally heated house, move dormant plants to a position with a temperature of 10–15°C (50–59°F). In cooler climates, remove plants from windowsills that may become very cold at night to prevent them suffering any damage.

Temperatures in a greenhouse should be kept between 10–32°C (50–90°F) for most cacti and succulents. Excessive heat can scorch the plants, especially those near the roof. In very hot weather, shade the greenhouse with blinds or apply a wash of shade paint to the glass. Good, draught-free ventilation is also essential for healthy plant growth and to reduce humidity, which can cause rot in many cacti. This applies even in winter if

the internal temperature is 16°C (61°F) or more. Tropical cacti and succulents will not thrive unless given warmer conditions; they need a temperature range of 21–32°C (70–90°F).

A few cacti and succulents tolerate outdoor temperatures as low as 0°C (32°F) for very short periods, but only grow well in a minimum of 5°C (41°F). In areas where the winter temperature falls below freezing regularly, grow plants outdoors in summer in containers or plunge them in their pots into seasonal beds. Before cold weather arrives, move them under cover. To protect plants from occasional frosts in normally frost-free areas, cover them with sacking, paper or plastic. Columnar plants are especially vulnerable. If cold damage occurs, it tends to attack only soft new growth, which can be cut out.

GROWING MEDIUMS

Although able to survive in solid clay or pure sand, cacti and succulents will be much healthier and more vigorous if grown in a soil or potting compost that is open in texture and free-draining, yet retains moisture. For pot plants and small beds, always use a gritty compost (for details, see p. 147); garden soil is likely to harbour pests and diseases.

Outdoors, it is useful to assess the soil and prepare it before planting. Most cacti and succulents like a slightly acid soil (pH5.5–6.5). If the soil is very acid, dig in garden lime, chalk or calcium. To make soil more acid, add plenty of peat, garden compost, flowers of sulphur or an acidifying chemical according to the supplier's instructions. Regular use of fertilizers also keeps soil slightly acid.

If the soil is sandy, add one part peat or well-rotted garden compost to three parts soil to aid moisture retention. Incorporate one part small sharp grit or pea-sized pebbles to three parts of the improved soil to help keep it open.

Heavy clay drains very poorly and planting holes can be waterlogged in rain, so build a raised bed at least 15 cm (6 in) above soil level to create a free-draining site but do not position it over an impermeable base. Fill the bottom with 5 cm (2 in) of drainage material such as gravel or rubble. Cover with old carpet or newspaper to stop compost clogging it up. Fill the bed with gritty topsoil or compost and firm, giving the surface a slight slope for good drainage.

WATER

Probably the most frequent cause of death in cultivated succulents and cacti is overwatering, which rots the plants. No matter how experienced the grower, a moisture meter (see p. 147) is the only sure way to gauge accurately how dry or wet the compost or soil is. Do not water until the gauge shows almost dry. Most cacti and succulents survive long droughts, so if in doubt, don't water them. In general, cacti and succulents need watering when in active growth (usually in spring and summer) and little or no water while dormant (mainly in winter).

In spring and autumn, water most plants every 1–2 weeks; plants in small pots may need more frequent watering. In summer, allow soil or compost nearly to dry out between waterings. It is vital not to overwater as most plants become dormant in very hot weather. They are unable to take up water and, if left in wet compost, rot from the roots up. This may not be apparent at the time, but the plants will collapse when cooler autumn weather arrives. In winter, in areas where the temperature remains above 10°C (50°F), water the plants sparingly from time to time to stop their roots drying out; in cooler regions, stop watering.

Water a large collection of plants from overhead, with a hose or an automatic greenhouse spray system. This is best done early in the morning or late in the day so that the plants can absorb the water, and surplus moisture on the leaves or stems, which could scorch them, can evaporate before the sun becomes too hot. With a few pot plants, it is more convenient to stand the pots in water until the compost surface is moist; then allow the pots to drain.

Outdoor plantings, window boxes and pots, especially those with a top-dressing, retain moisture longer than those under cover. The watering routine will depend on local conditions.

Jungle species often need a high humidity. To maintain this under cover, mist-spray occasionally. Other cacti and succulents prefer a dry atmosphere.

NUTRIENTS

Cacti and succulents are hungry plants that need regular feeding during the growing season with a balanced range of minerals. These include nitrogen (N) for vigorous top-growth, potassium (K) to encourage flowers and fruit, and phosphorus (P) for good root growth, as well as all the minor, or trace, elements. In the wild, cacti and succulents are able to absorb whatever minerals are in the soil only when they are dissolved in rain or dew. As a result of the sporadic and unbalanced availability of minerals, many cacti and succulents only just survive in the wild, but, with regular feeding, they flourish in cultivation.

Fertilizers may be organic or inorganic and are available in powder, granular, liquid or solid form. The advantage of inorganic fertilizers is that their chemical content is consistent. Some of the organic fertilizers, such as seaweed, are rich in the trace elements required for healthy growth, but not uniformly so, and others can be deficient in trace elements. It may be necessary therefore to supplement such fertilizers with extra minerals.

Cacti and succulents require feeding in two stages. Incorporate a base fertilizer, either in powder or granular form, into the compost or the soil at planting time or during the annual renovation of a permanent bed.

Thereafter, apply either liquid or solid fertilizers throughout the growing season, generally in spring and summer, to allow the plants' new growth to ripen in autumn. Fertilize summer-dormant plants, such as *Testudinaria*, in spring and autumn while they are in active growth.

Apply the liquid or solid fertilizer with routine waterings, but no more than once a week for desert plants or twice a week for jungle species.

Cacti and succulents respond well to liquid fertilizers comprising 15 per cent nitrogen, 15 per cent potassium, 30 per cent phosphorus and all the trace elements; apply this at half the strength recommended by the supplier for use with tomatoes. Tomato feed is useful in the short term, but is often quite low in nitrogen and, after prolonged use, can cause cacti and succulents to become stunted and woody. Cacti that are over-fed with nitrogen become thin and reluctant to flower, while succulents produce spindly lank growth.

KEEPING PLANTS HEALTHY

CACTI AND SUCCULENTS should survive quite happily if their basic requirements are met (see pp. 150–51), but a little attention will keep them healthy and looking their best. Check the plants once or twice a month and, when necessary, clean off the dust or tidy up the foliage. Cacti and succulents also benefit from occasional pruning to keep them in shape and, if grown in containers, from repotting every few years.

PRUNING

To look attractive and grow well, most succulents and some cacti, particularly epiphytes (see pp. 10–11), benefit from some shaping and restriction of their growth, to make them bushier and more compact. The other purpose of pruning is to remove any unproductive growth that may impair the vigour of the plant.

Prune shrubby succulents at the start of the growing season, winter-flowering succulents in summer, and epiphytic cacti such as *Epiphyllum* after flowering.

Always use clean, sharp pruning tools (see p. 146) to avoid infecting the plant through ragged cuts. Cut back shrubby plants just above a shoot or outward-facing bud, leaving no stub that could become diseased. Some creeping or mounding plants look healthier if old foliage beneath the new growth is removed. Cut back the longest stems of trailing plants that have outgrown their hanging baskets to encourage new bushier growth near the base.

Eventually, cacti and succulents that have been pruned regularly will become woody; use some of the prunings to root as cuttings and replace the old plant.

PRUNING AN EPIPHYTIC CACTUS

1 Cut back top-heavy stems that have branched from the tip. Use anvil secateurs to make a clean straight cut across the parent stem just below the leaf joint.

2 Stunted stems are unlikely to flower. Remove these and any old or diseased stems at the base of the plant, again cutting straight across the stem.

3 To stop dieback occurring, prune out stubs, or dead stem ends, cutting straight across the healthy part of each stem.

Scar tissue from old pruning cut

4 Prune back old stems that have flowered to new young shoots, making an angled cut that runs above and parallel to the leaf vein that feeds the young shoot.

BEFORE PRUNING
An overgrown plant looks unattractive, is less vigorous and is susceptible to pests and diseases.

5 After pruning, the plant may look a little shorn but it will quickly produce strong new flowering shoots and a much more elegant shape.

REPOTTING

All plants must be repotted periodically to allow for root growth, otherwise they become pot-bound and their growth is checked. How often depends mainly on the plants' growth rate, but all container-grown plants need repotting every two or three years to renew their compost even if they have not yet outgrown their pots. The compost in a pot will slowly compact, making it difficult for water and air to circulate to the plant roots; over time, watering also creates mineral imbalances in the compost.

The best time to repot is at the start of the growing season. Choose a clean new pot that is large enough in relation to the overall size of the plant in order to accommodate its new root growth (see Planting into Containers, p. 149). Most cacti and succulents, except tall-growing plants, are shallow-rooted so use pans rather than full-depth pots.

Examine the plant roots and control any pests (see p. 160). Plants that have not been repotted for years and those kept too wet or dry may have very poor roots, so take care not to overwater after repotting until new roots develop.

If using the same sort of compost as in the old pot, lightly break up the root ball to help the roots grow out into the new compost; if repotting into a different type, remove as much of the old compost as possible. The process is then the same as for planting in a container. Do not water the plant for a week or any damaged roots may rot. If the plant is very spiny, use the method shown below.

When teasing out the root ball, take care not to damage the fine feeding roots

REPOTTING A POT-BOUND PLANT

Prepare the plant for repotting by gently teasing out its compacted root ball, letting the old compost fall away. Cut out any overlong, old or damaged roots.

REPOTTING A VERY SPINY CACTUS

1 Use a pot at least 1 cm (½ in) larger than the plant. Scrub it with slightly soapy water and place a little compost in the base. Use another clean pot as a proxy plant and position it in the centre of the larger pot.

Proxy pot is exactly the same size as the existing one

2 Fill in between the pots with more compost to within 1 cm (½ in) of the rims. Firm the compost well and remove the smaller pot, so that it leaves its impression in the fresh compost.

3 Wear gloves as protection against the spines, if needed. Place the plant on its side and ease off the old pot. Remove the old compost from the top of the root ball and tease out the roots a little. Prune out dead roots. Control any pests or diseases.

4 Hold the plant by its root ball over the prepared new pot. Gently drop the plant into place and straighten it, if necessary. Top up with more compost, pushing it under the plant with a dibber; firm lightly. Cover with 1 cm (½ in) of top-dressing.

PLANT HYGIENE

Good hygiene maintains both the appearance and vigour of plants. House plants and outdoor plants in hot areas with low rainfall tend to become dusty; clean spiny plants with a soft brush (see p. 47) or thoroughly spray non-hairy plants with a hose or mist-sprayer. If the plant is very dirty, spray it with a teaspoon of liquid soap in 600 ml (1 pint) of water.

Deadhead plants after flowering, unless they have decorative seed pods, and remove any unsightly foliage. To prevent disease setting in, cut out any damaged areas of cactus stems with sharp secateurs or a knife, leaving a smooth clean wound surface that can heal easily.

Remove dead leaves or shoots, which harbour pests and diseases. Pull off leaves from rosette-shaped succulents or, with thumb and forefinger, pinch out shoots above a healthy joint.

PROPAGATION

PROPAGATING MOST CACTI and succulents is rewarding, easy and inexpensive. It is also the only way to obtain new plants of endangered species. Taking cuttings or dividing a plant often gives the quickest results and is a reliable means of reproducing hybrid plants. Raising plants from seed is slower but yields many new plants and makes it possible to cultivate new forms. Very slow-growing plants or difficult ones that need high temperatures are best grafted so that they grow into good-sized plants in only a few years. For details on which methods suit individual plants, see the Plant Selection Lists (pp. 166–7).

RAISING FROM SEED

Dry seed is available commercially but for best results use fresh seed. Allow the seed pods to ripen on the plants and collect the seed. Squash the wet seed from fleshy fruit on to a paper towel and leave the seed to dry. Sieve dry seed to remove any chaff that could cause rot. It is best to sow seed toward the end of winter so that the seedlings are as large as possible by the following winter.

SOWING SEED: Choose a 5 cm (2 in) pot, a 5 cm (2 in) deep seed tray or a 13 cm (5 in) pan, according to the quantity and size of the seed. When watering the compost, add some fungicide to stop the seedlings damping off (see p. 161).

1 Fill a pot almost to the brim with cactus potting compost and firm. Scatter the seed evenly over the surface (see inset). Stand the pot in tepid water until the compost surface is moist; then allow to drain. Cover thinly with small washed grit.

2 Place the labelled pot in a plastic bag or propagator. Leave in bright shade at a minimum temperature of 19°C (66°F), or 21–27°C (70–81°F) to speed germination.

PRICKING OUT: Move the seedlings out of their plastic bag or propagator, once the seed germinates (within 2–4 weeks). Grow them on at 10°C (50°F) in a bright airy position, but not in sun, which can scorch them. Wait several months to a year to prick them out; new roots are easily damaged and their growth checked. Plant seedlings less than 2.5 cm (1 in) across in a tray and larger ones in pots.

2 Gently separate each seedling from the clump, saving as much compost as possible with the roots. Cactus seedlings have very soft spines and can be handled safely without gloves but avoid touching the delicate roots.

3 Almost fill some 5 cm (2 in) or 6 cm (2½ in) pots with cactus potting compost. Plant one seedling in each pot and firm gently. Top-dress with a thin layer of small washed grit and label. After 3–4 days, water with a fungicide solution, diluted as recommended by the supplier.

1 Prick out seedlings only when they begin to crowd each other or the compost begins to cake. Use a widger to ease out a clump of seedlings with their compost. Take care not to damage the young roots.

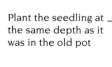

Plant the seedling at the same depth as it was in the old pot

CROSS-POLLINATION

Many cacti and succulents are unable to fertilize their own flowers. To produce seed, pollen must be transferred from the flowers of one plant to another. This is achieved outdoors by wind, insects, bats or birds, but under cover, plants must be cross-pollinated by hand. Pollinating two plants of the same species results in plants similar to the parents.

Before cross-pollinating a flower, isolate it or put a bag over it to protect it from contamination by pollen from other plants. Always label seed with details of its parentage because it takes several years for a new plant to flower.

To create new hybrid forms, transfer pollen from a flower of one species to a bloom of a different species in the same genus. Remove all the unripe stamens on the pollinated (female) flower to be sure of the new hybrid's parentage.

Stigma

Anther

Stamen

1 When the male anthers are ripe and laden with pollen, dab them gently with a small clean paint-brush until it is covered in pollen.

2 Transfer the pollen from the brush to the female stigma of a flower on another plant of the same species.

TAKING CUTTINGS

Cuttings provide a quick and easy means of propagating cacti and succulents, especially hybrids, which do not produce similar offspring from seed. Most plants can be increased from stem cuttings or stem sections and some succulents also reproduce from leaf cuttings. The best time to take cuttings is when a plant starts into active growth, which for most species is in spring. To reduce the risk of rot or disease, dust any wound of 13 cm (5 in) or more in diameter with a fungicide such as green sulphur. Allow the cuttings to heal and form a callus before they are inserted into pots. In summer, this may take only two days, but in winter it can take several months, depending on the type of plant.

LEAF CUTTINGS: Succulents such as *Gasteria* and some *Haworthia* root readily from leaf cuttings in 3–12 weeks. An alternative to rooting leaf cuttings in compost is to use a pot filled with only one-third compost and topped with two-thirds fine grit. Moisture evaporates from the compost to encourage rooting, while the grit stops the leaf rotting.

1 Carefully pull a young healthy leaf away from the parent plant or cut it off at the base with a clean sharp knife. Leave the leaf cutting (see inset) in a bright, warm, dry place for a day or two until a callus has formed over the wound.

2 Fill a small pot with cactus potting compost to within 2.5 cm (1 in) of the rim. Sit the cutting in the top of the compost and firm in. Fill the pot with small washed grit to keep the cutting upright.

3 Set the labelled pot in partial shade at a minimum of 18°C (64°F). Keep the compost slightly damp. When the new plantlets appear, separate them and pot up.

BUDDING LEAVES

The leaves of succulents such as *Crassula*, *Echeveria* and *Kalanchoe* can be easily pulled from the stem, together with a bud at the base of the leaf stalk. The bud is thus stimulated to form new roots and plantlets. *Echeveria* leaves growing from a flower stem usually come off more easily than those growing from the main rosette.

Remove a healthy leaf and leave in a slightly humid, shady place. Plantlets should form in 3–6 months (see above). When they are large enough, separate them and pot them up singly in 5 cm (2 in) pots of cactus potting compost.

TAKING CUTTINGS

STEM CUTTINGS: Most succulents can be propagated by stem cuttings but caudiciform species (see p. 10) are unsuitable as they are slow to root and often rot. Take cuttings at the end of the dormant period in spring (or autumn for winter-flowering plants). Overlong cuttings fail because they wilt before they can root. To stop the flow from stems that bleed when cut, dip them in water. With rosette-shaped plants, pull a young rosette cleanly from the parent and trim the stem to a length less than the rosette's width. Keep potted-up stem cuttings in an airy place in bright shade in a temperature range of 18–24°C (64–75°F). Mist-spray with water occasionally to keep moist.

1 Choose a healthy, sturdy stem whose removal will not disfigure the plant. Cut the stem just above a bud or shoot with a sharp knife. Do not leave a stub.

Parent plant should be healthy and vigorous

Cut straight across stem

2 Trim the stem so that the cutting is 5–10 cm (2–4 in) long. Remove any lower leaves, if necessary, so that the stem is clean at the base. Leave the cutting in a warm dry place for a couple of days until a callus forms over the wound.

3 Fill a small pot one-third full of cactus potting compost. Cover with some small washed grit. Stand the cutting in the centre of the pot. Fill in the pot with more grit and firm. The cutting should root in 2–6 weeks.

STEM SECTIONS: Many cacti, including epiphytic species (see pp. 10–11), can be economically propagated from a section of stem. Very slow-growing plants are not usually good subjects for sections because they tend to rot.

The length of the stem section will depend on the plant. Cuttings taken from tall columnar cacti can be 90 cm (3 ft) or more in length, but bear in mind that if the parent plant is fast-growing, very large cuttings will soon outgrow an indoor position. Pad-like jointed stems should be severed from the parent at a joint and a single pad used as a cutting.

Take stem sections at the end of their dormancy, which is usually in spring. Once planted, keep them slightly damp in a bright shady place at a temperature of 18–24°C (64–75°F). The sections should root from the stem base in 3–12 weeks, depending on the plant and season. Sections taken in spring that fail to root by autumn can take up to a year to do so; keep these dry in winter.

Clean sharp knife

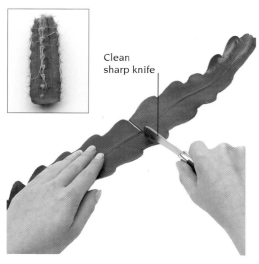

1 Cut a flat stem to a suitable length: 23 cm (9 in) sections are easy to handle and root rapidly. Sever a columnar stem at a point in proportion to its diameter (see inset). Leave in a warm dry place until it calluses. Use the smallest pot the section will stand up in without falling over and fill it one-third full of cactus potting compost.

2 Cover the compost with a thin layer of small washed grit and stand the stem section on it. Add grit up to the rim to support the section (above). Place each section as it would naturally grow, with the end that was nearest the parent stem in the pot (right). Label each section and stake it, if necessary.

DIVISION

In this technique, a vigorous plant is divided into several pieces, each of which has either its own roots or growing point. It is a simple and quick way to obtain new plants of a good size. Cacti and succulents that readily form stem or tuberous offsets lend themselves to this technique; some clump-forming species are also suitable. Usually, the best time to divide these types of cacti and succulents is at the beginning of the growing season in spring or early summer.

Some species of succulent that have swollen rootstocks can be increased in winter while the plants are dormant by cutting off segments from the rootstock. Before potting up the divided pieces, allow any cut surfaces to form a callus as a protection against infection by rot and other diseases.

Water all newly divided plants sparingly until they have become well established and show signs of active growth, otherwise their stems may rot in the damp compost.

CLUMPING OFFSETS: Succulents such as *Haworthia* and *Gasteria* and some cacti, for example *Mammillaria* and *Echinopsis*, produce many offsets in a dense clump. Mature offsets, which have begun to form their own roots, can be detached from the parent to grow into new plants. Once they have been potted up, leave the offsets at a minimum temperature of 18°C (64°F) in sun or bright shade, according to the plant's needs. Water sparingly until new growth appears.

If the offsets are tightly packed, it is easier to remove the parent clump from its pot or to dig it up, so that the offsets can be teased apart at the roots. Leave small offsets; they will grow much more quickly if still attached to the parent.

1 With a widger, carefully dig out an offset from around the base of the plant. Pull it away gently or cut across the joint with a clean sharp knife. Dust the wound with fungicide and leave to callus for a few days.

2 Almost fill a suitably sized pot with cactus potting compost. Insert the offset into the compost at the same depth as it was before and firm gently. Top-dress with small washed grit and label the pot.

OFFSET TUBERS: Some succulents such as *Senecio* and *Ceropegia* have tuberous roots and form offset tubers just below soil level around the parent. These can be gently detached or severed with a sharp knife and grown on. Allow any cut surfaces to callus for a few days before planting the offsets. When they begin to produce new top-growth, pot the offset tubers on or, in warm climates, plant them out.

1 Clear away any top-dressing, then dig carefully with a widger in the potting compost to locate an offset tuber. If necessary, sever it from the main tuber, using a clean sharp knife. Lift it out of the pot, taking care to protect any top-growth and new roots that have developed.

Top-growth of parent plant

Young roots on offset

2 Leave the offset in a warm dry place to callus. If the offset has roots, plant it in a pot of cactus potting compost. (If it has no roots, use a pot filled with one-third compost and two-thirds small washed grit.)

3 Cover the compost thinly with small washed grit. Label the pot. Place it in shade or bright light, depending on the plant, at a temperature of 18°C (64°F). Leave for a few days. Water sparingly until the plant is established.

DIVISION

DIVISION OF ROOTSTOCKS: This is used for a few clumping plants at the start of the growing season. It ensures that new plants grown from variegated cultivars of species such as *Sansevieria trifasciata* do not revert to the unvariegated form. Some *Sedum* and caudiciform succulents (see p. 10) have a swollen rootstock with several growing points. When the plant is dormant, cut the rootstock or tuber into pieces, each with its own growing point. Dust the cuts with a proprietary fungicide and allow to callus. Divisions of shrubby plants callus in days but any of caudiciform plants take a few weeks. Pot up each section and grow on in conditions that suit the plant's needs.

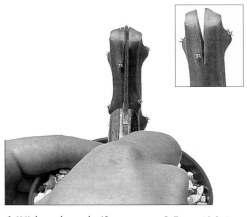

1 Dig up the parent plant or remove it from its container. Using a strong sharp knife, cut the rootstock into sections, each with at least one healthy growing point and some vigorous roots.

2 Cut out any part of the stock that is old and woody or damaged. Dust the cut surfaces with fungicide and allow to callus. Replant each section in a pot of cactus potting compost. Water after a few days.

GRAFTING

This process, used mainly with cacti, involves uniting a cutting (scion) from one species with the base of a more vigorous one (rootstock or stock). When grafted, many slow-growing and difficult species are easier to cultivate and bring into flower, and their growth rate can be increased by ten times. With a little practice and healthy plants, a success rate of 90 per cent is possible. The choice of split, flat or side grafting depends on the plant. Graft cacti at the start of the growing season from mid-spring to early summer for best results.

SPLIT GRAFTING: Suitable for cacti that have slender, leaf-like stems, such as *Schlumbergera* and other epiphytes, and some slender-stemmed succulents, this is also a good way to create a standard plant – one with a tree-like appearance.

3 Pare away the bottom 1 cm (½ in) of the stem section, carefully removing the skin from both sides to form a tapered scion. If necessary, trim the scion to the same diameter as the stock.

1 With a sharp knife, remove 2.5 cm (1 in) from the top of a healthy stock. Make a vertical cut 1–2 cm (½–¾ in) deep into the stem (see inset), ensuring that the cut passes through the central core tissue.

4 Gently insert the prepared scion (see inset) into the slit at the top of the stock. Check that the central core tissue of the scion is in close contact with that of the stock. The more snugly scion and stock fit, the more likely the graft will succeed.

2 To create a scion, select a length of healthy stem from the parent plant, about one or two sections long if it is a *Schlumbergera*. Make a straight clean cut through the leaf joint.

5 Secure the two parts in position with a sharp straight cactus spine or a clean needle. Then bind the graft firmly with raffia. Leave in a bright airy situation, at a temperature of least 10°C (50°F), for about four weeks until new growth is visible.

PROPAGATION | **159**

FLAT GRAFTING: Similar to split grafting but even easier, flat grafting can be used to propagate most types of cacti, including the brightly coloured neon cacti, which lack chlorophyll, and mutant cristate, or crested, forms.

Choose a healthy vigorous stock with a diameter similar to or a little larger than that of the intended scion; *Echinopsis* species, particularly those from the old genus *Trichocereus*, are a good choice. When preparing the graft, ensure your hands and the equipment are clean and take care not to touch either of the cut surfaces; they are very vulnerable to infection by fungal disease until the graft unites. Both the water-storing tissue and the central transport tissue, or core, of the scion and stock must be in contact for a successful graft, so if the diameters of the two plants are different, the scion may need to be positioned off-centre on the stock.

A gentle even pressure must be maintained for about two weeks to hold the scion and the stock together while the graft unites. A convenient method for grafts of small pot plants is to use two wide rubber bands. With taller pot plants or cacti that are growing in a bed, take two lengths of string and weight them at the ends, then drape them at right angles over the scion. If the cacti are spiny, cut a couple of strips from old nylon stockings; stretch them at right angles over the scion and hook the ends on to spines on either side of the stock.

1 With a clean sharp knife, cut horizontally through the stock about 2.5 cm (1 in) below the growing point. Remove the top. Check that some central core tissue is clearly exposed; if not, slice off another thin portion of the stock until the core is visible.

2 Bevel the edges of the cut, removing about 6 mm (¹/₄ in) of skin from all around the stock. This prevents the hard skin holding the scion off the stock when the fleshy stock tissue shrinks after grafting.

3 Cut through the scion at the base. Bevel 6 mm (¹/₄ in) of skin from around the cut edge of the scion (see inset). Place the cut surfaces of the scion and stock together so that their central core tissues touch.

4 Firmly rotate the scion to remove any air pockets. Secure the stock and scion in position with a pair of rubber bands. Place the grafted plant in a bright airy situation (but not in full sun) at a minimum temperature of 10°C (50°F).

5 If the graft is successful, the scion and stock should unite in about two weeks. Then feed and water as normal. Once there are signs of active growth – in about four weeks – remove the rubber bands.

SIDE GRAFTING

This is ideal for grafting very slender-stemmed plants, such as *Echinopsis chamaecereus*, which often have a very small central core. Cut the stock and scion obliquely, rather than horizontally, to expose more of the central core tissue and improve the chances of a successful union. Press the cut surfaces together, ensuring that both types of tissue overlap, and secure with one or two clean needles or cactus spines. Bind the graft with raffia, nylon stocking strips or rubber bands and, if necessary, support it with a thin cane and twine. Then treat the plant in the same way as a flat graft.

PLANT PROBLEMS

IF THEY ARE GROWN in appropriate conditions and properly cared for, cacti and succulents should remain healthy and vigorous and be no more prone to cultivation problems or attack from diseases or pests than any other type of plant. Inspect cacti and succulents now and then, perhaps when watering them, so that you can spot signs of trouble early on. Any symptoms or pests can then be treated before they become established and seriously affect the plant. Keep newly acquired succulents or cacti isolated for about two weeks before placing them with other plants. This allows any diseases or pests to become apparent and to be controlled before they have a chance to spread. When applying pesticides, fungicides or other treatments, always follow the manufacturer's instructions for use.

PESTS

Pests can be controlled by chemical insecticides or, in greenhouses, often by natural predators specific to each pest. Systemic insecticides are absorbed into the plant sap, poisoning any insects that feed on the plant, and are more efficient than a contact application. Use a systemic insecticide 2–3 times in the growing season as a preventative measure. The waxy skin of many cacti and succulents repels moisture, so water with a solution to drench the roots. If an infestation appears, use the insecticide weekly for 3–4 weeks.

As well as the pests shown here, cacti and succulents may be attacked by rodents and caterpillars, which nibble fleshy plants, and birds, which eat berries and steal woolly spines for nests. Roots are also eaten by root mealy bugs, which leave powdery white deposits along the roots. To save an infested plant, stand its root ball in a bath of soapy insecticide, then allow it to drain. Sciarid fly larvae, which look like tiny white worms, and microscopic nematodes, or eelworms, which leave galls on the roots, destroy the roots and base of a plant. Treat sciarid fly with a proprietary tar wash and prevent nematodes from spreading by burning the plant, its compost and pot.

VINE WEEVILS
Resistant to most chemicals, these increasingly troublesome, brown beetles nibble leaves, and their fat, white larvae eat roots and burrow into stems, causing the plant to collapse and die. When repotting, look for tunnels in the compost. If any exist, replace the compost.

MEALY BUGS
An infested plant is covered in tiny, woolly, white nests and sticky honeydew. The insects look like pale waxy woodlice. Treat with either a systemic or soapy contact insecticide or, in temperatures over 21°C (70°F), introduce the predator ladybird *Cryptolaemus montrouzieri*.

RED SPIDER MITES
Brown scars are a sign of spider mite attack on young growth. The tiny, yellow, red or brown mites resemble ground pepper, thrive in dry hot greenhouses and spin fine webs. Increase the humidity or use the predator mite *Phytoseiulus persimilis* in temperatures over 21°C (70°F).

SCALE INSECTS
Control these small, brown, limpet-like insects with systemic insecticide. They generally appear on the stems and lower leaves of a greenhouse or an indoor plant, and migrate up the stem. Plant growth is checked and the sticky honeydew encourages sooty mould.

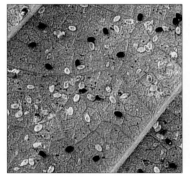

WHITEFLIES
These white, moth-like insects excrete honeydew on which sooty mould thrives, especially on soft-leaved succulents such as *Euphorbia*. Use an insecticidal spray or soap or, in the greenhouse, the wasp *Encarsia formosa*. This preys on young nymphs, which blacken when they die.

SLUGS AND SNAILS
These feed on leaves and fleshy stems, leaving unsightly holes and tell-tale slimy traces. They prefer damp shady places so often attack epiphytes. To eradicate persistent offenders, scatter slug pellets between the plants or apply a preparation based on aluminium sulphate.

DISEASES

Cacti and succulents suffer mainly from fungal diseases. Fungal spores abound in the atmosphere and attack plants in damp or wet conditions, especially in a shady spot with similar daytime and night-time temperatures. Some fungi actually grow through the plant skin. Most problems occur in late spring and autumn when condensation from cold nights fails to evaporate from plants if the next day is overcast.

As well as the diseases shown below, overwatering or damp conditions cause root or stem rot (treat as for basal stem rot) and damping off in seedlings, which makes them wilt and die. Avoid the latter by sowing seed thinly and lightly spraying the compost with a copper sulphate solution, which can also be used to treat white powdery mildew in dry conditions.

FUNGAL LEAF SPOT
The usually brown or grey spots may merge and cause leaf drop. Tiny fungal spore-heads develop where water beads lie on the leaf, leaving sunken brown scars. Burn all infected leaves, treat the plant with copper sulphate and, under cover, improve the ventilation.

SOOTY MOULD
Caused by a soil-borne fungus, this sooty black mould attacks plants, especially seedlings, that are damaged, weakened by very wet conditions or covered in honeydew. Burn infected seedlings and soil, treat plants with a systemic fungicide and control any pests present.

CORKY SCAB
Brown, bark-like spots that usually develop near the base of a stem are a result of past disease damage or poor cultivation. Do not confuse these spots with natural corking on very old plants. If growing conditions are improved, the spots should not reappear.

BASAL STEM ROT
Plants that are cold, damp or have poor roots are prone to rot. Rot fungus penetrates rapidly from the skin into the tissue, turning them soft and black. Cut off sound pot-plant stems for cuttings and burn the rest. Apply copper sulphate to permanent plantings.

CULTURAL DAMAGE

Although pests and diseases do affect cacti and succulents, the plants are much more likely to suffer physical damage caused by incorrect feeding and watering or adverse growing conditions, for example, inappropriate light, temperature, soil or humidity. A plant that is grown in an unsuitable position may produce unattractive distorted leaves or stems. Healthy growth can be retarded and permanent physical damage may result, which can lead to an insect infestation and disease, or even the death of the plant.

If a plant fails to flower once it has reached a size at which flowering normally begins, check carefully that the plant is being grown in an appropriate environment and that all its basic requirements have been met (see pp.150–51).

SCORCH DAMAGE
Hot stuffy greenhouses, strong winds or sudden bright sunshine on dewy plants can cause sunken brown patches, where the tissue has collapsed. When moving plants to less sheltered positions, harden them off in shade or protect them with fabric or a flexible mesh.

COLD DAMAGE
Plants subject for a long period to temperatures that are too low for them can suffer stem tip damage and scarring or even stem collapse. Rot often then attacks affected areas. Increase the temperature so that dead tissue can dry out or cut out all the damaged tissue.

ETIOLATION
Poor light, especially in heat, and incorrect feeding, causes plants to become pale-skinned with elongated stems or to have stunted leaves on spindly shoots. Healthy growth resumes once the plant is given sufficient light. Prune affected stems back to good tissue.

DROUGHT
If starved of water, leafy succulents shed their leaves, then start to die back from the stem tips or shed their branches, and eventually die. Watering usually reverses this process of decline. Cacti shrink into dormancy in a drought but rejuvenate rapidly once watered.

PLANT SELECTION LISTS

PLANTS FOR BEGINNERS

These include cacti and succulents that will stand some mistreatment. Many flower readily when only a few years old.

Adromischus, most species, including
  A. cooperi
  A. festivus
  A. maculatus
Aeonium, most species and hybrids, including
  A. arboreum
  A. haworthii
  A. tabuliforme
Agave, most species, including
  A. americana
  A. attenuata
Aloe aristata
  A. arborescens
  A. brevifolia
  A. ferox
  A. microstigma
  A. variegata
Aporocactus, most species and forms, including
  A. f. flagelliformis
Astrophytum ornatum
Cephalophyllum, most species and hybrids, including
  C. alstonii
  C. subulatoides
Cereus aethiops
  C. hildmannianus
  C. hildmannianus v. monstrose
  C. jamacaru
Ceropegia woodii
Cheiridopsis, most species, including
  C. candidissima
  C. pillansii
  C. purpurata
Cleistocactus hildegardiae
  C. strausii
  C. winteri
Cotyledon ladismithensis
  C. undulata
Crassula falcata
  C. ovata
  C. tetragona
Delosperma, most species, including
  D. minimum
  D. sutherlandii
  D. tradescantioides
Echeveria, most species, including
  E. agavoides
  E. derenbergii

E. elegans
E. harmsii
Echinocactus grusonii
Echinocereus cinerascens
  E. engelmannii
  E. scheeri
  E. stramineus
Echinopsis aurea
  E. backebergii
  E. chamaecereus, its forms and hybrids, including
    E. c. 'Fire Chief'
    E. c. 'Jubilee'
  E. densispina
  E. 'Forty-niner'
  E. huascha
  E. oxygona
Epiphyllum, most hybrids, including
  E. 'Carole'
  E. 'Fortuna'
  E. 'Hermossissimus'
  E. 'Jennifer Ann'
Euphorbia mammillaris
  E. milii
Faucaria, all species
Ferocactus, most species, including
  F. cylindraceus
  F. latispinus
  F. wislizeni
Frithia pulchra
Gasteria, most species, including
  G. armstrongii
  G. liliputana
  G. obtusa
  G. verrucosa
Gibbaeum petrense
Glottiphyllum, most species, including
  G. depressum
  G. oligocarpum
Gymnocalycium, most species, including
  G. andreae
  G. baldianum
  G. gibbosum
  G. horstii
  G. quehlianum
Haworthia, most common species, including
  H. attenuata
  H. cymbiformis
  H. obtusa
  H. reinwardtii
Kalanchoe, most species, including
  K. beharensis
  K. blossfeldiana
  K. daigremontiana
  K. pumila
  K. tomentosa

Lampranthus, most species, including
  L. citrinus
  L. haworthii
  L. spectabilis
Mammillaria, most species, including
  M. albilanata
  M. elongata
  M. zeilmanniana
Neoporteria curvispina
  N. subgibbosa
Opuntia ficus-indica
  O. lindheimeri
  O. neoargentina
Pachyphytum, all species and hybrids
Parodia concinna
  P. crassigibba
  P. herteri
  P. horstii
  P. leninghausii
  P. magnifica
  P. mammulosa
  P. ottonis
  P. scopa
Pereskia aculeata
Pleiospilos, most species, including
  P. bolusii
  P. nelii
  P. simulans
Rebutia, most species, including
  R. miniscula
  R. muscula
  R. senilis
Ruschia, most species, including
  R. crassa
  R. dualis
  R. macowanii
  R. mucronata
Schlumbergera, most hybrids, including
  S. 'Gold Charm'
  S. 'Lilac Beauty'
  S. 'Marie'
  S. 'Sonja'
  S. 'White Christmas'
Sedum, most hardy species
  S. morganianum
  S. nussbaumeranum
Sempervivum, most species and hybrids, including
  S. arachnoideum
  S. 'Bellot's Pourpre'
  S. montanum
  S. tectorum
Senecio aizoides
  S. articulatus
  S. fulgens
  S. haworthii

S. rowleyanus
S. stapeliiformis
Stenocactus, most species, including
  S. multicostatus
  S. phyllacanthus
Thelocactus bicolor
  T. setispinus
Trichodiadema, most species, including
  T. densum
  T. mirabile
Weberbauerocereus johnsonii

PLANTS FOR THE ENTHUSIAST

These present a challenge to the gardener because they are uncommon in cultivation and are usually difficult to grow well, except in ideal conditions.

Adenia, all species
Adenium, all species
Alluaudia, all species
Ariocarpus, all species
Arrojadoa, all species
Astrophytum asterias
Brachystelma, most species, including
  B. barberae
  B. modestum
Caralluma, most species, including
  C. burchardii
  C. lutea
  C. mammillaris
  C. retrospiciens
Ceropegia, most species, including
  C. elegans
  C. juncea
  C. multiflora
  C. rendallii
  C. sandersonii
Copiapoa cinerea
Cotyledon buchholziana
Cyphostemma, all species
Discocactus, all species
Epithelantha, all species
Escobaria, most species, including
  E. aguirreana
  E. dasyacantha
  E. lloydii
  E. minima
  E. missouriensis
  E. roseana
Euphorbia, most species, including
  E. decaryi
  E. lactea

E. muirii
E. obesa
Fouquieria, all species
Hoodia, all species
Huernia macrocarpa
Jatropha berlandieri
Leuchtenbergia principis
Mammillaria guelzowiana
  M. saboae
  M. theresae
  M. wrightii
Melocactus, most species, including
  M. bahiensis
  M. glaucescens
  M. matanzanus
  M. oreas
  M. salvadorensis
  M. zehntneri
Monadenium, most species
Neolloydia, all species
Pachypodium, most species, including
  P. bispinosum
  P. densiflorum
  P. lamerei
  P. namaquanum
  P. rosulatum
  P. succulentum
Parodia graessneri
  P. haselbergii
Pelecyphora, all species
Sarcocaulon, all species
Sclerocactus, all species
Stapelia, most species, including
  S. erectiflora
  S. flavirostis
  S. grandiflora
  S. revoluta
  S. variegata
Testudinaria elephantipes
  T. macrostachya
Trichocaulon, all species
Turbinicarpus, all species
Uebelmannia, all species

ARCHITECTURAL PLANTS

Because of their strong shapes, these plants make excellent focal points in a bed or a striking feature plant in a container.

Aeonium arboreum
  A. a. 'Atropurpureum'
A. haworthii
Agave americana, its varieties and forms
  A. parryi
  A. stricta
  A. victoria-reginae

Aloe arborescens
A. dichotoma
A. ferox
A. plicatilis
A. ramosissima
Cephalocereus, all species
Cereus, all species
Cleistocactus, all species
Cotyledon undulata
Crassula arborescens
C. falcata
C. ovata
C. tetragona
Cyphostemma bainesii
C. juttae
Dudleya, all species
Echeveria, many species and
hybrids, including
E. coccinea
E. gibbiflora
E. 'Painted Lady'
E. pulvinata
E. secunda
Echinocactus grusonii
Echinocereus cinerascens
E. pentalophus
Echinopsis bridgesii
E. bruchii
E. calochlora
E. deserticola
E. huascha
E. scopulicola
E. thelogona
Espostoa, all species
Euphorbia candelabrum
E. cooperi
E. evansii
E. horrida
E. milii
Ferocactus cylindraceus
F. histrix
F. wislizeni
Fouquieria, all species
Jatropha cordata
Kalanchoe beharensis
Lampranthus, all species
Opuntia basilaris
O. lindheimeri
O. monacantha
O. neoargentina
O. pilifera
O. scheeri
O. tunicata
Oreocereus, all species
Pachycereus, all species
Pachypodium geayi
P. lamerei
Parodia leninghausii
P. magnifica
Pedilanthus tithymaloides
Pereskia, all species
Pilosocereus, all species
Plumeria, all species and
hybrids
Sedum frutescens
S. spectabile 'Brilliant'
Senecio haworthii

GROUND-COVER PLANTS

Forming low mats or bushy mounds, these are useful for clothing the ground between large plants, either in the open garden or in greenhouse beds.

Carpobrotus, all species
Cephalophyllum, all species
Coleus, most succulent
species, including
C. arabicus
C. coerulescens
C. spicatus
Crassula, most species,
including
C. falcata
C. lactea
C. marginalis
C. multicava
Cyanotis somaliensis
Cylindrophyllum, most
species, including
C. comptonii
C. tugwelliae
Delosperma, all species
Drosanthemum, all species
Kalanchoe tubiflora
Lampranthus, most species,
including
L. aurantiacus
L. haworthii
L. pleniflorus
L. recurvus
L. spectabilis
Senecio citriformis
S. jacobsenii
S. kleiniiformis
S. rowleyanus

CLIMBING AND TRAILING PLANTS FOR SHADE

These plants usually prefer shady conditions and are good for clothing walls and banks or for growing in hanging baskets.

Aporocactus flagelliformis
A. martianus
Aporophyllum, all hybrids
Ceropegia, most species,
including
C. ballyana
C. elegans
C. nilotica
C. rendallii
C. sandersonii
C. woodii
Cynanchum, most species,
including
C. aphyllum
C. marnieranum
C. perrieri

Disocactus, all species
Epiphyllum, most species and
some hybrids, including
E. anguliger
E. 'Communion'
E. crenatum
E. 'Fortuna'
E. laui
E. oxypetalum
E. 'Professor Ebert'
E. 'Reward'
E. 'Space Rocket'
Harrisia, most species,
including
H. adscendens
H. gracilis
H. hahniana
H. martinii
H. pomanensis
H. tortuosa
Heliocereus, most species,
including
H. aurantiacus
H. cinnabarinus
H. schrankii
H. speciosus
Hylocereus, all species
Lepismium, all species
Rhipsalis, most species,
including
R. baccifera
R. cereuscula
R. hadrosoma
R. micrantha
R. oblonga
R. teres
Sarcostemma, most species,
including
S. aphyllum
S. australe
S. vanlessenii
S. viminale
Schlumbergera, most species
and hybrids, including
S. 'Christmas Charm'
S. 'Gold Charm'
S. 'Joanne'
S. 'Lilac Beauty'
S. russelliana
S. truncata
Selenicereus, all species
Senecio rowleyanus

PLANTS FOR A GREENHOUSE COLLECTION

Many groups of plants, including large but very slow-growing species, are suitable for growing in pots or small beds.

Small greenhouses

Adromischus, all species
Aeonium, all species
Agave parviflora
A. victoria-reginae

Aloe aristata
A. variegata
Aporocactus, all species and
hybrids
Ariocarpus, all species
Astrophytum, all species
Caralluma, all species
Cephalocereus senilis
Cereus hildmannianus
C. hildmannianus v.
monstrose
Ceropegia, most species,
including
C. dichotoma
C. woodii
Cleistocactus straussii
C. winteri
Conophytum, all species
Copiapoa, all species
Coryphantha, all species
Cotyledon ladismithensis
C. undulata
Crassula, most species,
including
C. deceptor
C. ovata
C. tetragona
Cyphostemma bainesii
C. juttae
Dudleya, all species
Echeveria, all species and
hybrids
Echinocactus grusonii
Echinocereus, all species
Echinopsis backebergii
E. chamaecereus and its
hybrids
E. oxygona
Epiphyllum, most hybrids,
including
E. 'Fortuna'
E. 'Hollywood'
E. 'Jennifer Ann'
Espostoa, all species
Euphorbia decaryi
E. horrida
E. mammillaris
E. obesa
Faucaria tuberculosa
Ferocactus, most species,
including
F. cylindraceus
F. hamatacanthus
F. latispinus
Frithia pulchra
Gasteria, most species,
including
G. batesiana
G. liliputana
G. obtusa
G. verrucosa
Gibbaeum, all species
Graptopetalum, all species
and hybrids
Gymnocalycium, all species
Haworthia, all species
Huernia, all species

Jatropha berlandieri
J. podagrica
Kalanchoe, most species,
including
K. blossfeldiana
K. pumila
K. tomentosa
Leuchtenbergia principis
Lithops, all species
Mammillaria, all species
Matucana, all species
Neoporteria, all species
Oreocereus, all species
Pachyphytum, all species and
hybrids
Parodia, all species
Rebutia, all species
Schlumbergera, all species and
hybrids
Sedum frutescens
S. furfuraceum
S. morganianum
Senecio haworthii
S. rowleyanus
S. stapeliiformis
Stapelia, all species
Stenocactus, all species
Testudinaria elephantipes
Thelocactus, all species
Weberbauerocereus johnsonii

Large greenhouses

Agave americana 'Variegata'
A. stricta
Aloe dichotoma
A. ferox
A. kedongensis
A. plicatilis
Carnegiea gigantea
Cephalocereus senilis
Cereus aethiops
C. hildmannianus
C. hildmannianus v.
monstrose
C. validus
Cleistocactus straussii
Crassula arborescens
C. ovata
Cyphostemma bainesii
C. juttae
Echinocactus grusonii
Echinopsis bruchii
E. calochlora
E. deserticola
E. scopulicola
Espostoa lanata
E. melanostele
Euphorbia milii
Ferocactus cylindraceus
F. wislizeni
Jatropha cordata
Kalanchoe beharensis
Lampranthus aurantiacus
L. haworthii
L. spectabilis
Opuntia neoargentina
O. tunicata

Oreocereus celsianus
  O. trollii
Pachycereus schottii
  P. schottii v. monstrose
Pachypodium lamerei
Pedilanthus tithymaloides
Pereskia aculeata
Pilosocereus leucocephalus f. palmeri
Selenicereus grandiflorus
  S. spinulosus
Testudinaria elephantipes
  T. macrostachya
Weberbauerocereus johnsonii

INDOOR POT PLANTS

Many small plants are especially suitable for small indoor displays; most flower easily.

Adenium obesum
Aeonium tabuliforme
Agave parviflora
  A. victoria-reginae
Aloe aristata
  A. bakeri
  A. variegata
Astrophytum, all species
Cephalocereus senilis
Cereus hildmannianus v. monstrose
Ceropegia woodii
Cleistocactus strausii
Conophytum, all species
Copiapoa hypogaea
Cotyledon undulata
Crassula 'Morgan's Beauty'
  C. ovata
  C. schmidtii
  C. tetragona
Echeveria, most species and hybrids, including
  E. affinis
  E. agavoides
  E. fimbriata
  E. 'Painted Lady'
  E. shaviana
Echinocactus grusonii
Echinocereus rigidissimus v. rubrispinus
  E. subinermis
Echinopsis backebergii
  E. chamaecereus
  E. chamaecereus f. lutea
  E. densispina
  E. 'Forty-niner'
  E. oxygona
Espostoa, all species
Euphorbia mammillaris
  E. milii
  E. obesa
Faucaria tuberculosa
Ferocactus cylindraceus
Frithia pulchra
Gasteria obtusa
Gibbaeum album

Graptopetalum bellum
Gymnocalycium baldianum
  G. bruchii
  G. mihanovichii 'Red Top'
  G. quehlianum
Haworthia, most species, including
  H. angustifolia
  H. arachnoidea
  H. attenuata
  H. cooperi
  H. venosa
Kalanchoe tomentosa
  K. tubiflora
Lithops, all species
Mammillaria, most species, including
  M. bocasana
  M. candida
  M. hahniana
  M. prolifera
  M. rhodantha
  M. schiedeana
Melocactus matanzanus
Neoporteria, most species, including
  N. clavata
  N. curvispina
  N. napina
  N. subgibbosa
  N. villosa
Oreocereus, all species
Pachyphytum oviferum
Pachypodium lamerei
Parodia, all species
Rebutia, all species
Sansevieria, most species, including
  S. caulescens
  S. cylindrica
  S. grandis
  S. intermedia
  S. parva
  S. trifasciata and forms
Schlumbergera, most species and hybrids, including
  S. abendrothii
  S. bicolor
  S. delicatus
  S. 'Ilona'
  S. 'Norris'
  S. russelliana
  S. truncata
  S. 'Westland'
Sedum furfuraceum
  S. daigremontianum
  S. morganianum
  S. nussbaumeranum
Sempervivum 'Oddity'
Senecio haworthii
  S. rowleyanus
  S. stapeliiformis
Stapelia flavirostis
  S. grandiflora
  S. variegata
Stenocactus, all species
Thelocactus, all species

FREE-FLOWERING PLANTS

If grown from seed or cuttings, most of these plants will provide a good display of flowers in under five years.

Aloe aristata
  A. variegata
Aporocactus, all species and hybrids
Astrophytum capricorne
  A. ornatum
Bergeranthus, most species
Bowiea, all species
Carruanthus, all species
Cephalophyllum, most species, including
  C. alstonii
  C. regale
  C. subulatoides
Cleistocactus strausii
  C. winteri
Coleus, most succulent species, including
  C. coerulescens
  C. spicatus
Conophytum, most species, including
  C. bilobum
  C. cupreatum
  C. ectypum
  C. minutum
  C. taylorianum
  C. wettsteinii
Crassula, most species, including
  C. falcata
  C. lactea
  C. marginalis
  C. multicava
  C. nealeana
  C. perfoliata
Cyanotis somaliensis
Delosperma, most species, including
  D. ashtonii
  D. lydenburgense
Drosanthemum, most species, including
  D. bicolor
  D. hallii
  D. speciosum
  D. tuberculiferum
Dudleya, most species and hybrids, including
  D. brittonii
  D. pulverulenta
Echeveria, most species and hybrids, including
  E. derenbergii
  E. harmsii
  E. nodulosa
  E. pulvinata
  E. setosa
  E. spectabilis

Echinocereus chloranthus
  E. knippelianus
  E. scheeri
Echinopsis backebergii
  E. chamaecereus
  E. densispina
  E. oxygona
Epiphyllum, most hybrids, including
  E. 'Baby'
  E. 'Best of All'
  E. 'Fantasy'
  E. 'King Midas'
  E. 'Thunder Cloud'
Euphorbia milii
Faucaria, all species
Frithia pulchra
Gasteria, most species, including
  G. batesiana
  G. liliputana
  G. obtusa
  G. verrucosa
Glottiphyllum, all species
Graptopetalum, most species and hybrids
Gymnocalycium, most species, including
  G. baldianum
  G. bruchii
  G. mihanovichii
  G. quehlianum
Haworthia, most species, including
  H. attenuata
  H. cuspidata
  H. glabrata
  H. reinwardtii
  H. tessellata
Jatropha podagrica
Kalanchoe, most species and hybrids, including
  K. citrina
  K. figueiredoi
  K. 'Flaming Katy'
  K. grandiflora
  K. manginii
  K. pumila
  K. 'Tessa'
Lampranthus, most species, including
  L. amoenus
  L. curvifolius
  L. haworthii
  L. magnificus
  L. roseus
  L. spectabilis
Lewisia, most species and hybrids, including
  L. cotyledon
  L. rediviva
Lithops, most species, including
  L. aucampiae
  L. karasmontana
  L. lesliei
  L. salicola

Mammillaria, most species, including
  M. elongata
  M. magnimamma
  M. matudae
  M. spinosissima
Opuntia neoargentina
Pachyphytum, most species and hybrids, including
  P. hookeri
  P. oviferum
Parodia, most species, including
  P. crassigibba
  P. herteri
  P. ottonis
Pleiospilos, most species, including
  P. bolusii
  P. nelii
  P. simulans
Rebutia, most species, including
  R. aureiflora
  R. marsoneri
  R. minuscula
Rhipsalis, many species, including
  R. cereuscula
  R. crispata
  R. pilocarpa
  R. teres
Schlumbergera, most hybrids, including
  S. 'Bristol Princess'
  S. 'Lilofee'
  S. 'Marie'
  S. 'Sonja'
Sedum, most species, including
  S. adolphii
  S. kamtschaticum
  S. morganianum
  S. spectabile
Sempervivum, most species and hybrids, including
  S. arachnoideum
  S. montanum
  S. tectorum
Stapelia, most species, including
  S. flavirostis
  S. variegata
Stenocactus, most species, including
  S. multicostatus
  S. phyllacanthus
  S. vaupelianus
Thelocactus bicolor
  T. setispinus
Titanopsis
  T. calcarea
  T. schwantesii
Trichodiadema, most species, including
  T. densum
  T. mirabile

WINTER-FLOWERING PLANTS

When many other plants are dormant or look dull, these plants flower and provide winter colour.

Aloe, many species, including
  A. arborescens
  A. bakeri
  A. comosa
  A. jacksonii
  A. krapohliana
  A. longistyla
  A. microstigma
  A. plicatilis
  A. tenuior
  A. thraskii
  A. variegata
  A. wickensii
Ceropegia woodii
Cotyledon ladismithensis
Crassula 'Blue Haze'
  C. 'Morgans Beauty'
  C. ovata
  C. schmidtii
  C. streyi
  C. tetragona
Echeveria, many hybrids and
  species, including
  E. coccinea
  E. gibbiflora
  E. grandifolia
  E. montana
  E. pulvinata
  E. 'Pulvicox'
  E. tenuis
  E. 'Zahnii'
Kalanchoe blossfeldiana
  K. tubiflora
Rhipsalis, many species,
  including
  R. cereuscula
  R. crispata
  R. paradoxa
Schlumbergera, most species
  and hybrids, including
  S. 'Joanne'
  S. 'Lilac Beauty'
  S. obtusangula
  S. opuntioides
  S. orrssichiana
  S. truncata

PLANTS TO GROW IN DIFFERENT CLIMATES

Warm climates

These plants need an all-year minimum temperature of 16°C (61°F) to flourish.

Adenium obesum
Brachystelma barberae
Caralluma, most species,
  including
  C. burchardii

C. dodsoniana
C. dummeri
C. hesperidum
C. joannis
C. longipes
C. lutea
C. mammillaris
C. pillansii
C. speciosa
C. turneri
Ceropegia, most species,
  including
  C. aristolochioides
  C. devecchii
  C. dimorpha
  C. distincta
  C. lingaris
Cyphostemma, most species,
  including
  C. bainesii
  C. juttae
  C. seitziana
  C. uter
Didierea, all species
Discocactus, all species
Disocactus, all species
Echinocactus grusonii
Echinopsis chamaecereus f.
  lutea
Epiphyllum, most species,
  including
  E. anguliger
  E. cartagense
  E. crenatum
  E. grandilobum
  E. oxypetalum
  E. thomasianum
Euphorbia, many succulent
  species, including
  E. aeruginosa
  E. cooperi
  E. cylindrifolia
  E. decaryi
  E. grandicornis
  E. lophogona
  E. milii
  E. poissonii
  E. sipolisii
  E. susannae
  E. tuberosa
Fouquieria, all species
Gymnocalycium mihanovichii
  'Red Top'
Hoodia gordonii
Hoya, most species,
  including
  H. coronaria
  H. cinnamomifolia
  H. imperialis
  H. multiflora
Jatropha, most succulent
  species, including
  J. cordata
  J. gossypifolia
  J. multifida
  J. podagrica
  J. tuberosa

Melocactus, all species
Monadenium, all species
Pachypodium, most species,
  including
  P. brevicaule
  P. densiflorum
  P. lamerei
  P. namaquanum
  P. rosulatum
  P. rutenbergianum
Pedilanthus tithymaloides
Pilosocereus, most species,
  including
  P. floccosus
  P. fulvilanatus
  P. glaucochrous
  P. leucocephalus
  P. magnificus
  P. royenii
Plumeria, all species and
  hybrids
Rhipsalis, most species,
  including
  R. cereoides
  R. crispata
  R. elliptica
  R. micrantha
  R. pachyptera
  R. pilocarpa
Sansevieria, most species,
  including
  S. aethiopica
  S. cylindrica
  S. kirkii
  S. raffillii
  S. singularis
  S. trifasciata
  S. trifasciata 'Hahnii'
Stapelia, most species,
  including
  S. acuminata
  S. englerana
  S. glanduliflora
  S. longidens
  S. longipes
  S. schinzii
  S. stultitioides

Temperate climates

Although they can withstand near-freezing temperatures for very short periods, these plants should be kept at a minimum temperature of 5°C (41°F).

Aeonium arboreum
  A. arboreum
    'Atropurpureum'
  A. haworthii
Agave americana 'Variegata'
  A. parryi
  A. parviflora
Aloe aristata
Aporocactus flagelliformis
Cereus hildmannianus v.
  monstrose

Delosperma, most species,
  including
  D. ashtonii
  D. cooperi
  D. hallii
  D. litorale
  D. parviflorum
  D. taylorii
  D. tradescantioides
Drosanthemum, most
  species, including
  D. barwickii
  D. bellum
  D. bicolor
  D. hallii
  D. hispidum
  D. speciosum
  D. striatum
  D. tuberculiferum
Echeveria elegans
Echinocereus, most species,
  including
  E. cinerascens
  E. engelmannii
  E. reichenbachii
  E. stramineus
  E. triglochidiatus
  E. viridiflorus
Gasteria, most species,
  including
  G. batesiana
  G. liliputana
  G. maculata
  G. nigricans
  G. obtusa
  G. verrucosa
Gibbaeum album
  G. petrense
Haworthia attenuata
  H. coarctata v. adelaidensis
  H. cymbiformis
Lampranthus, most species
  and hybrids, including
  L. amoenus
  L. aurantiacus
  L. haworthii
  L. roseus
  L. spectabilis
  L. stipulaceus
Lewisia cotyledon and hybrids
  L. tweedyi

Cold climates

A few species are hardy and can survive winter temperatures as low as –15°C (5°F) if they are kept dry or are protected by a layer of snow.

Sedum, many hardy species,
  including
  S. acre
  S. album
  S. cauticolum
  S. ewersii
  S. kamtschaticum

S. spectabile
S. spurium
Sempervivum, most species
  and hybrids, including
  S. 'Alpha'
  S. 'Apollo'
  S. 'Bengal'
  S. 'Commander Hay'
  S. 'Darkie'
  S. dolomiticum
  S. 'Fame'
  S. 'Grey Ghost'
  S. 'Hayling'
  S. montanum
  S. 'Red Beauty'
  S. 'Silver Spring'
  S. tectorum
  S. 'Wendy'

PLANTS THAT NEED CERTAIN LIGHT LEVELS

Full sun

These are desert plants that need dry conditions in full sun to thrive.

Adenium, all species
Agave, most species,
  including
  A. americana
  A. attenuata
  A. ferox
  A. filifera
  A. horrida
  A. lechuguilla
  A. parrasana
  A. parryi
  A. striata
  A. stricta
  A. toumeyana
  A. utahensis
  A. xylonacantha
Aloe dichotoma
  A. ferox
Ariocarpus, all species
Astrophytum, all species
Carnegiea gigantea
Cephalocereus, all species
Cleistocactus, all species
Conophytum, all species
Copiapoa, all species
Coryphantha, all species
Cyphostemma, all species
Echinocactus, all species
Echinocereus, most species,
  including
  E. maritimus
  E. nivosus
  E. rigidissimus
  E. triglochidiatus
Echinopsis, most species,
  including
  E. calochlora
  E. ferox
  E. formosa
  E. huascha

Echinopsis (cont.)
  E. mamillosa
  E. oxygona
Espostoa, all species
Euphorbia, most cactus-like
  species, including
  E. candelabrum
  E. cooperi
  E. evansii
  E. grandicornis
  E. horrida
Ferocactus, most species,
  including
  F. alamosanus
  F. cylindraceus
  F. latispinus
Gibbaeum, all species
Gymnocalycium baldianum
  G. horstii
  G. saglionis
Hoodia, all species
Jatropha berlandieri
  J. cordata
Lampranthus, all species
Leuchtenbergia principis
Lithops, all species
Mammillaria, most species,
  including
  M. bombycina
  M. candida
  M. geminispina
  M. zeilmanniana
Matucana, all species
Neoporteria, most species,
  including
  N. curvispina
  N. islayensis
  N. subgibbosa
Opuntia, most species,
  including
  O. invicta
  O. leptocaulis
  O. lindheimeri
  O. neoargentina
  O. tunicata
Oreocereus, all species
Pachycereus, all species
Pachypodium lamerei
  P. namaquanum
Parodia, most species,
  including
  P. chrysacanthion
  P. magnifica
  P. penicillata
Pilosocereus, all species
Rebutia, most species,
  including
  R. canigueralii
  R. marsoneri
  R. steinbachii
Sedum acre
  S. frutescens
  S. furfuraceum
Sempervivum, all species and
  hybrids
Senecio haworthii
Thelocactus, all species

Dry shade
These desert plants need
dry conditions in diffuse sun.

Adromischus, most species,
  including
  A. festivus
  A. hallii
  A. maculatus
Aeonium, most species,
  including
  A. simsii
  A. tabuliforme
Aloe antandroi
  A. brevifolia
  A. humilis
  A. millotii
  A. thompsonii
  A. variegata
Caralluma socotrana
Ceropegia, most species,
  including
  C. africana
  C. bulbosa
  C. woodii
Cotyledon ladismithensis
Crassula, most species,
  including
  C. lactea
  C. lycopodioides
  C. schmidtii
Echeveria, most species,
  including
  E. carnicolor
  E. ciliata
  E. harmsii
  E. setosa
Echinopsis chamaecereus f.
  lutea
Euphorbia decaryi
  E. francoisii
  E. neohumbertii and many
    other leafy species,
    including
    E. cap-saintemariensis
    E. didiereoides
    E. leuconeura
    E. tuberculata
Gasteria, all species
Graptopetalum bellum
x Graptoveria 'Debbi'
Haworthia, most species,
  including
  H. attenuata
  H. batesiana
  H. cymbiformis
  H. reinwardtii
  H. translucens
Huernia, most species,
  including
  H. hystrix
  H. macrocarpa
  H. pillansii
Kalanchoe, most species,
  including
  K. blossfeldiana
  K. manginii

  K. porphyrocalyx
  K. pumila
  K. schumacheri
Monadenium guentheri
  M. rhizophorum v.
    stoloniferum
Pedilanthus tithymaloides
Sansevieria trifasciata
  'Laurentii'
Sedum morganianum
Senecio rowleyanus
Stapelia, most species,
  including
  S. gettleffii
  S. schinzii
  S. trifida
  S. variegata

Moist shade
Jungle species require
shade and a humid
atmosphere.

Aporococtus flagelliformis
x Aporophyllum, most
  hybrids, including
  x A. 'Dawn'
  x A. 'Gigantea'
  x A. 'Sussex Flame'
  x A. 'Vivide'
Disocactus, all species
Epiphyllum, all species and
  hybrids
Heliocereus, all species
Hylocereus, all species
Rhipsalis, all species
Schlumbergera, all species
  and hybrids
Selenicereus, all species

PLANTS TO GROW FROM SEED
Many species can be
grown from seed, but
hybrids and cultivars will
not produce similar
offspring from seed.

Aloe, most species, including
  A. ferox
  A. tenuior
  A. variegata
Aloinopsis, all species
Astrophytum ornatum
Carpobrotus, all species
Cephalophyllum subulatoides
Cereus, all species
Cheiridopsis candidissima
  C. pillansii
  C. purpurata
Echinocactus grusonii
Echinocereus cinerascens
  E. engelmannii
  E. pectinatus
  E. pentalophus
  E. reichenbachii
  E. scheeri

Echinopsis ancistrophora
  E. backebergii
  E. eyriesii
  E. huascha
  E. oxygona
  E. thelegona
Faucaria, all species
Ferocactus, all species
Glottiphyllum, all species
Gymnocalycium, most
  species, including
  G. baldianum
  G. gibbosum
  G. quehlianum
Lampranthus, all species
Mammillaria, most species,
  including
  M. albilanata
  M. bocasana
  M. discolor
  M. duoformis
  M. elongata
  M. magnimamma
  M. microhelia
  M. prolifera
  M. rhodantha
  M. zeilmanniana
Matucana aureiflora
  M. intertexta
Neoporteria chilensis
  N. jussieui
  N. villosa
Oreocereus celsianus
  O. trollii
Parodia crassigibba
  P. horstii
  P. magnifica
  P. ottonis
Pilosocereus azureus
  P. magnificus
Rebutia, most species,
  including
  R. aureiflora
  R. marsoneri
  R. minuscula
Stenocactus, all species
Thelocactus bicolor
  T. setispinus

PLANTS TO PROPAGATE FROM CUTTINGS
This is a good way to
obtain identical offspring
from hybrids and cultivars.

Stem cuttings
Use this method for many
bushy succulents.

Aeonium, all species
Aloe, most branching species,
  including
  A. arborescens
  A. kedongensis
  A. jacksonii
Caralluma, all species

Ceropegia, most species,
  including
  C. dichotoma
  C. sandersonii
Cotyledon ladismithensis
  C. orbiculata
  C. undulata
Crassula, most species,
  including
  C. falcata
  C. ovata
Duvalia, all species
Echeveria, all species
Echinopsis, all species
Euphorbia, many species,
  including
  E. flanaganii
  E. mammillaris
  E. pentagona
  E. triangularis
Graptopetalum, all species
Hoya, all species
Huernia, all species
Kalanchoe, most species,
  including
  K. beharensis
  K. eriophylla
  K. tomentosa
Lampranthus, all species
Monadenium, all species
Senecio, most species,
  including
  S. aizoides
  S. coccineiflorus
  S. haworthii
Stapelia, all species
Trichodiadema, all species

Stem sections
All epiphytic cacti species
and hybrids and some
columnar cacti are suited to
this technique.

Aporocactus, all species
x Aporophyllum, all hybrids
Cereus, all species
Cleistocactus baumannii
  C. hildegardiae
  C. icosagonus
  C. samaipatanus
  C. winteri
Corryocactus, all species
Disocactus, all species
Echinopsis bridgesii
  E. pachanoi
  E. spachiana
Epiphyllum species and
  hybrids
Hatiora, all species
Heliocereus, all species
Hylocereus, all species
Lepismium, all species
Opuntia, all species
Pereskia aculeata
  P. bleo
  P. grandifolia

Pereskiopsis diguetii
  P. rotundifolia
Quiabentia verticillata
Rhipsalis, all species
Samaipaticereus corroanus
Schlumbergera, all hybrids
Selenicereus, all species
Tacinga funalis
Weberbauerocereus, all species

Leaf cuttings
Leafy succulents lend themselves to this technique.

Adromischus, all species
Cotyledon jacobseniana
  C. ladismithensis
  C. orbiculata
  C. tomentosa
  C. undulata
Crassula, many species, including
  C. anomala
  C. fragilis
  C. lactea
  C. liebuschiana
  C. macowaniana
  C. mesembryanthoides
  C. 'Morgan's Beauty'
  C. nealeana
  C. perforata
  C. rogersii
  C. rupestris
  C. schmidtii
  C. socialis
  C. susannae
  C. tecta
  C. watermeyeri
Echeveria, many species, including
  E. affinis
  E. agavoides
  E. amoena
  E. carnicolor
  E. ciliata
  E. derenbergii
  E. goldmanii
  E. nodulosa
  E. pulvinata
  E. rosea
  E. shaviana
  E. tenuis
Graptopetalum, all species
Kalanchoe, many species, including
  K. beauverdii
  K. daigremontiana
  K. eriophylla
  K. figueiredoi
  K. manginii
  K. marmorata
  K. orgyalis
  K. pinnata
  K. rhombopilosa
  K. rosei
  K. thyrsiflora

  K. tomentosa
  K. tubiflora
Pachyphytum, all species
Sedum, many species, including
  S. adolphii
  S. album
  S. anglicum
  S. comixtum
  S. hintonii
  S. nussbaumeranum
  S. pachyphyllum
  S. palmeri
  S. rubrotinctum
  S. rubrum
  S. stahlii

PLANTS TO PROPAGATE BY DIVISION
This method has a high level of success but it yields a fairly low number of new plants.

Clumping plants that produce offsets
Aloe albiflora
  A. bakeri
  A. bellatula
  A. brevifolia
  A. humilis
  A. jucunda
  A. millotii
  A. parvula
  A. rabaiensis
  A. rauhii
  A. thompsonii
  A. variegata
Crassula corallina
  C. lycopodioides
  C. marginalis
  C. marnierana
  C. multicava
  C. perforata
  C. schmidtii
  C. socialis
  C. teres
Echeveria agavoides
  E. amoena
  E. ciliata
  E. derenbergii
  E. elegans
  E. glauca
  E. runyonii
  E. setosa
  E. tenuis
  E. 'Zahnii'
Gasteria, most species, including
  G. acinacifolia
  G. armstrongii
  G. batesiana
  G. caespitosa
  G. liliputana
  G. maculata
  G. marmorata

  G. minima
  G. obtusa
  G. verrucosa
  G. zeyheri
Haworthia, most species, including
  H. arachnoidea
  H. attenuata
  H. batesiana
  H. coarctata
  H. cooperi
  H. cuspidata
  H. glauca
  H. herbacea
  H. limifolia
  H. reinwardtii
  H. retusa
  H. tessellata
Sedum acre
  S. dasyphyllum
  S. hirsutum
  S. humifusum
  S. kamtschaticum
  S. lydium
  S. maximowiczii
  S. spurium

Tuberous plants that produce offsets
Begonia incana
  B. natalensis
  B. shepherdii
Brachystelma, most species, including
  B. barberae
  B. cathcartense
  B. coddii
  B. foetidum
  B. modestum
  B. stellatum
Calibanus hookeri
Senecio coccineiflorus
  S. acaulis
  S. fulgens
  S. orbicularis
  S. oxyriifolius
  S. tropaeolifolius
  S. vallyi

Plants to divide at the rootstock
Sansevieria, all species and cultivars, including
  S. cylindrica
  S. grandis
  S. parva
  S. trifasciata 'Hahnii'
  S. thyrsiflora
Sedum, many species, including
  S. anacampseros
  S. cauticolum
  S. ewersii
  S. sieboldii
  S. spectabile
  S. tatarinowii
  S. telephium

PLANTS FOR GRAFTING
A specialized technique for slow-growing cacti or those requiring very warm temperatures. With succulents, graft the scions listed below only on to stocks of the same group.

Flat grafting
Cactus stocks
Cleistocactus samaipatanus
  C. winteri
Echinopsis, many species, including
  E. eyriesii
  E. oxygona
  E. pachanoi
  E. spachiana
  E. scopulicola
  E. thelegona
Hylocereus trigonus
  H. undatus
Myrtillocactus geometrizans
Opuntia, many species, including
  O. cochenillifera
  O. cylindrica
  O. ficus-indica
  O. robusta
Pereskiopsis diguetii (for small seedlings)
Cactus scions
Any species or hybrid cactus whose diameter is equal to or greater than its height, including
Ariocarpus, all species
Discocactus, all species
Melocactus, all species
Pediocactus, all species

Succulent stocks
Group 1
Euphorbia, many species, including
  E. canariensis
  E. candelabrum
  E. mammillaris
  E. resinifera
  E. submammillaris
Group 2
Ceropegia woodii (tuber)
Stapelia grandiflora
Group 3
Pachypodium lamerei
Nerium oleander
Succulent scions
Group 1
Euphorbia, all species
Group 2
Brachystelma, all species
Caralluma, all species
Ceropegia, all species
Hoodia, all species
Huernia, all species

Stapelia, all species
Trichocaulon, all species
Group 3
Adenium, all species
Pachypodium, all species
Plumeria, all species

Split grafting and side grafting
Use these techniques for very slender, flat-stemmed or columnar cacti.

Cactus stocks
Cleistocactus samaipatanus
  C. winteri
Harrisia 'Jusbertii'
Heliocereus speciosus
Selenicereus, all species
Cactus scions
Slender-stemmed cactus and seedlings, including
Ariocarpus seedlings
Austrocactus, all species
Echinocereus leucanthus
  E. schmollii
Echinopsis chamaecereus
  E. chamaecereus f. lutea
Peniocereus, all species

Epiphytic cactus stocks
Epiphyllum, any with thick triangular stems
Heliocereus speciosus
Hylocereus, all species
Selenicereus, all species
Epiphytic cactus scions
Aporocactus, any long-stemmed species to make standard "weeping" plants.
x Aporophyllum, any long-stemmed hybrids to make standard "weeping" plants.
Hatiora, all species
Schlumbergera, any species or hybrids to make standard "weeping" plants.

Succulent stocks
Group 1
Adenia globosa
Group 2
Portulacaria afra
Succulent scions
Group 1
Adenia, all species
Group 2
Ceraria, all species

GLOSSARY

AERIAL ROOTS Roots that grow from the plant stem above soil level; used to anchor the plant and, in *epiphytes*, for absorption of atmospheric moisture and nutrients.

ANNUAL 1. Living for only one season, applied to top-growth. 2. A plant that grows from seed, produces flowers and seed, and then dies in one growing season.

ANNULUS The raised ring around the centre of a succulent flower.

ANTHER The part of a *stamen* that produces pollen, usually carried on a *filament*.

AREOLE The cushion-like *growing point*, actually a modified leaf bud, on a cactus from which grow its spines, leaves, sideshoots or flowers.

BLEEDING When sap or *latex* flows freely from a damaged stem.

BLOOM 1. A flower. 2. A waxy, white or bluish-white coating on stems, succulent leaves or fleshy fruit.

BRACT A modified leaf at the base of a flower or flower cluster, which often protects the flower. Bracts can resemble normal leaves, be small and scale-like or large, brightly coloured and look like petals.

CALLUS The protective tissue formed over a wound, for example, at the base of cuttings.

CAPSULE A dry seed pod that splits open when ripe to release its seeds.

CAUDEX The swollen water-storage tissue, usually composed of both root and stem, of a succulent or woody plant.

CAUDICIFORM 1. Possessing a *caudex*. 2. With a swollen stem.

CEPHALIUM A densely spined crown, which produces the flowers and fruit. It is produced only by species of *Discocactus* or *Melocactus*.

CHLOROPHYLL The green pigment present in leaves or stems and used in *photosynthesis*.

CORKING Gradual ripening of stem from the base, to produce a bark-like texture.

CROSS-POLLINATION See *pollination*.

CULTIVAR Contraction of "cultivated variety". Derived from a *species*, a variant selected or bred only in cultivation.

CUTTING A cut or detached section of a plant, either from a leaf or stem, or an entire leaf, that is used for propagation.

DAMPING OFF The speedy wilting and collapse of seedlings due to fungal attack on the seedling stem at soil level.

DIEBACK The progressive death of a stem from the tip due to damage or disease.

DIVISION A method of propagation in which a single plant or a clump is divided into several sections, each with its own roots and a *growing point*.

DORMANCY A temporary cessation of a plant's active growth and a slowing-down of its other functions, usually in winter, in drought or in extreme heat or cold. Some succulents can produce flowers when otherwise dormant.

EPIPHYTE A plant that grows on the surface of another plant but is not a parasite. The plant obtains moisture and nutrients from the atmosphere, not the soil.

ERICACEOUS Applied to acid compost with a pH of 6.5 or less. It is generally used for lime-hating plants.

ETIOLATION Pale, sickly, excessive growth caused by insufficient light, incorrect feeding or overcrowding.

FAMILY A grouping of related *genera*. For example, the family of Cactaceae contains about 140 genera.

FIBROUS ROOT A fine, densely branching root, which absorbs moisture and nutrients from the soil.

FILAMENT The thread-like stalk supporting an *anther*; together they form the *stamen*.

FLAT GRAFTING See *grafting*.

FLOWERHEAD A mass of tiny flowers, or florets, that looks like a single large flower.

FORCING The technique of bringing a plant into growth or flower ahead of its natural season, usually by providing it with extra warmth or controlling the day length.

FORM Cultivated or naturally occurring variant of a *species*, differing only slightly from the *species*.

GENUS (plural, *genera*) A category in plant classification ranked between *family* and *species*, denoting a group of plants with several common characteristics.

GLAUCOUS Possessing a smooth, blue-white, blue-green or blue-grey *bloom*.

GLOCHIDS Barbed bristly *spines* or hairs, usually very fine and easily detached, on an *Opuntia* cactus.

GRAFTING A method of propagation in which an artificial union is made between different parts of two closely related plants; a *scion* from one is grafted on to a *stock* from another so that they grow into one plant. Methods include flat grafting, split grafting and side grafting.

GROWING POINT The tip of a shoot from which new growth emerges.

HARDY Able to withstand most climatic conditions all year without protection, often qualified with a minimum temperature, for example, -15° C (5° F).

HERBACEOUS A non-woody plant in which the top-growth dies down to a *rootstock* at the end of the growing season.

HYBRID A plant produced by crossing two different *species* within a *genus* or from two closely related genera (intergeneric hybrid).

HYBRIDIZATION The production, either in nature or in cultivation, of a *hybrid* by cross-pollination (see *pollination*).

INTERGENERIC HYBRID See *hybrid*.

LATEX The milky white sap, that exudes or bleeds from damaged stems of some succulents, for example, *Euphorbia*.

LEAF BRACT See *bract*.

LEAF CUTTING A *cutting* composed of a single leaf.

LOAM A medium soil with equal parts of sand, silt and clay, which is usually well-structured, fertile and moisture-retentive but also free-draining.

OFFSET 1. A young plant produced by the parent, usually at its base; also known as an offshoot. 2. To produce offsets.

OVARY The base of the female portion of a flower that develops into a fruit once fertilization has occurred.

PAN A shallow pot that is wider than it is deep, often used for potting established cacti and succulents.

PERENNIAL Living for three seasons or more.

pH The horticultural measure of the acidity or alkalinity of a soil or compost; pH7 is neutral, below pH7 is acid and above pH7 is alkaline. Cacti prefer a slightly acid soil.

PHOTOSYNTHESIS The production by a plant of compounds required for its growth, prompted by light acting on the plant's *chlorophyll*. Also needed in the process are water and carbon dioxide.

PINCHING OUT The removal of the *growing point* of a plant or its stems to induce the production of sideshoots or more flowerbuds.

PLANTLET A new young plant, which usually arises from the site of a wounded leaf or stem or is naturally borne on the leaf margins, for example, in some *Kalanchoe*.

POLLINATION (also known as cross-pollination) The transfer of pollen from the *anther* to the *stigma* on the same or a different flower by gravity, wind, birds, bats or insects in nature or by hand in cultivation.

PROPAGATOR A small case, usually heated, with a removable top of plastic or glass. It is used to provide a suitably moisture-retentive atmosphere for raising seedlings or rooting cuttings.

PSEUDOCEPHALUM A growth of long, hair-like spines, usually on one side of the upper stem of a columnar cactus, like a *cephalium*.

RIB A ridge on a cactus stem, usually vertical, that is formed from the skin.

ROOT BALL The root mass, together with its soil or compost, visible when a plant is lifted from its bed or taken from a pot.

ROOTSTOCK 1. A vigorous plant which provides the root system in *grafting*. Also known as a stock. 2. A plant's root system.

ROSETTE A group of leaves radiating from approximately the same point, often borne at ground level at the base of a very short stem, or at the tip of longer stems.

SCION A shoot or bud of one *species* which is united to the *stock* of another plant by *grafting*, for propagation.

SIDE GRAFTING See *grafting*.

SPECIES The unit of classification below a *genus*, denoting very closely related plants.

SPINE Modified leaf, which can be needle-like, barbed, curved, hair-like or bristly.

SPLIT GRAFTING See *grafting*.

STAMEN The male reproductive organ in a flower, comprising the *anther* and its supporting *filament*.

STANDARD A tree-like cactus obtained by grafting a trailing or arching species, for example *Schlumbergera*, on to a tall or columnar species.

STEM CUTTING A cutting taken from a portion of stem.

STIGMA The central part of the female portion of the flower that must receive pollen before fertilization can occur.

STOCK See *rootstock*.

STYLE The stalk that supports the *stigma* so that it is well placed to receive pollen.

SUCCULENT A plant with thick fleshy leaves and/or stems that are adapted to store water. This includes all cacti.

TAP ROOT The principal swollen, downward-growing root of a plant.

TERMINAL At the tip of a stem or branch, usually applied to a bud, rosette or flower.

TOP-DRESSING An inert material such as stone or grit, usually decorative, that is applied to the surface of the soil or compost around a plant, to aid drainage and to decrease soil erosion or moisture loss.

TUBER A swollen, usually underground storage organ, derived from a stem or root, that stores water and food during *dormancy*.

TUBERCLE A small wart-like swelling on cactus stems, formed by the horizontal division of a *rib*.

VARIETY A distinct variant, occurring in the wild, of a species.

WHORL A ring of three or more leaves or stems arising from the same point, usually on the stem of a plant.

WINDOW A layer of semi-transparent cells, containing calcium oxalate, at the tip of a *succulent* leaf. The window protects the *chlorophyll* in the plant body from being destroyed by strong sunlight by diffusing the light before it reaches the *chlorophyll*, so enabling *photosynthesis* to take place.

ZYGOMORPHIC Lopsided or symmetrical in only one plane, applied to a flower with an irregular face.

USEFUL ADDRESSES

NURSERIES

Abbey Brook Cactus Nursery
Bakewell Road, Matlock,
Derbyshire DE4 2QJ

Brookside Nursery
Elderberry Farm, Bognor Road,
Rowhook, Horsham,
West Sussex RH12 3PS

The Cactus Nursery
Westfield, Hastings,
East Sussex TN35 4QE

Cactuskwekerij Gebr. de Herdt
Schommeveg 3,
B 2310 Rijkevorsel,
Belgium

Connoisseurs' Cacti (mail order)
51 Chelsfield Lane,
Orpington,
Kent BR5 4HG

Exotica (succulents only)
Am Kloster 8,
D(W) 5140 Erkelenz-Golkrath,
Germany

Frans Noltee
Rotterdamseveg 88,
3332 AK Zwijndrecht,
Holland

W. G. Geissler
Kingston Road, Slimbridge,
Gloucester GL2 7BW

Holly Gate Cactus Nursery
Billingshurst Lane,
Ashington,
West Sussex RH20 3BA

Kakteen-Haage
Blumenstrasse 68,
D(O) 5023 Erfurt, Germany

Oak Dene Nurseries
10 Back Lane, West Royston,
Barnsley, Yorkshire S71 4SB

Pete and Ken's Cactus Nursery
Glencote, Saunders Lane, Ash,
Canterbury, Kent BR5 4HG

The Plant Lovers
Candlesby House, Candlesby,
Spilsby, Lincolnshire PE23 5RU

Southfield Nurseries
Borne Road, Morton, Borne,
Lincolnshire PE10 0RH

Succulent van Donkelaar
P.O. Box 15, Laantje 1,
4250 DA Werkendam, Holland

Uhlig Kakteen
Postfach 1107,
Hegnacher strasse,
D(W) Kernen-Rommelshausen,
Germany

Westfield Cacti
Kennford, Exeter,
Devon EX6 7XD

Whitestone Gardens Ltd
Sutton-under-Whitestonecliffe,
Thirsk, North Yorkshire YO7 2PZ

SEED SUPPLIERS

Gerhard Köhres
Wingertstrasse 33,
D(W) 6106 Erzhausen, Germany

D & V Rowland
200 Spring Road, Kempston,
Bedford MK42 8ND

Roy Young
23 Westland Chase,
West Winch, Kings Lynn,
Norfolk PE33 0QH

SOCIETIES

British Cactus and Succulent Society (B.C.S.S.)
1 Springwoods, Courtmoor, Fleet,
Hampshire GU13 9SU

Epiphytic Study Group
1 Belvedere Park, Great Crosby,
Lancashire L23 0SP

German Cactus Society (K. v. a. S.)
Deutsch Kakteen-Gesellschaffe e V,
Nordstrasse 18,
D (W) 2882 Ovelgonne 2, Germany

International Asclepiad Society
2 Keymer Court, Burgess Hill,
West Sussex RH15 0AA

The Mammillaria Society
8 Whitegables, 53 Carlisle Road,
Eastbourne,
East Sussex BN21 4JR

Mesembryanthemum Study Group
Brenfield, Bolney Road, Ansty,
West Sussex RH17 5AW

The Sempervivum Society
11 Wingle Tye Road,
Burgess Hill,
West Sussex RH15 9HR

PUBLICATIONS

The Cactus File (Journal)
Cirio Publishing Services Ltd,
25 Shamrock Way, Hythe,
Southampton,
Hampshire SO4 6DY

Cactus and Succulent Society of America (Journal)
P.O. Box 35034, Des Moines,
Iowa 50315, U.S.A.

International Shopping Guide, Cacti/succulents 1992/3
(Compiled and published
by Richard Wolf)
Steubenstrasse 33,
D(W) 6070 Langan,
Germany

Strawberry Press (Books)
227 Strawberry Drive, Mill Valley,
California 94941, U.S.A.

INDEX

Page numbers in **bold** refer to entries in the Plant Catalogue; *italic* page numbers refer to illustrations in other sections. Synonyms, or old plant names, of plants featured in the Plant Catalogue are cross-referenced to current names. Old names of genera that have been amalgamated into genera in the Plant Catalogue are also listed.

ACKNOWLEDGMENTS

ADDITIONAL CONTRIBUTORS
Claire Calman (pp. 38–45)
Keith Grantham (pp. 20–25)

AUTHOR'S ACKNOWLEDGMENTS
I would like to take this opportunity to thank all those people who, over the years, have shared their enthusiasm for these plants with me. Their generosity, help, guidance and useful pieces of information have all helped to increase my enjoyment from this hobby. I would also like to thank my family for their forbearance – jobs in the greenhouse always seem more necessary than those in the home or garden. Finally, I would like to thank Dorling Kindersley for the opportunity to present a selection of these interesting and colourful plants. Their photography, editorial and design teams have produced a magnificent book.

DORLING KINDERSLEY would like to thank Claire Calman, Joanna Chisholm, Serena Dilnot, Shona Grimbly, Elisabeth Haldane and Jackie Matthews for their editorial help; Isobel Maclean for the index; Kate Sarluis for design assistance; Diana Morris and Christine Rista for picture research; Chris Anderson, Helga Lien Evans, Helen Gatward, Tanya Hines, Teresa Pritlove and Thomas Read for general help; Emma Hutton, Joanna Figg-Latham, Karen Mackley and Debbie Rhodes for DTP; Miles Anderson, Trevor Cole, C.W.E. and S.N. Harland, David Hunt, Peter T. Mitchell, and Gordon Rowley for horticultural advice; for loaning plants: Miles Anderson at Bach's Cactus Nursery in Tucson, The Chelsea Gardener, Chuck Hansen at Arid Lands in Tucson, Jane Evans and Gene Joseph at Plants for the Southwest in Tucson and World's End Nurseries; for loaning props: Brats, The Chelsea Gardener, Classic Pot Emporium, Clifton Nurseries, Covent Garden General Store, Fulham Palace Garden Centre, Grahame

and Green, The Hungry Cowboy, London Graphics, Macondo South American Crafts, Marston & Langinger Showroom, Robert Dyas Hardware, Santa Fe Trading Post, Fiona Barkham at Suttons Seeds, and World's End Nurseries; Maria D'Orsi and Diana Mitchell for prop research; Juliet Payne, Chris Pietrzak and Merelina Dynoe White for transporting plants and props.

PICTURE CREDITS
KEY TO PICTURES
t = top; c = centre; b = bottom; l =left; r = right (Figures refer to page numbers.)

All photography by Peter Anderson except for: Arcaid, Richard Bryant 42–3; Prof. W. Barthlott 14tc; The Bodleian Library, Oxford 22tr; Bridgeman Art Library, London / Collection Georg Schafer, Schweinfurt 23tr; Bruce Coleman Limited, John Cancalosi 17tr, Eric Crichton 23bl, Hans Reinhard 16–17; Elizabeth Whiting & Associates / Tim Street-Porter 44–5; ET Archive Museum of Mankind 25cr; Roger Ferryman 20bl; The Garden Picture Library,

Linda Burgess 40bc, Ron Sutherland 42bl; Steve Gorton (DK Studio) 12tr, 24tl, 46–7, 75tr, 78–9, 81bl, 93bl, 95tl, 95bc, 117tr, 119tc, 146–7, 148–9, 150–51, 152–3, 156bl, 156br, 159br; Keith Grantham 12c, 18cl, 20cc, 21tc, 21cc, 25tc; Jerry Harpur 44bl; Harry Smith Horticultural Collection 97bc, 97tr, 97br, 120bc, 128br, 135tr, 139bl, 161cl; Terry Hewitt 72bl, 97bl, 98tr; *Houses and Interiors* 40tr; Hunt Institute for Botanical Documentation 21tc; Dave King 4br, 5, 28–9, 30–31, 32–3, 38–9, 48–9, 50–51; The Mansell Collection 20tl, 22bl; Susie Moore 16cl; Terence Moore 14b, 25bl; Nature Photographers / Paul Sterry 14–15; Clive Nichols 42tc; Jerry Pavia 44tc; Photos Horticultural / Michael Warren 97bc; Planet Earth Pictures / J. Provenza 18–19; Robert Harding Picture Library, James Merrell, IPC Magazines 1992 41.

ILLUSTRATORS David Ashby and Amy Lewis for Plant Catalogue profile artworks; Karen Cochrane for the map on pp. 20–21 and the diagram on p. 150.